ANVIL EDITIONS

# Hölderlin

Selected Verse

# HÖLDERLIN

EDITED, INTRODUCED AND TRANSLATED BY

MICHAEL HAMBURGER

Anvil Press Poetry

First published in 1961 by Penguin Books Ltd
This edition published in 1986
by Anvil Press Poetry Ltd
69 King George Street, London SE10 8PX
and 51 Washington Street, Dover, NH 03820

This book is published
with financial assistance from
The Arts Council of Great Britain

Set in Monotype Fournier
Printed and bound in Great Britain at
The Camelot Press Ltd, Southampton


*British Library Cataloguing in Publication Data*

Hölderlin, Friedrich
    Hölderlin: selected verse. – Rev. ed. –
    (Anvil editions)
    I. Title    II. Hamburger, Michael
    831'.6    PT2359.H2A6

    ISBN 0–85646–147–4
    ISBN 0–85646–148–2 Pbk


*Library of Congress Cataloging-in-Publication Data*

Hölderlin, Friedrich, 1770–1843.
    Hölderlin, selected verse.

    English and German.
    Rev. ed. of: Hölderlin. 1961
    Bibliography: p. xxvii
    Includes index.
    1. Hölderlin, Friedrich, 1770–1843 – Translations,
English.    I. Hamburger, Michael.    II. Hölderlin,
Friedrich, 1770–1843.    Hölderlin.    III. Title.
PT2359.H2A25    1985    831'.6    85–20479

# PUBLISHER'S NOTE

THIS series presents the work of major foreign poets in their original language, accompanied by prose translations. Its purpose is to help readers whose command of a language is not fluent enough to follow poems without constant recourse to a dictionary. It also aims to provide authoritatively edited texts or selections with expert introductions which will be useful to readers of any level of linguistic accomplishment.

Prose translations, aiming primarily to describe the content of poems with a high degree of denotative, lexical accuracy, are of course no substitute for creative verse translations, which we remain just as interested in publishing. Equally, verse translations which aim at independent literary qualities do not compete with the more modest, serviceable translations offered here. Their purposes are, quite simply, different, as a comparison of Michael Hamburger's separate treatments of Hölderlin, for example, will show. These editions can provide the stimulus for poets to embark on verse translations; many versions made since 1960 have doubtless been indebted to books like these published in the Penguin Poets. We hope, too, that these books will offer the more general pleasure, for readers who enjoy the challenge of languages, of approaching the work of great poets with the helping hand of an expert guide, and the safety-net firmly in place below them at the foot of the page.

PETER JAY

# CONTENTS

CONTENTS

CONTENTS

# INTRODUCTION

HÖLDERLIN'S best work is quite literally incomparable. We can try to fit it into one of many possible categories, trends, and movements, such as the German Neo-Hellenic movement of the eighteenth century, the humanist and Protestant traditions generally, or the school of mystical and messianic pietism that flourished in his native Swabia. We can speak of Hölderlin as a classical poet or as a Romantic, according to whether we are thinking of his art or his situation. Above all, we can look for his affinities with other poets of various nationalities and periods who shared his belief in the primarily religious function of poetry. Each of these approaches has its uses; but Hölderlin remains a poet quite unlike any other.

This uniqueness is difficult to explain or to characterize. Historically speaking, Hölderlin achieved a fusion of native and foreign qualities, of emotional and spiritual dynamism with 'stillness of beauty', as he called it, of pathos with precision, of directness with grandeur, unmatched by any other German poet. Humanly speaking, Hölderlin's distinction and tragedy arose from the very nature of his poetic gifts; he was too much of a poet, too little of anything else. Goethe said of Schiller that he was greater than other writers even when he was cutting his finger-nails; but Schiller was worldly and prosaic compared to Hölderlin, who lived by the imagination and perished by it. The tragic sense of fate, of his personal fate, is inseparable from Hölderlin's poetry; and it is certainly connected with another of his pecularities, the extraordinary speed and extent of his poetic development in the mere six or eight years granted to him between his first mature poems and his mental collapse.

Hölderlin's early poetry had been one of enthusiasm and aspiration; mainly religious at first, in the manner of his earliest master, Klopstock, mainly philosophical later, in the manner of his second master, Schiller. His diction, therefore, had tended towards the abstract and the rhetorical, his metaphors had been largely conventional. In the short odes of 1797 and 1798 he attained a purity, clarity, and economy of diction which excelled his German masters; in so far as he owed this achievement to any literary models at all, it was to the Greek and Latin poets whom he had studied, translated, loved, and emulated since his adolescence. Yet this was the beginning, not the end, of the development in question. To make it a little clearer it may be necessary to outline the bare facts of his life.

Johann Christian Friedrich Hölderlin was born in the small Swabian town of Lauffen on the Neckar on 20 March 1770. His father, the manager of estates belonging to the Lutheran Church, died soon after, in 1772. Two years later his mother remarried and the family moved to Nürtingen, where her second husband was burgomaster. Hölderlin attended the local grammar school until 1784. His step-father had died in 1779, leaving Hölderlin uncommonly dependent on his mother. He remained deeply attached to her, to his grandmother, and to his younger sister, as well as to his half-brother, Karl Gock. In 1784 Hölderlin entered the Lower Monastery School at Denkendorf, two years later the Higher Monastery School at Maulbronn. From 1788 to 1793 he studied for his ordination at the Theological Seminary at Tübingen; during these years he founded a Poetry Association together with his friends Neuffer and Magenau, who shared his sympathy with the French Revolution, and formed friendships with two other fellow students who were to become eminent philosophers, Hegel and Schelling. As early as 1787 he became engaged to Luise Nast, the cousin of a school friend, but broke off the engagement in 1790. At Tübingen he fell in love with Elise Lebret, but by this time he knew that he would not take up the career for which he was intended, and might never be in a position to support a wife. In the autumn of 1789 he had written to his mother asking her permission to leave the university; but he stayed on, wrote theses on the History of the Fine Arts in Greece and on the Parallels between the Proverbs of Solomon and Hesiod's *Works and Days*, as well as a great deal of poetry, obtained his degree of 'Magister', and passed his final examination in theology.

Even in his late childhood Hölderlin had been moody, hyper-sensitive, subject to extremes of depression and elation; he was devoted to his friends, but found it hard to be sociable in a general way. His ode *Mein Vorsatz* shows how well aware he was at an early age that his vocation set him apart even from his closest friends. If we also take into account his increasing Hellenism and his political radicalism in these years, it is not surprising that he preferred the humble drudgery, but relative independence, of a private tutor to the clerical profession for which he was intended, and which he would do almost anything to avoid. With the help of his friends and of Schiller, who remained Hölderlin's hero and patron for some years, he obtained the position of tutor to the son of Charlotte von Kalb; because of her literary interests and connexions, Hölderlin could not have found a more congenial and sympathetic employer. In her home at Waltershausen, where he lived from the winter of 1793 to the following summer, Hölderlin worked at an early version of his novel *Hyperion*; in the autumn he took his pupil to Jena, attended Fichte's philo-sophical lectures, saw a good deal of Schiller, and met several other distinguished writers, including Goethe. An early frag-ment of his novel was published by Schiller in his periodical *Thalia*.

Meanwhile Hölderlin's pupil proved intractable; Charlotte von Kalb sent them both to Weimar, then enabled Hölderlin to live independently at Jena and Nürtingen until the summer of 1795. He continued his work on *Hyperion*, on the philosophical 'hymns' of those years, dedicated to the 'ideals of humanity', and on a translation from Ovid.

In December he was appointed tutor to the children of J. F. Gontard, a wealthy banker at Frankfurt, whose wife Susette soon became the 'Diotima' of Hölderlin's poems. Recent re-search had suggested that Hölderlin had entered into a liaison at Waltershausen with Wilhelmine Mariane Kirms, a young widow who acted as a companion to Charlotte von Kalb, and that he may have been the father of her illegitimate daughter born in July 1795 (the child died of small-pox in the following year). If so, he looked upon this affair as a mere lapse on his part. His love for Susette was of a different order. The Diotima poems show more clearly than any comment what she meant to him; and the significant change in his style which coincided with her growing influence on him bears out all that the poems say.

In 1796 Susette, her four children, her mother-in-law, and Hölderlin were forced to leave Frankfurt for Westphalia to escape the invading French Army; Gontard remained in Frankfurt. At Kassel they were joined by Wilhelm Heinse, the author of *Ardhingello*, a novel that influenced Hölderlin's view of ancient Greece; it was to Heinse that he later addressed and dedicated the most Dionysian of his poems, the elegy *Brot und Wein*. In the following year Hegel also became a tutor at Frankfurt. Hölderlin met Goethe once more, at Schiller's recommendation, but the rather formal interview was not to Hölderlin's advantage, and Goethe was never to appreciate Hölderlin's gifts. The first volume of *Hyperion* was published in 1797. Hölderlin had now begun to write *Der Tod des Empedokles*, the tragedy which was to occupy him intermittently until 1800, though neither the two versions of this, nor his last version called *Empedokles auf dem Ätna*, were completed.

After an unpleasant scene in the autumn of 1798 Hölderlin left the Gontard household and settled at Homburg. He continued to correspond with Susette and to meet her in secret. At Homburg he made the acquaintance of Isaak von Sinclair, the most faithful and helpful of his friends in later years. It was Sinclair who introduced Hölderlin to the Landgrave of Hessen-Homburg. His daughter Princess Augusta of Homburg to whom Hölderlin dedicated an ode in 1799 and his translations from Sophocles in 1803, appears to have been in love with the poet, though he never knew it. 1799 was a productive but critical year: for the first and last time Hölderlin did his utmost to establish himself as an independent writer, to find the place which he thought was due to him in the intellectual and cultural life of Germany. He planned to edit a 'humanistic journal', *Iduna*, which would have been devoted to 'the unification and reconciliation of the sciences with life, of art and good taste with genius, of the heart with the head, of the real with the ideal', of civilization with nature – to the ends, in fact, which Hölderlin believed to be essential to the poet's religious and cultural function in the community. The failure of this plan, and of Hölderlin's appeal to Schiller to obtain an academic post for him, amounted to nothing less than his rejection by society. Its effect on him is apparent in his poems and letters of the next few years, as well as in his three Empedocles fragments. The second volume of *Hyperion* was published in 1799, and a number of his poems continued to appear in various periodicals and almanacs; but Hölderlin felt more and more isolated, more and more remote from the literature and culture of his time. At Homburg Hölderlin also renewed his Greek studies in a more critical and methodical manner, and began to formulate his own critical theories, mainly concerning the differences between ancient and modern literature and the laws governing epic, dramatic, and lyric poetry. His unfinished poem of 1799, *Wie wenn am Feiertage* ..., remained his only attempt to imitate the strict metrical scheme of the Pindaric ode, which he modified in his later 'hymns'.

In the spring of 1800 he went home to Nürtingen, then stayed at Stuttgart as the guest of his friend Landauer. He returned to Nürtingen for the rest of the year, and set out for Hauptwyl in Switzerland in January 1801, to take up another post as tutor. He was back at Nürtingen by April and spent the rest of that year at his mother's home and at Stuttgart. In January 1802 he left for his last appointment as a private tutor, at Bordeaux; there, too, he spent only a few months, returning home early in July in a state of mind judged to be insane, and later described as 'dementia praecox' or schizophrenia. Susette had died on 22 June.

He recovered sufficiently to complete his translations of Sophocles' *Oedipus Rex* and *Antigone*, which were published with Hölderlin's critical commentary in 1804, to continue his translation of Pindar's odes, and to write the last of his own 'hymns'. In the autumn of 1802 Sinclair took him to Regensburg, where Hölderlin came under the influence of the Land-grave of Homburg, Sinclair's employer; it was at the Landgrave's suggestion that Hölderlin wrote *Patmos*. His changing attitude is also reflected in the dedication of the Sophocles translations to Princess Auguste: 'Apart from these, if time permits, I will sing the parents of our princes, their seats, and the angels of our holy country.' After his return to Nürtingen, so greatly improved in health that his mother believed Sinclair to have effected a com-plete cure, he also prepared for publication the group of shorter poems which he called *Nachtgesänge*, published in 1804. In July 1804 Sinclair took Hölderlin to Homburg, where he had pre-viously obtained the appointment of Court Librarian for him, though it was Sinclair who supported Hölderlin financially at this time. Despite Sinclair's care and protection, Hölderlin had to be removed to a Tübingen clinic in 1806. In the following year he was entrusted to a carpenter, Zimmer, at Tübingen, and spent the remaining thirty-six years of his life in the carpenter's house on the Neckar embankment.

One of many reports of his madness will have to suffice here. It is by Zimmer himself, in a letter to Hölderlin's mother, and refers to the little poem on page 253. 'His poetic spirit still shows itself to be active,' Zimmer wrote; 'for instance in my house he saw the drawing of a temple. He told me to make one out of wood. I replied that I have to work for my living, that I am not fortunate enough to live in philosophic calm like him, immediately he replied, "Oh I am a wretched creature", and in the same minute he wrote the following verses on a wooden board with his pencil:

> The lines of life are various; they diverge and cease
> Like footpaths and the mountains' utmost ends;
> What here we are, elsewhere a god amends
> With harmonies, eternal recompense and peace.'

Hölderlin died suddenly and peacefully on 7 June 1843, at the age of seventy-three.

Some of Hölderlin's very early poems, those written before 1793, are both more original and closer to his mature work than the philosophical hymns in rhymed stanzas which immediately preceded his maturity. The two early odes included here are less impressive than the apocalyptic *Die Bücher der Zeiten*, but this interesting poem proved too long and too rhetorical to serve as an introduction to the later work, as the two early odes do in several respects. The earlier one, *Mein Vorsatz*, is in the Alcaic metre which was to become Hölderlin's favourite ode form, and it gives us a glimpse of Hölderlin's late adolescence, his ambitions, conflicts, and scruples. The Kepler ode, in a metre derived from one of Klopstock's freely improvised ode forms, shows the local patriotism to which Hölderlin was to return by a long and devious route – a route leading through classical antiquity and the cosmopolitan humanism of his time.

Perhaps the total absence here of the Tübingen and Waltershausen hymns calls for an apology. These are considerable poems in their way, but they are poems concerned with abstract ideas, and one cannot enjoy these poems without sharing the particular idealism which they expound. 'Thought by itself makes no poet at all,' Leigh Hunt remarked, and Hölderlin soon came to regard his philosophical interests as a danger and a distraction. There were times in his life when, like Coleridge, he complained of being a 'thought-bewildered man'. Here we have to remember the character of German metaphysics in Hölderlin's time, and the degree to which it was affected by a crisis which extended to imaginative literature also. Briefly, it amounted to a gruelling awareness of the disparity between mind and world, idea and reality, reflection and spontaneous impulse, art and nature – art in a wider sense that embraced what we now call civilization, all that is the result of conscious endeavour, science, and ingenuity. Like Schiller before him, Hölderlin had to find his own way out of this maze; and it was only at Frankfurt that idea and reality converged for him in the person of a real woman in whom he also saw the ideal Diotima of Plato's *Symposium*.

For a while the idealism of his Tübingen and Waltershausen

years found its fulfilment in a single being 'upon whom my mind can dwell, and will dwell, for thousands of years, and yet recognize how all our thought and understanding fall short of nature', as he wrote in a letter of 1796. Yet even in the odes of the next few years there is a tragic undertone. In the ode to the Fates it is the presentiment that his happiness cannot last, simply because it is too great; and all the circumstances, of course, made its continuation unlikely. In the ode on Man it is the knowledge of human destiny in general, of the civilizing urge in men that divides them from nature and drives them from one achievement to the next. More important still, Hölderlin could never be content with personal happiness; his conception of the poet's vocation demanded an incessant awareness of the community as a whole, and this awareness became not less, but more acute during his Frankfurt period. His enforced separation from Susette merely confirmed his worst fears; for his Diotima, too, was a victim of the barbaric society which he castigated in his novel.

Hyperion is a young Greek who wishes to liberate his country from the Turks. The novel consists of letters, mainly written by Hyperion to his friend Bellarmine, a German, and to Diotima, whom he loves. All the hero's endeavours and aspirations are thwarted. Diotima dies, Hyperion is betrayed by his confederates and disillusioned with political action. He leaves Greece for Germany, curses that country for its inhumanity and philistinism, and turns to nature for consolation. 'Want and fear and might are your masters,' Hyperion says to the Germans; 'these divide you, these drive you together with blows. Hunger you call love, and where you see nothing, there your gods dwell. Gods and love?' A true society, Hölderlin implies, sees its gods everywhere, in all its activities and institutions. That is what he meant by religion. In the good society the poet acts as a mediator between gods and men, imparting the revelations granted to him to the community. This function is both priest-like and reminiscent of the Old Testament prophets; but in its emphasis on direct inspiration it conflicts with established religion, with the regular priesthood who insist on the authority of tradition. This conflict is prominent in the first version of Hölderlin's Empedocles tragedy; in the second version, included here, and in the last, Hölderlin has modified his antagonism to tradition and to the priesthood. The same change was to affect his poetry.

*Hyperion* sheds light not only on the development of Hölderlin's religious and political ideals during these important formative years, on his pantheism and Hellenism and his view of the poet's functions, but on a peculiar dialectic also to be found in his odes, elegies, and hymns. This is a dialectic of feeling as much as of thought; out of two conflicting moods and themes Hölderlin creates a synthesis that both reconciles and transcends them. It is a process akin to Hegel's philosophical method and to Goethe's morphological concepts, 'polarity' and 'intensification'; in music, it is related to sonata form.

The basic dualism of the age has already been mentioned. 'Man is a god when he dreams, a beggar when he reflects' is how Hyperion puts it. It is the alternation of these states, producing cycles of dejection and exaltation in the hero, that gives *Hyperion* its peculiar structure. Yet there is a gradual progression towards synthesis, just as there is in the longer odes and elegies, culminating in Hyperion's pantheistic communion with nature: 'O well-springs of the earth! O flowers and forests and eagles, O brotherly light! How old and new is our love! We are free, and do not resemble one another timidly from without; how could the theme of life refrain from changing? Yet we all love Aether, and in our deepest depths we are alike.

'We also, we also have not been parted, Diotima, though the tears I wept for you cannot understand it. We are living sounds and mingle in your harmony, Nature! Who draws us apart? Who can separate lovers?

'... As the quarrels of lovers, so are the dissonances of the world. In the midst of strife there is reconciliation, and all that is parted reunites.'

All Hölderlin's aspirations at this time were directed towards the reconciliation of basic antinomies, principally that between civilization and nature, familiar from the writings of Rousseau. In an early preface to *Hyperion* Hölderlin summed up his hopes as follows: 'There are two ideals of our existence: a state of extreme ingenuousness, in which our needs themselves are in concord, both with our abilities and with everything related to us, solely through the organization of nature, without our interference; and a state of extreme culture, where the same would take place with infinitely multiplied, varied, and intensified needs and abilities, through the organization which we are able to give to ourselves.' The culture of his time and country had not yet reached the second stage; hence the endless dualisms and conflicts. Some five years later, in connexion with his *Empedocles*, he went further than this: 'In pure life, nature and art are only harmoniously opposed; art is the bloom, the perfection of nature. Nature only becomes divine by its connexion with heterogeneous, but harmonious art.'

True to this correspondence between nature and art, even the structure of Hölderlin's works was governed by the law of cyclic growth and progression. His short ode *Lebenslauf* applies the same law to human life. Elsewhere he uses an astronomical term, 'the eccentric course', to describe the pattern that underlay his own development and the development of each of his works. Hence his habit of returning to early themes and even to finished poems in later years, not merely to improve or elaborate on them, but to join the old to the new, the downward motion to the upward, to trace the full cycle of growth. Hence, too, the extraordinarily small vocabulary of this great poet, who achieved variety by the modulation, rather then the multiplicity, of themes and concepts. True, the vocabulary grew very much larger towards the end of his creative period, corresponding to the wider range of themes in his last hymns and fragments of hymns, with their centrifugal trend towards history and away from myth, towards the specific and away from the general; but even this development was subject to the law of cyclic progression.

It is his submission to this law that explains Hölderlin's integrity and originality. Nothing in his work was forced, nothing was self-conscious, even when he had begun to recognize and formulate such principles as the 'modulation of tones', and to apply them more deliberately than before. What he wrote about his *Hyperion* applies to all his mature work: 'On no account would I wish that it were original. For originality is novelty to us; and nothing is dearer to me than the things that are as old as the world itself. To me originality means sincerity and intensity, depth of feeling and intellect. But precisely this, it seems to me, is most out of favour in our time. ...' Not only in his time, one may add; and in one of his few extant letters written after his return from Bordeaux, Hölderlin could claim with perfect truthfulness: 'My dear friend, I think that we shall not comment on the poets before our time, but that the mode of song will assume an entirely different character, and that we are not appreciated for this reason, that, for the first time since the Greeks, we are beginning once more to sing nationally and naturally, that is, originally.'

The development in Hölderlin's poetry between 1797 and 1803, which in many ways prefigures the development of all European poetry in the next century and a half, was due to continuous tension and intensification, not to any desire for novelty as such, far less the wish to shock, mystify, or astonish. Even Hölderlin's relation to ancient Greece was a dialectic one, subject to the same tensions and progressions as his other preoccupations. To begin with, he saw through the prevalent conception of ancient Greece as a model of restraint, symmetry, and decorum to the tragic, orgiastic, and savage foundations; long before Nietzsche he recognized the Dionysian, as well as the Apollonian, nature of the Greeks. Indeed, he came to reverse the conventional view by stating that what was proper to the Greeks was their 'holy pathos', or 'holy drunkenness' as he calls it elsewhere, though Homer was 'spirited enough to acquire occidental Junonian sobriety', its complement. The moderns, on the other hand, should turn to the ancient Greeks to learn 'holy pathos', because cold sobriety is what is proper to them. The matter is complicated by Hölderlin's discovery, explained in the same letter of 1801, that 'the free use of what is proper to one is the most difficult thing of all'; it 'must be learnt just as much as what is foreign to one'.

Secondly, Hölderlin's relation to ancient Greece was always conditioned by his Christian heritage and sensibility, and by that attachment to the person of Christ of which he speaks in his hymns. Despite his attempt to reconcile Christ with Dionysus in *Brot und Wein*, to relate him to the gods, demi-gods, and heroes of ancient Greece, he continually comes up against the uniqueness of Christ. It is impossible here to elucidate the complexities of this relationship as it appears in successive poems, and I shall have to confine myself to commenting on a few concepts essential to all the later poems.

After the unqualified pantheism of *Hyperion*, Hölderlin evolved a form of syncretic monotheism which incorporates elements of Greek polytheism, pantheism, and Christianity. He posited a supreme and timeless deity, 'the God of gods', and a succession of temporal divinities of whom Christ was the last to reveal himself. In addition, he posited alternating periods of Day and Night, divine revelation and retraction, partly dependent on the capacity of men to bear the dazzling brightness of God. Like Milton's, Hölderlin's constant purpose in these later works was to 'justify the ways of God to Men', though in a manner that did full justice to his own tragic sense of life and experience of 'God's absence'. Yet his conception of the 'searing beam', the unbearable brightness of God, is firmly rooted in Biblical, esoteric, and poetic tradition. *Paradise Lost* provides close parallels; so does the poetry of William Blake, who wrote in *The Little Black Boy*:

> And we are put on earth a little space
> That we may learn to bear the beams of love.

Related to the concept of Night, or divine retraction, is that of 'wilderness', which occurs when men are left to their own devices, without the direct guidance and manifestation of the divine. 'Wilderness', in turn, entails the temptation to Titanic arrogance, the temptation to forget the divine laws and the limits of human power. Our present age, which began with the death of Christ, is one of Night and wilderness. Yet this Night and wilderness are tempered by the Christian gospel, by the 'cloud of witness' that diffused the brightness of Christ so as to make it bearable to men until they are ready for another epiphany. In some of the poems it is suggested that this epiphany will include both the second coming of Christ and the return of the ancient gods. Nature still has an important place in this scheme; and in the last hymns and fragments there is a growing concern with representative men and landscapes, the concrete manifestation of ancient and modern history.

Hölderlin now sets out to relate divine history to human history and topography. In place of Man and Nature, he deals with individuals, nations, and regions, never forgetting their connexion with the whole. His business now is to 'see that the existing be well construed'. This is what he meant by singing 'nationally and naturally'. After 'colonizing' ancient Greece, ideally and spiritually, that is, he is ready to attempt the most difficult task of all, that of 'going to the source', of 'learning what is proper to one'. The last hymns are poems of home-coming, not only in a topographical or narrowly patriotic sense, but in the sense that Hölderlin now confronts the religious and political character of his own country, its past, present, and future. Once again he completes the cycle that was his 'course of life'; the end is a return to the beginning.

During the whole of this development Hölderlin also revised his view of the poet's function. The most significant change occurred during the crisis of 1799, and it can be traced in the successive versions of the Empedocles tragedy. There can be little doubt that Hölderlin thought himself guilty of the offence committed by his Empedocles, the tragic *hubris* of the seer who acknowledges no authority other than that of his own vision, and who betrays divine mysteries to the uninitiated. Hence the terrible self-accusation of *Wie wenn am Feiertage ...*, in which

Hölderlin describes himself as a 'false priest' and alludes to the Tantalus myth. Hence, too, the increasing reticence and impersonality of his poems, his reluctance to speak openly of the mysteries. Hölderlin's homecoming is also a deliberate and voluntary limitation of his own scope and vision; prophecy is always preceded by interpretation, and both are subject to a severe discipline of the imagination.

Stylistically, this self-limitation corresponds to the more concrete character of Hölderlin's diction and imagery. His early work had been that of a poet more aural than visual, more rhetorical than descriptive. Even in the superbly controlled and lucid odes of 1797 and 1798 he retained his fondness for generic terms like 'flower', 'tree', 'bird', for figures rather than images. In his late hymns and fragments all is vivid, sensuous, and specific to a degree that explains the impact of these poems on writers of the Symbolist, Expressionist, and Imagist schools. Their syntax is equally remarkable. It combines the directness of common speech with the most daring use of ellipse and inversion, not for rhetorical, but for imaginative ends. Hölderlin explained one aspect of this innovation when he remarked: 'It is common practice to have inversions of word order within the period. But clearly much greater effects can be obtained by the inversion of the periods themselves. The logical order of periods, in which the basis (the basic period) is followed by its development, the development by its culmination, the culmination by its purpose, and the subsidiary clauses are merely appended to the main clauses to which they primarily apply – all this can only very rarely serve the poet's ends.' Hölderlin was also aware that the diction and structure of his later poems make unusual demands on the reader; but to his modest excuse that 'he could not help it' one must add that the ambiguities and obscurities of these poems are amply compensated by their 'raids on the inarticulate', their unique contribution to the possibilities of language, feeling, and thought.

Lastly, a word about this selection. Apart from the two very early odes, it concentrates on Hölderlin's most characteristic work, the poetry of his middle years. A very substantial part of this has been included, much of it not previously translated into English. The *Empedocles* fragment also has not previously appeared in English.

I have given my reasons for not including any of Hölderlin's early philosophic 'hymns'; the problem of drawing the line on the other side, that of his so-called madness, was more difficult, since many of the fragments that preceded his total collapse contain passages of startling beauty and profundity. It is worth mentioning that two early translators of Hölderlin, Pierre Jean Jouve in France and David Gascoyne in England, treated these fragments, and the poems of Hölderlin's madness proper, as Hölderlin's most important achievement; but their emphasis reflected a trend in the poetry of that time, the Surrealism of the twenties and early thirties. For similar reasons an admirer of Ezra Pound's *Cantos* might pick out such fragmentary sketches as the following:

So Mahommed,* Rinaldo,
Barbarossa, as a liberal spirit,

The Emperor Heinrich.
But we are mixing up
the periods

    Demetrius Poliorcetes
Peter the Great
        Heinrich's
crossing of the Alps and that
with his own hand he gave the people food
and drink and his son Conrad died of poison
Example of one who changes an age
reformer
Conradin etc.
all as representative

of conditions.

*Hear the horn of the watchman by night
After midnight it is, at the fifth hour

Such parallels with recent developments are certainly interesting, but they have not determined this selection. As far as Hölderlin is concerned, these late fragments point to the historical interests which his retreat into ingenuousness prevented him from pursuing further. The subjects of his projected and fragmentary poems include Christopher Columbus, Luther, Shakespeare, Ovid's Return to Rome, Tasso to Leonora.

The poems of Hölderlin's last phase are more fully represented than the fragments, though, being largely rhymed, they do not lend themselves so well to literal prose versions. The charm of such a poem as *The Walk* (page 256), with its naïve enumeration of visual phenomena and its delightful metre, cannot be rendered in prose. This poem, too, anticipates a style that was to be cultivated in this century by no less radical an innovator than the late Gottfried Benn (1886–1956). At their best, that is, at their least 'philosophical', these poems are more than a touching postscript to Hölderlin's greatest work; something like their childlike immediacy, now luminously fresh, now pitiably trite, is also to be found in John Clare's asylum poems. The fictitious signature and dates under some of the last short verses are explained by Hölderlin's estrangement from his former identity; in conversation, too, he would call himself Scardanelli, Scaliger Rosa, or Buonarotti.

As for the translations, they are intended to be accurate above all; but in order to be accurate one must first be sure of the precise meaning, and this is by no means always an easy matter in Hölderlin's case. The late hymns especially are still capable of arousing violent controversies, such as that provoked by the recent discovery of one of them, *Friedensfeier*. Whether he likes or not, the translator is sometimes forced to commit himself to one interpretation or another – in some cases even to one reading of the text or another. Variant readings could not be included here, and explicatory notes had to be reduced to the indispensable minimum. The reader who requires more comment and guidance – but ignorance has much to be said for it where experts differ so radically – should get some help from the book list that follows.

I have done my best to keep these prose versions plain; but where the rhythm or metre of a line seemed inseparable from what it states, I have sometimes reproduced it without sacrificing literal accuracy. The reader of these versions will therefore receive an intimation at least of Hölderlin's Alcaic, Asclepiadean, and elegiac metres, of the mainly iambic verse of the *Empedocles* fragment, and the irregular rhythms of the hymns. The 'problems' of verse translation are infinite, insoluble, and tedious to all but the translator; I shall not enter into them here. If these versions have any merit, it can only be because even the bare prosaic bones of such poetry have a quality greater than all the resources of elegance and euphony.

### TEXTUAL AND BIBLIOGRAPHICAL NOTE

THE German text follows that established by Friedrich Beissner in vols. I and II of the *Grosse Stuttgarter Ausgabe* of Hölderlin's works (Kohlhammer Verlag, Stuttgart, 1943–51), with the exception of the preliminary versions of *Friedensfeier*, which are based on the reading by Wolfgang Binder and Alfred Kelletat (*Hölderlins Friedensfeier*. Lichtdruck der Reinschrift und ihrer Vorstufen. J. C. B. Mohr, Tübingen, 1959). The text of *Der Tod des Empedokles* is based on the Hellingrath and Zinkernagel editions. Hölderlin's spelling has been modernized and standardized, but not his punctuation or his inconsistent use of the eliding apostrophe. My grateful acknowledgements are due to Fräulein Ursula Trefzer for her help in preparing the text.

The following critical and biographical works on Hölderlin in English are recommended:

INTRODUCTION

BUTLER, E. M. *The Tyranny of Greece over Germany*. Cambridge (University Press), 1935. Chapter on Hölderlin.

PEACOCK, RONALD. *Hölderlin*. London (Methuen), 1938. Mainly critical.

STANSFIELD, AGNES. *Hölderlin*. Manchester (University Press), 1943. Mainly biographical.

STAHL, E. L. *Hölderlin's Symbolism*. Oxford (Blackwell), 1945.

MUIR, EDWIN. *Essays on Literature and Society*. London (Hogarth Press), 1949. Two essays on Hölderlin's poetry.

SALZBERGER, L. S. *Hölderlin*. Cambridge (Bowes & Bowes), 1952. Brief general study.

BOWRA, C. M. *Inspiration and Poetry*. London (Macmillan), 1955. Chapter on Hölderlin's later hymns.

HAMBURGER, MICHAEL. *Reason and Energy*. London (Routledge & Kegan Paul), 1957. Chapter on Hölderlin's later poetry. Revised edition, London (Weidenfeld & Nicolson), 1970.

UNGER, RICHARD. *Hölderlin's Major Poetry*. Bloomington (Indiana University Press), 1975.

The following verse translations have appeared in book form:

GASCOYNE, DAVID. *Hölderlin's Madness*. London (Dent), 1938.

PROKOSCH, FREDERICK. *Some Poems of Hölderlin*. New Directions, New York, 1943.

HAMBURGER, MICHAEL. *Poems of Hölderlin*. London (Nicholson & Watson), 1943. New version: London (Harvill Press), 1952. *Hölderlin: Poems & Fragments*. London (Routledge & Kegan Paul), 1966; Cambridge (University Press), 1980.

LEISHMAN, J. B. *Selected Poems of Friedrich Hölderlin*. London (Hogarth Press), 1944 and 1954.

MIDDLETON, CHRISTOPHER. *Selected Poems of Friedrich Hölderlin and Eduard Mörike*. Chicago (University of Chicago Press), 1972.

TRASK, WILLARD A. *Hyperion*. New York (Signet), 1965.

# TWO EARLY POEMS

# MEIN VORSATZ

O FREUNDE! Freunde! die ihr so treu mich liebt!
   Was trübet meine einsame Blicke so?
     Was zwingt mein armes Herz in diese
       Wolkenumnachtete Totenstille?

Ich fliehe euren zärtlichen Händedruck,
   Den seelenvollen, seligen Bruderkuß.
     O zürnt mir nicht, daß ich ihn fliehe!
       Schaut mir in's Innerste! Prüft und richtet! –

Ists heißer Durst nach Männervollkommenheit?
   Ists leises Geizen um Hekatombenlohn?
     Ists schwacher Schwung nach Pindars Flug? ists
       Kämpfendes Streben nach Klopstocksgröße?

Ach Freunde! welcher Winkel der Erde kann
   Mich decken, daß ich ewig in Nacht gehüllt
     Dort weine? Ich erreich' ihn nie den
       Weltenumeilenden Flug der Großen.

---

## MY RESOLUTION

O FRIENDS, my friends who love me so loyally! What is it that so troubles my lonely glances? What is it that forces my heart into this cloud-benighted, deathly stillness?

I flee the tender pressure of your hands, the soulful, blissful brotherly kiss. Oh don't be angry with me for fleeing them. Look deep into my inmost self. Examine it and judge! –

Is it hot thirst for manly perfection? Is it a creeping avarice for the reward of hecatombs? Is it a feeble urge towards Pindar's flight? Is it contentious striving for Klopstock's greatness?

Ah, friends, what corner of the earth can obscure me, so that, for ever wrapped in night, I may weep there? Never shall I attain it, that flight of the great which speeds round the earth in a moment.

Doch nein! hinan den herrlichen Ehrenpfad!
Hinan! hinan! im glühenden kühnen Traum
Sie zu erreichen; muß ich einst auch
Sterbend noch stammeln; vergeßt mich, Kinder!


KEPLER *

Unter den Sternen ergehet sich
Mein Geist, die Gefilde des Uranus
Überhin schwebt er und sinnt; einsam ist
Und gewagt, ehernen Tritt heischet die Bahn.


Wandle mit Kraft, wie der Held, einher!
Erhebe die Miene! doch nicht zu stolz,
Denn es naht, siehe es naht, hoch herab
Vom Gefild, wo der Triumph jubelt, der Mann,


But no! Upward along that glorious path to fame! Upward, upward, in the ardent and reckless dream of reaching those men; even if dying one day I shall have to stammer: forget me, children!


KEPLER

Amidst the stars my spirit walks, hovers over the fields of Uranus, and ponders; solitary and daring is my course, demanding a brazen stride.

Mightily, like the hero, wander about! Lift up your face! But not too proudly, for there approaches, look, there approaches down from the fields high up, where triumph exults, that man

---

\* Johannes Kepler (1571–1630), the great astronomer, was born at Weil in Swabia and was one of the heroes of Hölderlin's local patriotism. The 'thinker in Albion', of course, is Isaac Newton, who profited by Kepler's researches, especially by those that led to an improved telescope. It is clear from Hölderlin's use of astronomical terms that his interest in the great Swabian extended to Kepler's scientific works.

Welcher den Denker in Albion,
    Den Späher des Himmels um Mitternacht
        Ins Gefild tiefern Beschauns leitete,
            Und voran leuchtend sich wagt' ins Labyrinth,

Daß der erhabenen Themse Stolz
    Im Geiste sich beugend vor seinem Grab,
        Ins Gefild würdigern Lohns nach ihm rief:
            «Du begannst, Suevias Sohn! wo es dem Blick

Aller Jahrtausende schwindelte;
    Und ha! ich vollende, was du begannst,
        Denn voran leuchtetest du, Herrlicher!
            Im Labyrinth, Strahlen beschwurst du in die Nacht.

Möge verzehren des Lebens Mark
    Die Flamm' in der Brust – ich ereile dich,
        Ich vollends! denn sie ist groß, ernst und groß,
            Deine Bahn, höhnet des Golds, lohnet sich selbst.»

Who led the thinker in Albion, the spy of the midnight heavens, into the field of deeper contemplation, and who, lighting the way, ventured into the labyrinth,

So that the pride of exalted Thames, bowing in spirit before his grave, called after him into the field of more worthy reward: 'You began, Swabia's son, where the gaze

Of all the millennia grew dizzy; and hah! I complete what you began; for it was you, glorious one, that lighted the way in the labyrinth, conjuring beams into the night.

Though the flame in my breast devour the marrow of life, I shall catch you up, I shall complete it! For it is great, solemn and great, your course, scorning gold, rewarding itself.'

Wonne Walhallas! und ihn gebar
  Mein Vaterland? ihn, den die Themse pries?
    Der zuerst ins Labyrinth Strahlen schuf,
      Und den Pfad, hin an dem Pol, wies dem Gestirn.


Heklas Gedonner vergäß' ich so,
  Und, ging' ich auf Ottern, ich bebte nicht
    In dem Stolz, daß er aus dir, Suevia!
      Sich erhub, unser der Dank Albions ist.


Mutter der Redlichen! Suevia!
  Du stille! dir jauchzen Äonen zu,
    Du erzogst Männer des Lichts ohne Zahl,
      Des Geschlechts Mund, das da kommt, huldiget dir.


Bliss of Walhalla! And did my homeland give birth to him? Him, whom the Thames praised? Who was the first to cast beams into the labyrinth, and traced the path of the stars to the Pole.

Thus I should forget the thundering of Hekla and, if I walked on adders, I should not quake in the pride that from you, Swabia, he arose, and the thanks of Albion is ours.

Mother of the truthful, Swabia! You, the quiet! The aeons cry out to you in joy; you reared numberless men of light; the mouth of the generation that is to come pays homage to you.

# POEMS OF HIS
# MATURITY

.

# FÜNF EPIGRAMME

## Guter Rat

HAST du Verstand und ein Herz, so zeige nur eines von beiden,
Beides verdammen sie dir, zeigest du beides zugleich.

## Advocatus Diaboli

TIEF im Herzen haß ich den Troß der Despoten und Pfaffen
Aber noch mehr das Genie, macht es gemein sich damit.

## Die Vortrefflichen

LIEBE Brüder! versucht es nur nicht, vortrefflich zu werden
Ehrt das Schicksal und tragts, Stümper auf Erden zu sein
Denn ist einmal der Kopf voran, so folget der Schweif auch
Und die klassische Zeit deutscher Poeten ist aus.

# FIVE EPIGRAMS

## Good Advice

IF you have both a head and a heart only show one of the two; both will
be condemned if you show both at once.

## Advocatus Diaboli

DEEP down in my heart I hate the gang of despots and clerics; but what
I hate still more is genius that joins forces with them.

## The Excellent Ones

DEAR brothers, don't try to excel; honour fate and submit to being
bunglers on this earth; for once the head has ventured forth, the tail will
follow; and the classical age of German poets is over.

*Die beschreibende Poesie*

Wißt! Apoll ist der Gott der Zeitungsschreiber geworden
Und sein Mann ist, wer ihm treulich das Factum erzählt.

*Falsche Popularität*

Oder Menschenkenner! er stellt sich kindisch mit Kindern
Aber der Baum und das Kind suchet, was über ihm ist.

## DIOTIMA

Komm und besänftige mir, die du einst Elemente versöhntest
  Wonne der himmlichen Muse das Chaos der Zeit,
Ordne den tobenden Kampf mit Friedenstönen des Himmels
  Bis in der sterblichen Brust sich das entzweite vereint,
Bis der Menschen alte Natur die ruhige große,
  Aus der gährenden Zeit, mächtig und heiter sich hebt.
Kehr' in die dürftigen Herzen des Volks, lebendige Schönheit!
  Kehr' an den gastlichen Tisch, kehr' in die Tempel zurück!

*Descriptive Poetry*

Learn this: Apollo has become the god of journalists, and the man for
him is the one who faithfully reports the facts.

*False Popularity*

Oh the worldly wise! With children he pretends to be childish; but the
tree and the child look for what is above them.

## DIOTIMA

Bliss of the heavenly muse, now come and soothe for me, as once you
reconciled elements, the chaos of this age! Temper the raging battle with
Heaven's peaceful music until in the mortal heart all that is severed unites,
until the ancient nature of man, the calm and noble, rises mighty and serene
from this troubled age. Enter once more into the needy hearts of the
people, living beauty, return to the banqueting hall, and return to the

Denn Diotima lebt, wie die zarten Blüten im Winter,
Reich an eigenem Geist sucht sie die Sonne doch auch.
Aber die Sonne des Geists, die schönere Welt ist hinunter
Und in frostiger Nacht zanken Orkane sich nur.

## BUONAPARTE

HEILIGE Gefäße sind die Dichter,
Worin des Lebens Wein, der Geist
Der Helden sich aufbewahrt,

Aber der Geist dieses Jünglings
Der schnelle, müßt' er es nicht zersprengen
Wo es ihn fassen wollte, das Gefäß?

Der Dichter laß ihn unberührt wie den Geist der Natur,
An solchem Stoffe wird zum Knaben der Meister.

Er kann im Gedichte nicht leben und bleiben,
Er lebt und bleibt in der Welt.

---

temples! For Diotima lives; like delicate blossoms in winter, rich in inherent spirit, yet she seeks the sun. But the sun of the spirit, the lovelier world, has gone down, and only quarrelling gales clash in the frosty night.

## BUONAPARTE

THE poets are holy vessels in which the wine of life, the spirit of heroes is preserved.

But the spirit of this youth, the quick – would it not burst the vessel that tried to contain it?

Let the poet leave him untouched like the spirit of Nature, for such material reduces masters to apprentices.

He cannot live and last in a poem; he lives and lasts in the world.

## EMPEDOKLES

DAS Leben suchst du, suchst, und es quillt und glänzt
Ein göttlich Feuer tief aus der Erde dir,
  Und du in schauderndem Verlangen
    Wirfst dich hinab, in des Ätna Flammen.

So schmelzt' im Weine Perlen der Übermut
Der Königin; und mochte sie doch! hättst du
  Nur deinen Reichtum nicht, o Dichter
    Hin in den gährenden Kelch geopfert!

Doch heilig bist du mir, wie der Erde Macht,
Die dich hinwegnahm, kühner Getöteter!
  Und folgen möcht' ich in die Tiefe,
    Hielte die Liebe mich nicht, dem Helden.


## AN DIE PARZEN

NUR einen Sommer gönnt, ihr Gewaltigen!
Und einen Herbst zu reifem Gesange mir,
  Daß williger mein Herz, vom süßen
    Spiele gesättiget, dann mir sterbe.


### EMPEDOCLES

YOU look for life, you look, and a divine fire wells up and gleams at you from the deeps of Earth, and in your quivering desire you cast yourself down into Etna's flames.

So did the Queen's exuberance dissolve pearls in wine, and well she might! If only you, O poet, had not offered up your wealth to the seething chalice!

But you are holy to me as the might of Earth that bore you away, bold victim! And, did not love hold me back, gladly I'd follow the hero down to the depth.

### TO THE FATES

ONLY one summer grant me, you mighty ones, and only one autumn for mellow song, so that my heart, sated with its sweet playing, more willingly then may die.

Die Seele, der im Leben ihr göttlich Recht
Nicht ward, sie ruht auch drunten im Orkus nicht;
Doch ist mir einst das Heil'ge, das am
Herzen mir liegt, das Gedicht gelungen,

Willkommen dann, o Stille der Schattenwelt!
Zufrieden bin ich, wenn auch mein Saitenspiel
Mich nicht hinab geleitet: Einmal
Lebt ich, wie Götter, und mehr bedarfs nicht.

## DIOTIMA

Du schweigst und duldest, und sie versteh'n dich nicht,
Du heilig Leben! welkest hinweg und schweigst,
Denn ach, vergebens bei Barbaren
Suchst du die Deinen im Sonnenlichte,

Die zärtlichgroßen Seelen, die nimmer sind!
Doch eilt die Zeit. Noch siehet mein sterblich Lied
Den Tag, der, Diotima! nächst den
Göttern mit Helden dich nennt, und dir gleicht.

The soul which in life did not obtain its divinely appointed right, down in Orcus too finds no rest; but if once I have accomplished that which is holy and dear to me, the poem,

Then welcome, O silence of the world of shades! Contented I shall be, even if my lyre does not accompany me on that downward journey; *once* I lived as the gods live, and that suffices.

## DIOTIMA

You are silent and suffer in patience, and they do not understand you, holy being! You wilt away and are silent, for, oh, in vain among barbarians you seek your own kind in the sunlight,

Those tender, noble souls that are no more! Yet time speeds on. Yet shall my mortal song see the day which, Diotima, next to the gods, together with heroes, names you, and resembles you.

13

## AN IHREN GENIUS

S END' ihr Blumen und Frücht' aus nieversiegender Fülle,
Send' ihr, freundlicher Geist, ewige Jugend herab!
Hüll' in deine Wonnen sie ein und laß sie die Zeit nicht
Sehn, wo einsam und fremd sie, die Athenerin, lebt,
Bis sie im Lande der Seligen einst die fröhlichen Schwestern,
Die zu Phidias Zeit herrschten und liebten, umfängt.

## ABBITTE

H EILIG Wesen! gestört hab' ich die goldene
Götterruhe dir oft, und der geheimeren,
Tiefern Schmerzen des Lebens
Hast du manche gelernt von mir.

O vergiß es, vergib! gleich dem Gewölke dort
Vor dem friedlichen Mond, geh' ich dahin, und du
Rúhst und glänzest in deiner
Schöne wieder, du süßes Licht!

## TO HER GENIUS

S END her flowers and fruit from your inexhaustible fullness, kindly spirit,
send her eternal youth from above! Wrap her up in your delights and let
her not see the time when lonely and alien she, the Athenian, will live,
until in the land of the blessed one day she embraces her happy sisters, those
who ruled and loved when Phidias was in his prime.

## PLEA FOR FORGIVENESS

H OLY being, often I have disturbed your golden and god-like quiet, and
you have learnt many of life's more secret, more deep-seated griefs from
me.

Oh, forget it, forgive me! Like those clouds up there in front of the
peaceful moon, I shall move on, and you, sweet light, shall rest and gleam
in your beauty as before.

## EHMALS UND JETZT

IN jüngern Tagen war ich des Morgens froh,
    Des Abends weint' ich; jetzt, da ich älter bin,
        Beginn ich zweifelnd meinen Tag, doch
            Heilig und heiter ist mir sein Ende.


## LEBENSLAUF

HOCH auf strebte mein Geist, aber die Liebe zog
    Schön ihn nieder; das Leid beugt ihn gewaltiger;
        So durchlauf ich des Lebens
            Bogen und kehre, woher ich kam.


## DIE KÜRZE

"WARUM bist du so kurz? liebst du, wie vormals, denn
    «Nun nicht mehr den Gesang? fandst du, als Jüngling,
        doch,
        «In den Tagen der Hoffnung,
            «Wenn du sangest, das Ende nie!»


## THEN AND NOW

IN younger days I was happy in the morning, wept in the evening; now
that I am older, I begin my day in doubt, but its end is holy to me and
serene.

## THE COURSE OF LIFE

HIGH up my spirit aspired, but love well and truly drew it down; suffering
bowed it still more; so I follow the arc of life and return to where I began.

## BREVITY

'WHY are you now so brief? Are you less fond of singing than you used
to be? Since as a youth, in the days of hope, you could never bear to put
an end to your singing!'

15

Wie mein Glück, ist mein Lied. – Willst du im Abendrot
Froh dich baden? hinweg ists! und die Erd' ist kalt,
   Und der Vogel der Nacht schwirrt
     Unbequem vor das Auge dir.


## MENSCHENBEIFALL


Ist nicht heilig mein Herz, schöneren Lebens voll,
   Seit ich liebe? warum achtetet ihr mich mehr,
     Da ich stolzer und wilder,
       Wortereicher und leerer war?


Ach! der Menge gefällt, was auf den Marktplatz taugt,
   Und es ehret der Knecht nur den Gewaltsamen;
     An das Göttliche glauben
      Die allein, die es selber sind.


As my fortune, so is my song. – Would you gaily bathe in the glow of
the setting sun? It is gone! And the earth is cold, and the bird of night whirs
awkwardly down towards your eyes.

## HUMAN APPLAUSE

Has not my heart been holy, filled with rarer life, since I began to love?
Why did you prize me more when I was prouder and wilder, more full of
words and more empty?

Oh, the crowd likes that which sells in the market-place, and the slavish
honour no one but the violent; only those who themselves are god-like
believe in gods.

## DIE HEIMAT

Froh kehrt der Schiffer heim an den stillen Strom
Von fernen Inseln, wo er geerntet hat;
  Wohl möcht' auch ich zur Heimat wieder;
    Aber was hab' ich, wie Leid, geerntet? –

Ihr holden Ufer, die ihr mich auferzogt,
  Stillt ihr der Liebe Leiden? ach! gebt ihr mir,
    Ihr Wälder meiner Kindheit, wann ich
      Komme, die Ruhe noch Einmal wieder?

## DER GUTE GLAUBE

Schönes Leben! du liegst krank, und das Herz ist mir
Müd vom Weinen und schon dämmert die Furcht in mir,
  Doch, doch kann ich nicht glauben,
    Daß du sterbest, so lang du liebst.

## HOME

Happy the boatman returns home to the quiet river from distant islands where he has harvested; and I too would like to go home again; but what have I harvested, other than suffering? –

Dear river-banks, you that brought me up, do you soothe the sufferings of love? Oh, you woods of my childhood, when I return, will you give me peace once more?

## GOOD FAITH

Precious being, you are sick, and my heart is weary with weeping, and already I feel a flicker of fear, and yet, yet I cannot believe that you will die as long as you love.

HÖLDERLIN

## IHRE GENESUNG

DEINE Freundin, Natur! leidet und schläft und du
Allbelebende, säumst? ach! und ihr heilt sie nicht,
    Mächt'ge Lüfte des Äthers,
      Nicht ihr Quellen des Sonnenlichts?

Alle Blumen der Erd', alle die fröhlichen,
    Schönen Früchte des Hains, heitern sie alle nicht
    Dieses Leben, ihr Götter!
      Das ihr selber in Lieb' erzogt? –

Ach' schon atmet und tönt heilige Lebenslust
    Ihr im reizenden Wort wieder wie sonst und schon
    Glänzt das Auge des Lieblings
      Freundlichoffen, Natur! dich an.

## HER RECOVERY

NATURE, your friend is suffering, and sleeps, and you, the all-animating, delay? Oh, and you do not heal her, mighty breezes of Aether, nor you, the sunlight's sources?

All the flowers of Earth, all the glad and beautiful fruit of the orchard – will none of them brighten this life, you gods? This life which you yourselves lovingly reared? –

Oh, holy delight in living already breathes and rings out again in her charming speech, as before, and already, Nature, your darling's eye, kindly and candid, gleaming responds to you.

## DAS UNVERZEIHLICHE

WENN ihr Freunde vergeßt, wenn ihr den Künstler höhnt,
　　Und den tieferen Geist klein und gemein versteht,
　　　　Gott vergibt es, doch stört nur
　　　　　　Nie den Frieden der Liebenden.


## AN DIE JUNGEN DICHTER

LIEBE Brüder! es reift unsere Kunst vielleicht,
　　Da, dem Jünglinge gleich, lange sie schon gegärt,
　　　　Bald zur Stille der Schönheit;
　　　　　　Seid nur fromm, wie der Grieche war!


Liebt die Götter und denkt freundlich der Sterblichen!
　　Haßt den Rausch, wie den Frost! lehrt und beschreibet nicht!
　　　　Wenn der Meister euch ängstigt,
　　　　　　Fragt die große Natur um Rat.


### THE UNPARDONABLE

IF you forget your friends, if you mock the artist, and pettily, vulgarly interpret the deeper mind, God forgives you; but never, never disturb the peace of lovers.

### TO THE YOUNG POETS

DEAR brothers, perhaps our art will ripen soon – since, youth-like, it has long been fermenting – ripen to stillness of beauty; only be pious, as was the Greek!
　　Love the Gods and think kindly of mortals! Hate drunkenness as you hate frost! Neither moralize nor describe! If your master intimidates you, ask great Nature for her advice.

## AN DIE DEUTSCHEN

Spottet ja nicht des Kinds, wenn es mit Peitsch' und Sporn
Auf dem Rosse von Holz mutig und groß sich dünkt,
    Denn, ihr Deutschen, auch ihr seid
      Tatenarm und gedankenvoll.

Oder kömmt, wie der Strahl aus dem Gewölke kömmt,
Aus Gedanken die Tat? Leben die Bücher bald?
    O ihr Lieben, so nimmt mich,
      Daß ich büße die Lästerung.

## SONNENUNTERGANG

Wo bist du? trunken dämmert die Seele mir
Von aller deiner Wonne; denn eben ist's,
    Daß ich gelauscht, wie, goldner Töne
      Voll, der entzückende Sonnenjüngling

## TO THE GERMANS

Never laugh at the child when with whip and spurs on his wooden horse he thinks himself brave and great, for, you Germans, you too are poor in deeds and rich in fancies.

Or, as the lightning ray from clouds, from fancies does action issue? Will books soon come to life? O my dear ones, then seize me, make me repent the blasphemy.

## SUNSET

Where are you? Drunken my dazzled soul grows faint with all your gladness, for only now I listened while profuse of golden tones, the enrapturing youth, the sun-god

Sein Abendlied auf himmlischer Leier spielt';
Es tönten rings die Wälder und Hügel nach.
    Doch fern ist er zu frommen Völkern,
        Die ihn noch ehren, hingweggegangen.


## SOKRATES UND ALCIBIADES

"WARUM huldigest du, heiliger Sokrates,
«Diesem Jünglinge stets? kennest du Größeres nicht?
    «Warum siehet mit Liebe,
        «Wie auf Götter, dein Aug' auf ihn?»

Wer das Tiefste gedacht, liebt das Lebendigste,
Hohe Jugend versteht, wer in die Welt geblickt
    Und es neigen die Weisen
        Oft am Ende zu Schönem sich.

Intoned his evening song on a heavenly lyre; the woods and hills around him re-echoed it, but far from here, to pious people who still revere him, he has departed.

## SOCRATES AND ALCIBIADES

'HOLY Socrates, why do you always look up to this young man? Are not greater things known to you? Why do you gaze at him with love, as you would at the gods?'

He who has pondered the deepest truths, loves what is most alive. He who has seen something of the world, understands the high aspirations of youth. And often in the end the wise will bow to the beautiful.

21

## DER MENSCH

Kaum sproßten aus den Wassern, o Erde, dir
Der jungen Berge Gipfel und dufteten
    Lustatmend, immergrüner Haine
        Voll, in des Ozeans grauer Wildnis

Die ersten holden Inseln; und freudig sah
Des Sonnengottes Auge die Neulinge
    Die Pflanzen, seiner ew'gen Jugend
        Lächelnde Kinder, aus dir geboren.

Da auf der Inseln schönster, wo immerhin
    Den Hain in zarter Ruhe die Luft umfloß,
        Lag unter Trauben einst, nach lauer
            Nacht, in der dämmernden Morgenstunde

Geboren, Mutter Erde! dein schönstes Kind; –
    Und auf zum Vater Helios sieht bekannt
        Der Knab', und wacht und wählt die süßen
            Beere versuchend, die heil'ge Rebe

## MAN

Hardly out of your waters, O Earth, the peaks of young mountains were sprouting; and, breathing delight, full of evergreen groves, in the ocean's grey wilderness

    The first beautiful islands gave out their fragrance; and joyfully the Sun-god's eye looked upon the newly arrived, the plants, the smiling children of his eternal youth, born from within you.

    Then on the loveliest of the islands, where unceasing the breeze flowed with tender calm around the orchard, once under grapes, after a mild night, born in the twilight of morning,

    Mother Earth, there lay your loveliest child; and up to Father Helios the boy gazes familiar, and wakes and, tasting the sweet berries, chooses the holy vine

Zur Amme sich; und bald ist er groß; ihn scheun
  Die Tiere, denn ein anderer ist, wie sie
    Der Mensch; nicht dir und nicht dem Vater
      Gleicht er, denn kühn ist in ihm und einzig

Des Vaters hohe Seele mit deiner Lust,
  O Erd'! und deiner Trauer von je vereint;
    Der Göttermutter, der Natur, der
      Allesumfassenden möcht' er gleichen!

Ach! darum treibt ihn, Erde! vom Herzen dir
  Sein Übermut, und deine Geschenke sind
    Umsonst und deine zarten Bande;
      Sucht er ein Besseres doch, der Wilde!

Von seines Ufers duftender Wiese muß
  Ins blütenlose Wasser hinaus der Mensch,
    Und glänzt auch, wie die Sternennacht, von
      Goldenen Früchten sein Hain, doch gräbt er

For his nurse; and soon has grown up; the animals shun him, for different from them is man; neither you nor his father he resembles, for boldly in him and uniquely
His father's noble soul has always been combined with your delight, O Earth, and your sorrow; his desire no less than to be like the Mother of the Gods, like Nature, the all-embracing!
Ah, that is why his arrogance drives him away from your heart, and your presents, Earth, are in vain, and your tender bonds; since he seeks something better, the wild one!
From the fragrant meadows of his shores man must go out into the blossomless water; and though like the starry night, with golden fruit his orchard gleams, yet he digs

Sich Höhlen in den Bergen und späht im Schacht
  Von seines Vaters heiterem Lichte fern,
    Dem Sonnengott auch ungetreu, der
      Knechte nicht liebt und der Sorge spottet.

Denn freier atmen Vögel des Walds, wenn schon
  Des Menschen Brust sich herrlicher hebt, und der
    Die dunkle Zukunft sieht, er muß auch
      Sehen den Tod und allein ihn fürchten.

Und Waffen wider alle, die atmen, trägt
  In ewigbangem Stolze der Mensch; im Zwist
    Verzehrt er sich und seines Friedens
      Blume, die zärtliche, blüht nicht lange.

Ist er von allen Lebensgenossen nicht
  Der seligste? Doch tiefer und reißender
    Ergreift das Schicksal, allausgleichend,
      Auch die entzündbare Brust dem Starken.

Himself caves in the mountains and searches the shaft, far from his father's cheering light, unfaithful also to the Sun-god, who has no love for slaves and laughs at all cares.

For more freely breathe the birds of the forest, though the breast of man may heave more proudly, and he can see the dark future, yet he must see death also and alone must fear it.

And man bears weapons against all who breathe in his ever-timorous pride; in conflict he consumes himself, and the delicate flower of his peace does not bloom for long.

Of all his fellow creatures is he not the most blessed? Yet more deeply too, with more sweeping might does Fate, the all-compensating, grip this strong one's inflammable breast.

## HYPERIONS SCHICKSALSLIED

Iʜʀ wandelt droben im Licht
  Auf weichem Boden, selige Genien!
    Glänzende Götterlüfte
    Rühren euch leicht,
      Wie die Finger der Künstlerin
      Heilige Saiten.

Schicksallos, wie der schlafende
  Säugling, atmen die Himmlischen;
    Keusch bewahrt
    In bescheidener Knospe
    Blühet ewig
    Ihnen der Geist,
      Und die seligen Augen
      Blicken in stiller
      Ewiger Klarheit.

## HYPERION'S SONG OF FATE

Yoᴜ walk above in the light upon soft floors, O blessèd Genii! Radiant breezes, divine, touch you lightly, as the girl artist's fingers touch holy strings.

  Fateless as the sleeping infant the Heavenly breathe; chastely preserved in modest bud, their spirits bloom eternally, and their blissful eyes gaze with tranquil, eternal clearness.

Doch uns ist gegeben,
   Auf keiner Stätte zu ruhn,
      Es schwinden, es fallen
         Die leidenden Menschen
            Blindlings von einer
               Stunde zur andern,
                  W:e Wasser von Klippe
                     Zu Klippe geworfen,
                        Jahrlang ins Ungewisse hinab.


Da ich ein Knabe war,
   Rettet' ein Gott mich oft
      Vom Geschrei und der Rute der Menschen,
         Da spielt' ich sicher und gut
            Mit den Blumen des Hains,
               Und die Lüftchen des Himmels
                  Spielten mit mir.

Und wie du das Herz
Der Pflanzen erfreust,
Wenn sie entgegen dir
Die zarten Arme strecken,


But we are destined to find no resting-place; and suffering mortals
dwindle and fall blindly from one hour to the next, hurled like water from
ledge to ledge, downwards for years to the vague abyss.

In my boyhood days a god often saved me from the shouts and the rod
of mankind; then safe and virtuous I played with the orchard flowers, and
the breezes of Heaven played with me.
   And as you delight the hearts of plants when towards you they extend
their delicate arms,

So hast du mein Herz erfreut
Vater Helios! und, wie Endymion,
War ich dein Liebling,
Heilige Luna!

O all ihr treuen
Freundlichen Götter!
Daß ihr wüßtet,
Wie euch meine Seele geliebt!

Zwar damals rief ich noch nicht
Euch mit Namen, auch ihr
Nanntet mich nie, wie die Menschen sich nennen
Als kennten sie sich.

Doch kannt' ich euch besser,
Als ich je die Menschen gekannt,
Ich verstand die Stille des Äthers
Der Menschen Worte verstand ich nie.

Mich erzog der Wohllaut
Des säuselnden Hains
Und lieben lernt' ich
Unter den Blumen.

Im Arme der Götter wuchs ich groß.


So you delighted my heart, Father Helios, and like Endymion I was
your darling, holy Luna.

O all you faithful and kindly gods! Would that you knew how my soul
loved you then!

True, at that time I did not yet call you by name, and you never named
me as men do, as though they knew one another;

Yet I knew you better than ever I have known men; I understood the
Aether's stillness, the words of men I never understood.

I was reared by the euphony of the rustling grove, and learned to love
amidst the flowers.

In the arms of the Gods I grew up.

## ABSCHIED

W ENN ich sterbe mit Schmach, wenn an den Frechen nicht
Meine Seele sich rächt, wenn ich hinunter bin
Von des Genius Feinden
Überwunden, ins feige Grab,

Dann vergiß mich, o dann rette vom Untergang
Meinen Namen auch du, gütiges Herz! nicht mehr
Dann erröte, die du mir
Hold gewesen, doch eher nicht!

Aber weiß ich es nicht? Wehe! du liebender
Schutzgeist! ferne von dir spielen zerreißend bald
Auf den Saiten des Herzens
Alle Geister des Todes mir.

O so bleiche dich denn Locke der mutigen
Jugend! heute noch, du lieber als morgen mir,
. . . . .

. . . . .
... hier wo am einsamen
Scheidewege der Schmerz mich,
Mich der Tötende niederwirft.

## FAREWELL

IF I should die disgraced, if on the insolent my soul does not take ven-
geance, if to a coward's grave I go down, vanquished by the enemies of the
spirit,
    Then forget me, oh, then you also, kind heart, no longer save my name
from oblivion: then blush, you that have loved me, but only then!
    But don't I know it? Alas, my loving guardian spirit, when I am far
from you, soon all the spirits of death, tearing them, will play on the strings
of my heart.
    Blanch, then, locks of brave youth! Today let it be, rather than to-
morrow...
    ... here, at the lonely crossroads where pain, murderous pain, hurls me
down.

## DER ZEITGEIST

Zu lang schon waltest über dem Haupte mir
  Du in der dunkeln Wolke, du Gott der Zeit!
    Zu wild, zu bang ist's ringsum, und es
      Trümmert und wankt ja, wohin ich blicke.

Ach! wie ein Knabe, seh' ich zu Boden oft,
  Such' in der Höhle Rettung von dir, und möcht'
    Ich Blöder, eine Stelle finden,
      Alleserschütt'rer! wo du nicht wärest.

Laß' endlich, Vater! offenen Aug's mich dir
  Begegnen! hast denn du nicht zuerst den Geist
    Mit deinem Strahl aus mir geweckt? mich
      Herrlich an's Leben gebracht, o Vater! –

Wohl keimt aus jungen Reben uns heil'ge Kraft;
  In milder Luft begegnet den Sterblichen,
    Und wenn sie still im Haine wandeln,
      Heiternd ein Gott; doch allmächt'ger weckst du

## THE SPIRIT OF THE AGE

Too long already above my head you rule in your dark cloud, you god of the age! Too desolate, too awe-struck it is around me, and wherever I look, all shakes and bursts asunder.

Oh, like a boy often I cast down my eyes, seek to escape you in caves, and, timid, look for a place where you are not, you the all-convulsing!

Father, at last let me meet you with open eyes! Was it not you who at first roused my spirit from out of me with your beam! Gloriously brought me to life, O Father! –

True, from young vines holy power sprouts for us; in mild air, and when quietly they wander in the orchard, brightening a god meets mortals; yet more almightily you awaken

Die reine Seele Jünglingen auf, und lehrst
  Die Alten weise Künste; der Schlimme nur
    Wird schlimmer, daß er bälder ende,
      Wenn du, Erschütterer! ihn ergreifest.

## ABENDPHANTASIE

VOR seiner Hütte ruhig im Schatten sitzt
  Der Pflüger, dem Genügsamen raucht sein Herd.
    Gastfreundlich tönt dem Wanderer im
      Friedlichen Dorfe die Abendglocke.

Wohl kehren izt die Schiffer zum Hafen auch,
  In fernen Städten, fröhlich verrauscht des Markts
    Geschäft'ger Lärm; in stiller Laube
      Glänzt das gesellige Mahl den Freunden.

Wohin denn ich? Es leben die Sterblichen
  Von Lohn und Arbeit; wechselnd in Müh' und Ruh'
    Ist alles freudig; warum schläft denn
      Nimmer nur mir in der Brust der Stachel?


The pure souls of young men, and teach wise arts to the aged; only the bad man grows worse, so that sooner his end will come, when you, the convulsing, take possession of him.

## EVENING FANTASY

THE ploughman sits calmly in front of his cottage, in the shade; satisfied with his lot he sees the smoke rise from his stove. The vesper bell rings out hospitably to the rambler entering a peaceful village.

Now too the boatmen return to the harbour; in distant cities, merrily the market's busy uproar subsides; in a quiet garden bower a sociable meal brightly beckons to the assembled friends.

But where shall I go? Mortals live by wages and work; alternating between labour and rest, all is joyful; why must I alone be afflicted with a thorn that never ceases to goad my heart?

Am Abendhimmel blühet ein Frühling auf;
Unzählig blühn die Rosen und ruhig scheint
Die goldne Welt; o dorthin nimmt mich
Purpurne Wolken! und möge droben

In Licht und Luft zerrinnen mir Lieb' und Leid! –
Doch, wie verscheucht von töriger Bitte, flieht
Der Zauber; dunkel wirds und einsam
Unter dem Himmel, wie immer, bin ich –

Komm du nun, sanfter Schlummer! zu viel begehrt
Das Herz; doch endlich, Jugend! verglühst du ja,
Du ruhelose, träumerische!
Friedlich und heiter ist dann das Alter.

## DES MORGENS

Vom Taue glänzt der Rasen; beweglicher
Eilt schon die wache Quelle; die Buche neigt
Ihr schwankes Haupt und im Geblätter
Rauscht es und schimmert; und um die grauen

---

A spring bursts into bloom in the evening sky; unnumbered the roses flower, and calmly gleams the golden world; O take me there, you crimson clouds! and up there

In light and air let my love and my sorrow dissolve! But, as though dispelled by my foolish entreaty, the magic breaks: it grows dark, and lonely beneath the heavens I stand, as always –

Come, then, mild sleep! Too much the heart desires; but in the end youth too, the restless, dreamy will burn itself out. Old age will then be peaceful and serene.

## IN THE MORNING

The lawn is glistening with dew; more nimble now, awake, the stream speeds on; the beech inclines her nodding head and there's a rustle and glitter in her foliage; around the grey

31

Gewölke streifen rötliche Flammen dort,
　　Verkündende, sie wallen geräuschlos auf;
　　　　Wie Fluten am Gestade, wogen
　　　　　　Höher und höher die Wandelbaren.


Komm nun, o komm, und eile mir nicht zu schnell,
　　Du goldner Tag, zum Gipfel des Himmels fort!
　　　　Denn offner fliegt, vertrauter dir mein
　　　　　　Auge, du Freudiger! zu, so lang du


In deiner Schöne jugendlich blickst und noch
　　Zu herrlich nicht, zu stolz mir geworden bist;
　　　　Du möchtest immer eilen, könnt ich,
　　　　　　Göttlicher Wanderer, mit dir! – doch lächelst


Des frohen Übermütigen du, daß er
　　Dir gleichen möchte; segne mir lieber dann
　　　　Mein sterblich Tun und heitre wieder
　　　　　　Gütiger! heute den stillen Pfad mir.


Clouds reddish flames are flickering; heralds they are, and noiselessly they rise up; like breakers by the shore, higher and higher these mutable ones are rolling.

Now come, oh, come, and not too quickly, O golden day, hurry off to the peaks of heaven! For more openly, more familiarly, my vision flies up to meet you, O joyous one, as long as

Youthfully you gaze in your beauty and have not grown too glorious, too proud for me. Speed as you will, I'd say, if only I could go with you, divine wanderer! – but you smile

At my glad exuberance in wishing to be like you. Then, rather bless my mortal endeavours, you kindly one, and as ever, brighten my quiet path for me.

## DER MAIN

Wohl manches Land der lebenden Erde möcht'
Ich sehn, und öfters über die Berg' enteilt
    Das Herz mir, und die Wünsche wandern
        Über das Meer, zu den Ufern, die mir

Vor andern, so ich kenne, gepriesen sind;
    Doch lieb ist in der Ferne nicht Eines mir,
        Wie jenes, wo die Göttersöhne
            Schlafen, das trauernde Land der Griechen.

Ach! einmal dort an Suniums Küste möcht'
Ich landen, deine Säulen, Olympion!
    Erfragen, dort, noch eh der Nordsturm
        Hin in den Schutt der Athenertempel

Und ihrer Götterbilder auch dich begräbt;
    Denn lang schon einsam stehst du, o Stolz der Welt,
        Die nicht mehr ist! – und o ihr schönen
            Inseln Ioniens, wo die Lüfte

## THE RIVER MAIN

True, there's many a country of the living Earth that I long to see, and often over the mountains my heart speeds away, and my wishes wander across the sea, to shores which
    More than others known to me, have been praised; but in the distance not one is dear to me as that where the sons of gods lie asleep, the mourning land of the Greeks.
    Oh, that once I could land on Sunium's shore, ask my way to your columns, Olympion, there, and before the northern gale buries you too in the rubble of the Athenian temples
    And their statues of the gods! For long you have stood in solitude, O pride of the world that is no more! – And O you lovely isles of Ionia, where the breezes

33

Vom Meere kühl an warme Gestade wehn,
  Wenn unter kräft'ger Sonne die Traube reift,
    Ach! wo ein goldner Herbst dem armen
      Volk in Gesänge die Seufzer wandelt,

Wenn die Betrübten izt ihr Limonenwald
  Und ihr Granatbaum, purpurner Äpfel voll
    Und süßer Wein und Pauk' und Zithar
      Zum labyrinthischen Tanze ladet –

Zu euch vielleicht, ihr Inseln! gerät noch einst
  Ein heimatloser Sänger; denn wandern muß
    Von Fremden er zu Fremden, und die
      Erde, die freie, sie muß ja leider!

Statt Vaterlands ihm dienen, so lang er lebt,
  Und wenn er stirbt – doch nimmer vergeß ich dich,
    So fern ich wandre, schöner Main! und
      Deine Gestade, die vielbeglückten.

Gastfreundlich nahmst du Stolzer! bei dir mich auf
  Und heitertest das Auge dem Fremdlinge,
    Und still hingleitende Gesänge
      Lehrtest du mich und geräuschlos Leben.

Blow cool from the sea upon warm beaches, and the grape ripens under a powerful sun; oh, where a golden autumn turns the poor people's sighs into song,

Now that the lemon grove and pomegranate tree, full of purple apples, and sweet wine and kettle drum and zither invite them to the labyrinthine dance –

To you perhaps, you islands, still one day a homeless singer shall come; for from strangers to strangers he has to roam; and Earth, the free, alas, must

Serve him in place of a homeland as long as he lives, and when he dies – but never, far as I may wander, shall I forget you, beautiful Main, and your banks, the variously favoured.

Hospitably, proud one, you welcomed me and brightened the stranger's eye, and taught me songs that quietly glide along, and taught me to live in silence.

O ruhig mit den Sternen, du Glücklicher!
Wallst du von deinem Morgen zum Abend fort,
Dem Bruder zu, dem Rhein; und dann mit
Ihm in den Ozean freudig nieder!

## FÜNF EPIGRAMME

### Προς Εαυτον

Lern im Leben die Kunst, im Kunstwerk lerne das Leben,
Siehst du das eine recht, siehst du das andere auch.

### Sophokles

Viele versuchten umsonst das Freudigste freudig zu sagen
Hier spricht endlich es mir, hier in der Trauer sich aus.

### Der zürnende Dichter

Fürchtet den Dichter nicht, wenn er edel zürnet, sein
Buchstab
Tötet, aber es macht Geister lebendig der Geist.

O peacefully with the stars, fortunate one, you travel on from your
morning to evening, towards your brother, the Rhine; and then together
with him, joyfully down into the ocean!

## FIVE EPIGRAMS

### Προς Εαυτον (*To Himself*)

In life learn your art, in the work of art learn life; if you see the one aright,
you will see the other too.

### Sophocles

Many tried in vain joyfully to utter the extremity of joy; here at last, in
mourning, I see it expressed.

### The Angry Poet

Do not fear the poet in his noble anger; his letter kills, but his spirit gives
life to spirits.

### Die Scherzhaften

IMMER spielt ihr und scherzt? ihr müßt! o Freunde! mir geht
dies
In die Seele, denn dies müssen Verzweifelte nur.

### Wurzel alles Übels

EINIG zu sein, ist göttlich und gut; woher ist die Sucht denn
Unter den Menschen, daß nur Einer und Eines nur sei?

## MEIN EIGENTUM

IN seiner Fülle ruhet der Herbsttag nun,
   Geläutert ist die Traub und der Hain ist rot
     Vom Obst, wenn schon der holden Blüten
       Manche der Erde zum Danke fielen.

Und rings im Felde, wo ich den Pfad hinaus
   Den stillen wandle, ist den Zufriedenen
     Ihr Gut gereift und viel der frohen
       Mühe gewähret der Reichtum ihnen.

### The Jokers

ALWAYS playing and joking? You *must!* O friends, that troubles my very
soul, for none feels this compulsion but those in despair.

### The Root of All Evil

TO be at one is divine and good; but whence comes the mania of men that
there is only *the one* and only *one thing?*

## MY POSSESSIONS

NOW in its plenty the autumn day reposes, pure and mellow is the grape,
and the orchard red with fruit, though many a lovely blossom fell as an
offering of thanks to Earth.

    And in the fields around me, as now I saunter out along the quiet path,
their goods have grown for contented men, and wealth grants them much
happy labour.

Vom Himmel blicket zu den Geschäftigen
Durch ihre Bäume milde das Licht herab,
Die Freude teilend, denn es wuchs durch
Hände der Menschen allein die Frucht nicht.

Und leuchtest du, o Goldnes, auch mir, und wehst
Auch du mir wieder, Lüftchen, als segnetest
Du eine Freude mir, wie einst, und
Irrst, wie um Glückliche, mir am Busen?

Einst war ichs, doch wie Rosen, vergänglich war
Das fromme Leben, ach! und es mahnen noch,
Die blühend mir geblieben sind, die
Holden Gestirne zu oft mich dessen.

Beglückt, wer, ruhig liebend ein frommes Weib,
Am eignen Herd in rühmlicher Heimat lebt,
Es leuchtet über festem Boden
Schöner dem sicheren Mann sein Himmel.

Mildly from heaven the light glances down at the busy ones through their trees, sharing their pleasure, for not human hands alone made the fruit grow ripe.

And will you shine for me too, golden light, and, breeze, will you blow for me again, as though to bless a joy for me, as once you did, and meander around my bosom, as you do to those who are happy?

Once I was too, but brief as roses was my pious life; oh, and they that still remain in flower for me, the beloved stars, too often remind me of it.

Fortunate he who, loving a pious wife, lives at his own hearth in a homeland of good fame; above firm ground to the settled man more gloriously gleams his heaven.

Denn, wie die Pflanze, wurzelt auf eignem Grund
Sie nicht, verglüht die Seele des Sterblichen,
Der mit dem Tageslichte nur, ein
Armer, auf heiliger Erde wandelt.

Zu mächtig ach! ihr himmlischen Höhen zieht
Ihr mich empor, bei Stürmen, am heitern Tag
Fühl ich verzehrend euch im Busen
Wechseln, ihr wandelnden Götterkräfte.

Doch heute laß mich stille den trauten Pfad
Zum Haine gehn, dem golden die Wipfel schmückt
Sein sterbend Laub, und kränzt auch mir die
Stirne, ihr holden Erinnerungen!

Und daß mir auch zu retten mein sterblich Herz,
Wie andern eine bleibende Stätte sei,
Und heimatlos die Seele mir nicht
Über das Leben hinweg sich sehne,

For like the plant, if in its own soil it does not take root, the soul of that mortal fades who with the daylight only, a pauper wanders on holy Earth.

Too mightily, O heavenly heights, you draw me upwards; during gales, on a cloudless day, I feel your changes in my heart, consuming me, you mutable powers of gods.

Today, though, let me walk the familiar path towards the orchard whose dying leaves garnish the crests with gold; and wreathe my forehead too, dear memories!

And that my mortal heart also may yet be saved, as for others, may be a durable dwelling-place, and, homeless, my soul may not yearn to transcend this life,

Sei du, Gesang, mein freundlich Asyl! sei du
   Beglückender! mit sorgender Liebe mir
     Gepflegt, der Garten, wo ich, wandelnd
       Unter den Blüten, den immerjungen,

In sichrer Einfalt wohne, wenn draußen mir
   Mit ihren Wellen allen die mächt'ge Zeit
     Die Wandelbare fern rauscht und die
       Stillere Sonne mein Wirken fördert.

Ihr segnet gütig über den Sterblichen
   Ihr Himmelskräfte! jedem sein Eigentum,
     O segnet meines auch und daß zu
       Frühe die Parze den Traum nicht ende.

Song, be my kindly refuge, you, the giver of joy, be tended with loving
care, the garden where wandering among blossoms, the ever-youthful,
   I live in safe ingenuousness while outside with all his breakers mighty
Time, the ever-changing, roars in the distance, and the more quiet sun
aids my endeavours.
   You bless benevolently each mortal man's possessions from above, you
heavenly powers; oh bless mine also and grant that not too early the Fates
put an end to my dreaming.

# DER TOD DES EMPEDOKLES
## EIN TRAUERSPIEL IN FÜNF AKTEN
*Zweite Fassung*

\*

*Personen*

EMPEDOKLES

PAUSANIAS

PANTHEA

DELIA

HERMOKRATES

MEKADES

AMPHARES ⎫
DEMOKLES ⎬ Agrigentiner
HYLAS ⎭

Der Schauplatz ist teils in Agrigent, teils am Ätna

# THE DEATH OF EMPEDOCLES
## FRAGMENT OF A TRAGEDY IN FIVE ACTS
*Second Version*

\*

*The Persons*

EMPEDOCLES

PAUSANIAS

PANTHEA

DELIA

HERMOCRATES

MECADES

AMPHARES ⎫
DEMOCLES ⎬ Citizens of Agrigentum
HYLAS ⎭

The Scene partly at Agrigentum, partly at the foot of Etna

40

## ERSTER AKT
### ERSTER AUFTRITT

*Chor der Agrigentiner in der Ferne. Mekades. Hermokrates*

MEKADES: Hörst du das trunkne Volk?

HERMOKRATES: Sie suchen ihn.

MEKADES: Der Geist des Mannes
Ist mächtig unter ihnen.

HERMOKRATES: Ich weiß, wie dürres Gras
Entzünden sich die Menschen.

MEKADES: Daß einer so die Menge bewegt, mir ist's,
Als wie wenn Jovis Blitz den Wald
Ergreift, und furchtbarer.

HERMOKRATES: Drum binden wir den Menschen auch
Das Band ums Auge, daß sie nicht
Zu kräftig sich am Lichte nähren.
Nicht gegenwärtig werden
Darf Göttliches vor ihnen,
Es darf ihr Herz
Lebendiges nicht finden.
Kennst du die Alten nicht,
Die Lieblinge des Himmels man nennt?

## ACT ONE
### SCENE ONE

*Chorus of Agrigentines in the distance Mecades, Hermocrates*

MECADES: Do you hear the frenzied people?

HERMOCRATES: They look for him.

MECADES: The spirit of that man is powerful among them.

HERMOCRATES: I know; like withered grass the minds of men catch fire.

MECADES: That one man should so move a whole nation, seems to me like
when Zeus' lightning seizes the forest, only more terrible still.

HERMOCRATES: And that is why we bind that band around the eyes of
men, so that not too richly light shall nourish them. Never must the
divine be wholly present to them, nor their minds grasp that which is
wholly alive. Do you not know those ancients who are called the

HÖLDERLIN

Sie nährten die Brust
An Kräften der Welt
Und den Hellaufblickenden war
Unsterbliches nahe,
Drum beugten die Stolzen
Das Haupt auch nicht,
Und vor den Gewaltigen konnt'
Ein Anderes nicht bestehn,
Es ward verwandelt vor ihnen.

MEKADES: Und er?

HERMOKRATES: Das hat zu mächtig ihn
Gemacht, daß er vertraut
Mit Göttern worden ist.
Es tönt sein Wort dem Volk,
Als käm es vom Olymp;
Sie dankens ihm,
Daß er vom Himmel raubt
Die Lebensflamm', und sie
Verrät den Sterblichen.

MEKADES: Sie wissen nichts, denn ihn.
Er soll ihr Gott,
Er soll ihr König sein.

darlings of Heaven? They nourished their hearts on the world's own powers, and to the brightly up-gazing the immortal was near; that too is why these proud ones did not bow their heads, and before those mighty ones nothing other than they could remain as it was: it was transformed by their force.

MECADES: And he?

HERMOCRATES: What has made him too mighty is that he became familiar with gods. His word rings out to the people as though it came from Olympus; they thank him for stealing the flame of life from Heaven and betraying it to mortals.

MECADES: They have no thought but for him; they want him to be their god, their king. They say that Apollo built the Trojans their city, but

Sie sagen, es hab' Apoll
Die Stadt gebaut den Trojern,
Doch besser sei, es helf'
Ein hoher Mann durchs Leben.

Noch sprechen sie viel Unverständiges
Von ihm und achten kein Gesetz
Und keine Not und keine Sitte.

Ein Irrgestirn ist unser Volk
Geworden, und ich fürcht',
Es deute dieses Zeichen
Zukünft'ges noch, das er
Im stillen Sinne brütet.

HERMOKRATES: Sei ruhig, Mekades!
Er wird nicht.

MEKADES: Bist du denn mächtiger?

HERMOKRATES: Der sie versteht,
Ist stärker denn die Starken,
Und wohlbekannt ist dieser Seltne mir.

Zu glücklich wuchs er auf;
Ihm ist von Anbeginn
Der eigne Sinn verwöhnt, daß ihn
Geringes irrt; er wird es büßen,
Daß er zu sehr geliebt die Sterblichen.

that it is even better if an exalted man leads mortals through life. Many
other incomprehensible things they say about him, and respect no law,
no necessity, and no custom. Our people have turned into a dizzy comet,
and I fear that this sign points to other things yet to come which he is
silently hatching out in his mind.

HERMOCRATES: Never fear, Mecades! He will not.

MECADES: Why, are you stronger, then?

HERMOCRATES: Who understands them is stronger than the strong. And
I know this rare one well. Too happily he grew up; from the beginning
his will was pampered so that little things confound him; he will regret
that he loved mortal men too much.

MEKADES: Mir ahndet selbst,
  Es wird mit ihm nicht lange dauern,
  Doch ist es lang genug,
  So er erst fällt, wenn ihm's gelungen ist.
HERMOKRATES: Und schon ist er gefallen.
MEKADES: Was sagst du?
HERMOKRATES: Siehst du denn nicht? es haben
  Den hohen Geist die Geistesarmen
  Geirrt, die Blinden den Verführer.
  Die Seele warf er vor das Volk, verriet
  Der Götter Gunst gutmütig den Gemeinen,
  Doch rächend äffte leeren Widerhalls
  Genug denn auch aus toter Brust den Toren.
  Und eine Zeit ertrug er's, grämte sich
  Geduldig, wußte nicht,
  Wo es gebrach; indessen wuchs
  Die Trunkenheit dem Volke; schaudernd
  Vernahmen sie's, wenn ihm vom eignen Wort
  Der Busen bebt', und sprachen:
  So hören wir nicht die Götter!
  Und Namen, so ich dir nicht nenne, gaben
  Die Knechte dann dem stolzen Trauernden.


MECADES: I too have a feeling that he will not last long; yet it will be long
  enough, if he falls only when he has attained his end.
HERMOCRATES: But he has fallen already.
MECADES: What are you saying?
HERMOCRATES: Is it not clear enough? The poor in mind have con-
  founded that noble mind, the blind have misled their false leader. He
  threw his soul before the people, good-naturedly betrayed the favour of
  gods to the vulgar; but in revenge his dead heart's hollow echo has aped
  and mocked the fool incessantly. And for a time he suffered it, pined, but
  patiently, not knowing what was wrong; meanwhile the people's frenzy
  grew; shuddering they heard his bosom shaken by the resonance of his
  own words, and said: it is not thus we listen to gods! And called that
  proudly mourning one such names as I shall not repeat to you. And in

Und endlich nimmt der Durstige das Gift,
Der Arme, der mit seinem Sinne nicht
Zu bleiben weiß und Ähnliches nicht findet,
Er tröstet mit der rasenden
Anbetung sich, verblindet, wird wie sie,
Die seelenlosen Aberglaubigen;
Die Kraft ist ihm entwichen,
Er geht in einer Nacht, und weiß sich nicht
Herauszuhelfen, und wir helfen ihm.

MEKADES: Des bist du so gewiß?

HERMOKRATES: Ich kenn' ihn.

MEKADES: Ein übermütiges Gerede fällt
Mir bei, das er gemacht, da er zuletzt
Auf der Agora war. Ich weiß es nicht,
Was ihm das Volk zuvor gesagt; ich kam
Nur eben, stand von fern: ihr ehret mich,
Antwortet' er, und tuet recht daran;
Denn stumm ist die Natur,
Es leben Sonn und Luft und Erd und ihre Kinder
Fremd umeinander,
Die Einsamen, als gehörten sie sich nicht.
Wohl wandeln immerkräftig

the end the thirsty takes the poison, that wretch whose spirit knows no resting place and looks in vain for equals – he consoles himself with raving idolatry, grows blind, becomes as they are, that superstitious rabble void of soul; his power has left him, he walks in a dark night and cannot think how to get out of it, and we shall help him.

MECADES: Are you quite sure of that?

HERMOCRATES: I know him.

MECADES: A piece of arrogant talk occurs to me which he perpetrated when he last appeared at the Agora. I cannot say just what the people had said to him before, I had only just arrived, and stood at some distance from him. 'You honour me,' he answered, 'and rightly so; for Nature is dumb. Sun, Air, and Earth, and all her children like strangers live together, the solitary ones, as though they were not related. True, the immortal and untrammelled cosmic Powers, ever strong, in the

Im Göttergeiste die freien
Unsterblichen Mächte der Welt
Rings um der andern
Vergänglich Leben,
Doch wilde Pflanzen
Auf wilden Grund
Sind in den Schoß der Götter
Die Sterblichen alle gesäet,
Die Kärglichgenährten, und tot
Erschiene der Boden, wenn Einer nicht
Des wartete, lebenerweckend,
Und mein ist das Feld. Mir tauschen
Die Kraft und Seele zu Einem
Die Sterblichen und die Götter.
Und wärmer umfangen die ewigen Mächte
Das strebende Herz und kräftger gedeihn
Vom Geiste der Freien die fühlenden Menschen,
Und wach ist's! denn ich
Geselle das Fremde,
Das Unbekannte nennet mein Wort,
Und die Liebe der Lebenden trag'
Ich auf und nieder; was Einem gebricht,
Ich bring' es vom andern, und binde
Beseelend, und wandle

spirit of the gods revolve around those others' ephemeral life, yet, like
wild plants on ground as wild, we mortals on to the lap of the gods have
all been sown, we the scantily nourished, and the soil would seem dead
if One were not there to tend it, awakening life; and mine is that field.
My strength and my soul mortals and gods combine to fuse into One.
And more warmly these everlasting Powers embrace the aspiring heart,
and feeling men more richly thrive for the spirit of those untrammelled
ones, and suddenly all's awake! For what is strange I conjoin, the un-
known my word can name, and the love of the living I carry up and
down; what one lacks I fetch from the other, and, soul-infusing, bind

Verjüngend die zögernde Welt,
Und gleiche keinem und Allen.
So sprach der Übermütige.

HERMOKRATES: Das ist noch wenig. Ärgers schläft in ihm.
Ich kenn ihn, kenne sie, die überglücklichen
Verwöhnten Söhne des Himmels,
Die anders nicht, denn ihre Seele, fühlen.
Stört einmal sie der Augenblick heraus –
Und leichtzerstörbar sind die Zärtlichen –
Dann stillet nichts sie wieder, brennend
Treibt eine Wunde sie, unheilbar gärt
Die Brust. Auch er! so still er scheint,
So glüht ihm doch, seit ihm das arme Volk
Den hohen Geist ...
Im Busen die tyrannische Begierde.
Er oder wir! Und Schaden ist es nicht,
So wir ihn opfern. Untergehen muß
Er doch!

MEKADES: O reiz ihn nicht! schaff ihr nicht Raum und laß
Sie nicht ersticken, die verschloss'ne Flamme!
Laß ihn! gib ihm nicht Anstoß! findet den
Zu frecher Tat der Übermütge nicht,

---

each to each, and, rejuvenating, transform the hesitant world, and re-semble none and all.' Thus spoke the arrogant one.

HERMOCRATES: That's a mere trifle. Worse lies dormant in him. I know him, know his kind, the over-fortunate, spoilt sons of Heaven who have no sense for anything but their own souls. If once the moment shakes them, jars on them – and these too delicate ones are easily shattered – then nothing reassures them, but a burning wound drives them about, incurably their inner being seethes. He too! Calm though he may appear, yet since the wretched people [confused] his noble spirit, tyrannical de-sire has glowed within his heart. He or ourselves? And we shall do no harm by sacrificing him. For perish he must!

MECADES: Do not provoke him! Do not clear a space, nor let it choke, the flame that's well confined! Leave him alone! Give him no cause to act! If in his arrogance he himself finds none for insolent deeds, and if in

Und kann er nur im Worte sündigen,
So stirbt er, als ein Tor, und schadet uns
Nicht viel. Laß träumend ihn nur fliegen!
Ein kräftger Gegner macht ihn furchtbar,
Dann fühlt er seine Macht, dann ...

HERMOKRATES: Du fürchtest ihn und alles, armer Mann!

MEKADES: Ich mag die Reue nur mir gerne sparen,
Mag gerne schonen, was zu schonen ist.
Das braucht der Priester nicht, der alles weiß,
Der Heil'ge, der sich alles heiliget.

HERMOKRATES: Begreife mich, Unmündiger! eh du
Mich lästerst. Fallen muß der Mann; ich sag'
Es dir und glaube mir, wär er zu schonen,
Ich würd es mehr, wie du! Denn näher bin
Ich ihm, wie du. Doch lerne dies:
Verderblicher denn Schwert und Feuer ist
Der Menschengeist, der götterähnliche,
Wenn er nicht schweigen kann, und sein Geheimnis
Unaufgedeckt bewahren. Bleibt er still
In seiner Tiefe ruhn, und gibt, was not ist,
Wohltätig ist er dann; ein fressend Feuer,
Wenn er aus seiner Fessel bricht.

words alone he can transgress, then as a fool he dies and does us little harm. Day-dreaming let him soar! A strong opponent makes him terrible, then he will feel his power, and then ...

HERMOCRATES: You fear him, and fear everything, poor man!

MECADES: No, but I like to save myself remorse, and like to spare whatever can be spared; different in that from the omniscient priest, the holy man who can make holy all he undertakes.

HERMOCRATES: Understand me, you callow youth, before you insult me. The man must fall, I tell you. And if he could be spared, believe me, I would spare him more than you would. For I am closer to him than you are. But learn this: more ruinous than sword or fire is human spirit, godlike though it is, if it cannot keep silent and preserve its secret unexposed. As long as in its depth it lies at rest, gives what is needed, it is salutary, but a devouring fire when from its fetters it breaks loose. Away with

Hinweg mit ihm, der seine Seele bloß
Und ihre Götter gibt, verwegen
Unauszusprechendes aussprechen will,
Und sein gefährlich Gut, als wär es Wasser,
Verschüttet und vergeudet; schlimmer ist's,
Wie Mord, und du, du redest für diesen?
Beschwätzen möchtest du Notwendiges?
Bescheide dich! Sein Schicksal ist's. Er hat
Es sich gemacht, und sterben soll,
Vergehn, wie er, in Weh und Torheit jeder,
Der Göttliches verrät, und allverkehrend
Verborgenherrschendes
In Menschenhände liefert!
Er muß hinab!

MEKADES: So teuer büßen muß er, der sein Bestes
    Aus voller Seele Sterblichen vertraut?

HERMOKRATES: Er mag es, doch es bleibt die Nemesis
    Nicht aus. Mag große Worte sagen, mag
    Entwürdigen das keuschverschwiegne Leben,
    Ans Tageslicht das Gold der Tiefe ziehn;
    Er mag es brauchen, was zum Brauche nicht
    Den Sterblichen gegeben ist, ihn wird's
    Zuvor zugrunde richten; hat es ihm

him who would lay bare his soul and his soul's gods, recklessly seeks to utter the unutterable, squanders and spills his dangerous wealth as though it were water. Why, it is worse than murder, and you of all men, you plead for him? With idle chatter hope to cheat the inevitable? Resign yourself! It is his fate. He's brought it on himself; and die like him, perish in pain and folly shall every man who betrays the divine and, all-perverting, delivers up into human hands that which rules us in secret! He shall not live!

MECADES: So dear, then, must he pay who in the fullness of his soul entrusts the best he has to mortals?

HERMOCRATES: He may, but Nemesis, too, infallibly will come. May speak great words and may dishonour life that was ever chastely veiled in silence, raise to the light of day the gold of the deeps; he may make use of that which is not given to mortals for their use, yet it will be his

Den Sinn nicht schon verwirrt? ist ihm
Bei seinem Volke denn die volle Seele?
Die Zärtliche, wie ist sie nun verwildert!
Wie ist er nun ein Eigenmächtiger
Geworden, dieser Allmitteilende,
Der gütge Mann! wie ist er so verwandelt
Zum Frechen, der wie seiner Hände Spiel
Die Götter und die Menschen achtet.

MEKADES: Du redest schrecklich, Priester, und es dünkt
Dein dunkel Wort mir wahr. Es sei!
Du hast zum Werke mich. Nur weiß ich nicht,
Wo er zu fassen ist. Es sei der Mann
So groß er will, zu richten ist nicht schwer;
Doch mächtig sein des Übermächtigen,
Der wie ein Zauberer die Menge leitet,
Es dünkt ein andres mir, Hermokrates.

HERMOKRATES:
Gebrechlich ist sein Zauber, Kind, und leichter,
Denn nötig ist, hat er es uns bereitet.
Es wandte zur gelegnen Stunde sich
Sein Unmut um, der stolze, stillempörte Sinn
Befeindet jetzt sich selber, hätt' er auch
Die Macht, er achtet's nicht, er trauert nur

downfall long before. Has it not confused his mind already? Is his entire
soul his to give to the people? Oh, how that tender soul has run to
waste! And he become a law unto himself whose one desire was to com-
municate all, kind as he is! How utterly insolent he's grown, who now
regards both gods and men as playthings for his hands.

MECADES: Priest, you speak terribly, and your dark words seem true to
me. So be it, then! You may depend on me. My only doubt is how we
should set about it. Let a man be never so great, to judge him is not hard;
but to prevail against a man supreme, who sways the multitude like some
magician, that is another thing, Hermocrates.

HERMOCRATES: Frail is his magic, child, and he has made it easier for us
than he need have done. At a moment most opportune his anger turned,
and now his proud, quietly indignant mind makes war on itself; even
if he had the power, he would not notice it, but only mourns, sees noth-

Und siehet seinen Fall, er sucht
Rückkehrend das verlorne Leben,
Den Gott, den er aus sich hinweggeschwätzt.
Versammle mir das Volk; ich klag' ihn an,
Ruf' über ihn den Fluch; erschrecken sollen sie
Vor ihrem Abgott, sollen ihn
Hinaus verstoßen in die Wildnis,
Und nimmer wiederkehrend soll er dort
Mir's büßen, daß er mehr, wie sich gebührt,
Verkündiget den Sterblichen.

MEKADES: Doch wes beschuldigest du ihn?

HERMOKRATES: Die Worte, so du mir genannt,
Sie sind genug.

MEKADES: Mit dieser schwachen Klage
Willst du das Volk ihm von der Seele ziehn?

HERMOKRATES: Zu rechter Zeit hat jede Klage Kraft
Und nicht gering ist diese.

MEKADES: Und klagtest du des Mords ihn an vor ihnen,
Es wirkte nichts.

ing but his downfall, and turns back to look for the life he has lost, the god he has driven out of himself by his prattling. Assemble the people for me, I shall accuse him, pronounce the curse upon him, and they shall be horrified by their idol, shall drive him out into the wilderness, and, never again returning, there he will do penance for having proclaimed more than is fitting for mortals.

MECADES: But what will you charge him with?

HERMOCRATES: The words you told me just now; they will suffice.

MECADES: What, with this feeble charge you hope to wean the people from his spirit?

HERMOCRATES: Any accusation has force enough – at the right time; and this one is not slight.

MECADES: Though you were to accuse him of murder in their presence, it would have no effect.

HERMOKRATES: Dies eben ist's! die offenbare Tat
Vergeben sie, die Aberglaubigen,
Unsichtbar Ärgernis muß es sein, ins Auge muß es
Sie treffen; das bewegt die Blöden.

MEKADES: Es hängt ihr Herz an ihm, das bändigest,
Das lenkst du nicht so leicht! Sie lieben ihn!

HERMOKRATES: Sie lieben ihn? ja wohl! solang er blüht'
Und glänzt' ...
... naschen sie.
Was sollen sie mit ihm, nun er
Verdüstert ist, verödet? Da ist nichts,
Was nützen könnt und ihre lange Zeit
Verkürzen, abgeerntet ist das Feld,
Verlassen liegt's und nach Gefallen gehn
Die Stürme drüber hin und unsre Pfade.

MEKADES: Empör ihn nur! empör ihn! siehe zu!

HERMOKRATES: Ich hoffe, Mekades! er ist geduldig.

MEKADES: So wird sie der Geduldige gewinnen!

HERMOKRATES: Nichts weniger!

MEKADES: Du achtest nichts, so wirst du dich
Und mich und ihn und alles noch verderben.

HERMOCRATES: Precisely! the flagrant act they will forgive, those super-
stitious ones; so it must be invisible, yet hit them in the eye: that will
move the timid crowd.

MECADES: Their hearts are attached to him; these you will not tame and
guide so easily! They love him!

HERMOCRATES: They love him? Yes, indeed, as long as he thrives and
shines. ... What use have they for him now he is darkened, desolate?
Now there is nothing they can get out of him and while away their bore-
dom; that field has been despoiled, it lies abandoned, and gales are free to
cross it – and our paths.

MECADES: Incite him, then, incite him; see what happens!

HERMOCRATES: I hope, Mecades, that he will prove patient.

MECADES: In that case it's his patience that will win them.

HERMOCRATES: Never!

MECADES: You pay no heed to anything, and so will ruin me and him and
all our projects.

HERMOKRATES: Das Träumen und das Schäumen
  Der Sterblichen, ich acht' es wahrlich nicht!
  Sie möchten Götter sein und huldigen
  Wie Göttern sich, und eine Weile dauert's!
  Sorgst du, es möchte sie der Leidende
  Gewinnen, der Geduldige?
  Empören wird er gegen sich die Toren,
  An seinem Leide werden sie den teuern
  Betrug erkennen, werden unbarmherzig
  Ihm's danken, daß der Angebetete
  Doch auch ein Schwacher ist, und ihm
  Geschiehet recht, warum bemengt er sich
  Mit ihnen.
MEKADES: Ich wollt', ich wär aus dieser Sache, Priester!
HERMOKRATES: Vertraue mir und scheue nicht, was not ist.
MEKADES: Dort kömmt er. Suche nur dich selbst,
  Du irrer Geist! indes verlierst du alles.
HERMOKRATES: Laß ihn! hinweg!

HERMOCRATES: The dreaming and the scheming of mortals – quite true,
I do not heed it! Gods they would like to be, and as to gods pay homage
to themselves, and for a while it lasts! Are you afraid the suffering man
will sway them, or the patient? No, but to fury he will rouse the fools,
and by his suffering they'll recognize the rare imposture, mercilessly pay
their idol back for being weak as they are; and it serves him right, for
getting involved with them.
MECADES: I wish I were well out of this business, priest!
HERMOCRATES: Rely on me, and do not shun what must be.
MECADES: There he comes. – Go on, then, seek yourself, you spirit astray,
and meanwhile you lose all.
HERMOCRATES: Leave him alone! Away!

## ZWEITER AUFTRITT

EMPEDOKLES: In meine Stille kamst du leisewandelnd,
Fandst drinnen in der Halle Dunkel mich aus,
Du Freundlicher! du kamst nicht unverhofft,
Und fernher, wirkend über der Erde, vernahm
Ich wohl dein Wiederkehren, schöner Tag!
Und meine Vertrauten, euch, ihr schnellgeschäftgen
Kräfte der Höh! – und nahe seid auch ihr
Mir wieder, seid wie sonst, ihr Glücklichen,
Ihr irrelosen Bäume meines Hains!
Ihr ruhetet und wuchst und täglich tränkt'
Des Himmels Quelle die Bescheidenen
Mit Licht, und Lebensfunken sät' der Äther
Befruchtend auf die Blühenden aus!
O innige Natur! ich habe dich
Vor Augen, kennest du den Freund noch,
Den Hochgeliebten, kennest du mich nimmer,
Den Priester, der lebendigen Gesang,
Wie frohvergossnes Opferblut, dir brachte?
O bei den heil'gen Brunnen,
Wo Wasser aus Adern der Erde

## SCENE TWO

EMPEDOCLES: Into my stillness quietly wandering you came, deep in the darkness of the hall you sought me out, you kindly one! Nor yet un-hoped for you came, but from the distance active above the earth clearly I heard you returning, glorious Day! And you my familiars, you the quick industrious Powers of the Heights! – and you are near to me again, as once you were, you happy ones, you the unalterable trees of my grove! You rested and you grew, and Heaven's source daily watered the undemanding ones with light, and vital sparks did Aether, life-giving, scatter upon the blossoming! O inmost Nature! close to my eyes again, do you still know your friend, the fondly loved, do you no longer know me, the priest who offered you living song like a glad sacri-fice of votive blood? Oh, by the sacred springs where waters from the veins of Earth collect and the thirsty refresh themselves on summer days

Sich sammeln, und die Dürstenden
Am heißen Tage sich erquicken auch in mir,
In mir, ihr Quellen des Lebens, strömtet
Aus Tiefen der Welt ihr einst
Zusammen, und es kamen
Die Dürstenden zu mir – wie ist's denn nun?
Vertrauert? bin ich ganz allein?
Und ist es Nacht hier außen auch am Tage?
Der höher, denn ein sterblich Auge, sah,
Der Blindgeschlagne tastet nun umher,
... und wandeln soll
Er nun so fort, der Langverwöhnte,
Der selig oft mit allen Lebenden
Ihr Leben, ach! in heilig schöner Zeit,
Sie wie das Herz gefühlt von einer Welt
Und ihren königlichen Götterkräften!
Verdammt in seiner Seele soll er nun
Dahingehn, ausgestoßen? freundlos er,
Der Götterfreund? an seinem Nichts
Und seiner Nacht sich weiden immerdar,
Unduldbares duldend, gleich den Schwächlingen, die
Ans Tagewerk im scheuen Tartarus
Geschmiedet sind. Was, daherab bin ich
Gekommen? Um nichts? ha! Eines,

– in me also, in me, you sources of life, from the depths of the world once you welled up and merged, and the thirsty came to me – how is it now? All saddened? and all alone? And is it night out here in daytime too? He who looked higher than ever did mortal eye, now blinded gropes about and evermore is to wander thus, who long was spoilt, who blissful often with all the living in holy and happy days felt their life, ah, felt it as the heart of a whole world and of its regal Powers, the Powers of gods. Damned in his soul, is he now to perish, an outcast wholly friendless he, who was the friend of gods? For ever feast upon his nothingness, his night, suffer the insufferable like those weaklings welded to their daily toil in the wastes of Tartarus? What, am I come to this? For no reason? Yet one thing, one thing you could not take from me! Fool, for

Eins mußtet ihr mir lassen! Tor, bist du
Derselbe doch und träumst, als wärest du
Ein Schwacher. Einmal noch! noch Einmal
Soll mir's lebendig werden, und ich will's!
Fluch oder Segen! Täusche nur die Kraft,
Demütiger, dir nimmer aus dem Busen!
Weit will ich's um mich machen, tagen soll's
Von eigner Flamme mir! Du sollst
Zufrieden werden, armer Geist,
Gefangener! sollst frei und groß und reich
In eigner Welt dich fühlen! –
Weh! einsam! einsam! einsam!
Und nimmer find ich
Euch, meine Götter,
Und nimmer kehr ich
Zu deinem Leben, Natur!
Dein Geächteter! weh! hab ich doch auch
Dein nicht geachtet, dein
Mich überhoben; hast du einst
Umfangend doch mit den warmen Fittichen,
Du Zärtliche, mich vom Schlafe gerettet,
Den Törigen? ihn
Mitleidig schmeichelnd zu deinem Nektar
Gelockt, damit er trank und wuchs

you are the same and only dream that you are feeble. Once more, but
once again it shall become alive for me, and that's my will! A curse or a
blessing! Else, humble one, remain what you are and never beguile the
strength to spring from your heart! I will have space about me, it shall
be day though my own flame illumines it! You shall be satisfied, poor
spirit, prisoner! Free, great, and rich you shall feel in your own world! –
Oh, lonely, lonely, lonely. And nevermore I can find you, my gods, and,
Nature, never return to your life! Your exile, woe! And why did I not
heed you, raised myself above you, though once enclosing me in your
warm wings, your tenderness saved me from sleep, fool that I am! Com-
passionately flattering you lured him to your nectar that he might drink

Und blüht', und mächtig geworden und trunken
Dir nun ungestraft höhnt – O Geist,
Geist, der mich groß gemacht! du hast
Dir deinen Herrn, hast, alter Saturn!
Dir einen neuen Jupiter
Gezogen, einen schwächern nur und frechern.
Denn schmähen kann die böse Zunge dich nur.
Ist nirgend ein Rächer, und muß ich denn allein
Den Hohn und Fluch in meine Seele sagen?
Muß einsam sein? auch so?

### DRITTER AUFTRITT
*Pausanias. Empedokles*

. . . . .

EMPEDOKLES: Ich fühle nun des Tages Neige, Freund!
Und dunkel will es werden mir und kalt!
Es gehet rückwärts, Lieber! nicht zur Ruh,
Wie wenn der beutefrohe Vogel sich
Das Haupt verhüllt zu frischerwachendem
Zufriednem Schlummer, anders ist's mit mir!
Erspare mir die Klage! laß es mir!

and grow and bloom, and grown strong and drunken, mock you now
with impunity – O spirit, spirit that made me great, you have reared
your own master, an aged Saturn have reared a new Jupiter for yourself,
only a feeble one, and more insolent, who can only revile you with his
malicious tongue. Is there no avenger anywhere, and must I then pour all
this scorn and execration into my own soul, unaided? Must I be lonely?
Even there?

### SCENE THREE
*Pausanias, Empedocles*

. . . . .

EMPEDOCLES: I feel the day declining now, my friend. And it grows dark
for me, and cold! A lapse it is, dear friend, a lapse not into rest, as when
the bird well pleased with the day's booty covers his head for freshly
wakening, contented slumber; different it is with me! But spare me the
complaint! Leave it unspoken!

57

.....

PAUSANIAS: ... Ich faß es nicht.

Sehr fremde bist du mir geworden,
Mein Empedokles! Kennest du mich nicht?
Und kenn ich nimmer dich,
Du Herrlicher? konntest so
Zum Rätsel werden, edel Angesicht,
Und so zur Erde beugen darf der Gram
Die Lieblinge des Himmels? Bist du denn
Es nicht? Und sieh! wir danken dir es alle,
Und so in goldner Freude mächtig war
Kein anderer, wie du, in seinem Volke.

EMPEDOKLES: Sie ehren mich? o sag es ihnen doch,
Sie sollen's lassen. Übel steht
Der Schmuck um eine finstre Stirne
Mir an, und welkt doch auch
Das grüne Laub dem ausgerissnen Stamme!

PAUSANIAS: Noch stehst du ja und frisch Gewässer spielt
Um deine Wurzel dir, es atmet mild
Um deine Gipfel nicht Vergängliches.
Und nähren dich die Götterkräfte denn nicht?

EMPEDOKLES: Du mahnest mich der Jugendtage, Lieber!

PAUSANIAS: Noch schöner dünkt des Lebens Mitte mir.

.....

PAUSANIAS: ... I cannot grasp it. You have grown strange to me, Empedocles, strange and remote. Do you not know me now? And do I no longer know you, most glorious one? Could you become such an enigma to me, noble countenance, and thus down to earth may sorrow bow the darlings of Heaven? Are you, then, not he? And, look, we thank you for it, all of us, and none in golden joy was ever mighty as you were, to his people.

EMPEDOCLES: They honour me, you say? Oh, tell them, then, tell them to cease. Ill-befitting around a dark brow is the ornament to me, and do not green leaves wither on the uprooted trunk?

PAUSANIAS: But still you stand and crystal waters play about your roots; and mildly too what is imperishable breathes about your crests. And are you not nourished by the powers of gods?

EMPEDOCLES: It is my youth you call to mind, dear friend.

PAUSANIAS: The noon of life seems lovelier still to me.

EMPEDOKLES: Und gerne sehen, wenn es nun
Hinab sich neigen will, die Augen
Der Schnellhinschwindenden noch einmal
Zurück. O jene Zeit!
Ihr Liebeswonnen, da die Seele mir
Von Göttern, wie Endymion, geweckt,
Die kindlich schlummernde, sich öffnete,
Lebendig sie, die Immerjugendlichen,
Des Lebens große Genien empfand.
O schöne Sonne! Menschen hatten mich
Es nicht gelehrt, mich trieb unsterblich liebend
Mein heilig Herz Unsterblichem entgegen,
Entgegen dir! ich konnte Göttlichers
Nicht finden, stilles Licht! und so wie du
Das Leben nicht an deinem Tage sparst
Und sorgenfrei und froh, du Glückliches!
Der goldnen Fülle dich
Entledigest, so gönnt auch ich, der Deine,
Die beste Seele gern
Den Sterblichen und furchtlos offen gab
Mein Herz, wie du, der ernsten Erde sich,
Der schicksalvollen; ach! ihr treu zu bleiben,
Gelobt ich, und in Jünglingsfreude ihr
Mein Leben so zu eignen bis zuletzt.

EMPEDOCLES: And gladly, now that soon it will decline, do we, the swiftly evanescent, turn back our eyes once more. O time of youth! Your ecstasies of love when by the gods my spirit, like Endymion, was awakened, and after childlike sleep was opened up, alive, responded to the ever-youthful, the genii of Life in their magnificence. Beautiful sun! It was not men that taught me, but my own holy heart, immortally loving, impelled me towards the Immortal; and towards you! I could find nothing here more god-like, silent light! And just as you never stint life in your full day, but free from care and joyful, fortunate one, expend your golden wealth, so I, your own, was glad to lavish the best of souls on mortals, and, fearlessly open, my heart, like yours, devoted itself to serious Earth, the fateful; and, alas, I vowed to be loyal to her and, a youth, ever to dedicate my life to her as now. And often I affirmed it at the trysting hour,

Ich sagt ihr's oft in trauter Stunde zu,
Band so den teuern Todesbund mit ihr.
Dann rauscht' es anders, denn zuvor, im Hain,
Und zärtlich tönten ihrer Berge Quellen –
Und ihrer Liebe Blumen gab sie mir;
Mit ihren Zweigen
Umschlang sie mir das Haupt. –
PAUSANIAS: Ach solche Jugend! Vom Gedanken glänzt
Das Auge dem Trauernden noch auf.
EMPEDOKLES: All deine Freuden, Erde! wahr, wie sie,
Und warm und voll, aus Müh' und Liebe reifen,
Sie alle gabst du mir. Und wenn ich oft
Auf stiller Bergeshöhe saß und staunend
Der Menschen wechselnd Irrsal übersann,
Zu tief von deinen Wandlungen ergriffen,
Und nah mein eignes Welken ahndete,
Dann atmete der Äther, so wie dir,
Mir heilend um die liebeswunde Brust,
Und, wie Gewölk der Flamme, lösten
Gereiniget die Sorgen mir sich auf,
Im hohen Blau.
PAUSANIAS: O Sohn des Himmels!


thus knotting fast the dear bond of death. Then through this grove a
different rustle ran, and tenderly her mountain sources murmured – and
her love's flowers she gave to me, and wound her slender branches
around my head.
PAUSANIAS: Such was that youth that even now his eye gleams through
his sadness at the thought of it.
EMPEDOCLES: Yes, all your pleasures, Earth, which true, as she, and
warm and full, through toil and love mature, all these you gave to me.
And often when on some calm mountain top I sat and, marvelling, re-
flected on the mutable ways of men, too deeply troubled by your trans-
formations, and felt the nearness of my own sere age, then Aether
breathed around me, as on you, a healing balm to soothe the wounds of
love and, like the fire's clouds, my griefs rose up and, purified, dissolved
in the celestial blue.
PAUSANIAS: O son of Heaven!

EMPEDOKLES: Ich war es, ja! und möcht' es nun erzählen,
Ich Armer! möcht es einmal noch
Mir in die Seele rufen,
Das Wirken deiner Geniuskräfte,
Der herrlichen, deren Genoss ich war, o Natur!
Daß mir die stumme, todesöde Brust
Von deinen Tönen allen widerklänge!
Bin ich es noch? o Leben! und rauschten sie,
All deine geflügelten Melodien, und hört
Ich deinen alten Einklang, große Natur?
Ach! ich, der Einsame, lebt ich nicht
Mit dieser heilgen Erd' und diesem Licht
Und dir, von dem die Seele nimmer läßt,
O Vater Äther! und mit allen Lebenden,
Der Götterfreund, im gegenwärtigen
Olymp? Ich bin hinausgeworfen, bin
Ganz einsam, und das Weh ist nun
Mein Tagsgefährt' und Schlafgenosse mir.
Bei mir ist nicht der Segen, geh!
Geh! frage nicht! denkst du, ich trauere?
O sieh mich an, und wundre des dich nicht,
Du Guter, daß ich daherab
Gekommen bin; des Himmels Söhnen ist,

EMPEDOCLES: I was, indeed, and now would tell the story, wretch that I
am, once more recall it to my soul, the working of those spiritual
Powers, the glorious, whose companion I was, O Nature! O that my
dumb breast, desolate as death, could now re-echo all your various
music! Am I that still? O Life! and did they sound, all your winged
melodies, and did I hear that pristine harmony, O Nature? Ah, did not I,
the lonely, live with this holy Earth, and with this light, and you, from
whom the soul can never bear to be parted, O Father Aether! and with
all the living – I, the friend of gods, familiar in Olympus? But they have
cast me out, and I am utterly alone, and woe's my playmate and my bed-
fellow. Leave me, I have no blessing to bestow! Ask me no questions,
leave me! Do you think I mourn? Oh, look at me, and do not wonder,
kindly friend, to see how far I'm fallen: for to the sons of Heaven, if

Wenn überglücklich sie geworden sind,
Ein eigner Fluch beschieden.

PAUSANIAS: Weh! solche Reden! Du? ich duld' es nicht,
Du solltest so die Seele dir und mir
Nicht ängstigen. Ein böses Zeichen dünkt
Es mir, wenn so der Geist, der immerfrohe, sich
Der Mächtigen umwölket.

EMPEDOKLES: Fühlst du's? Es deutet, daß er bald
Zur Erd' hinab im Ungewitter muß.

PAUSANIAS: O laß den Unmut, Lieber!
Was tat er euch, o dieser Reine,
Daß ihm die Seele so verfinstert ist?
Ihr Todesgötter! haben die Sterblichen denn
Kein Eigenes nirgendswo, und reicht
Das Furchtbare denn ihnen bis ans Herz
Und herrscht es in der Brust der Stärkeren noch,
Das ewige Schicksal? Bändige den Gram
Und übe deine Macht; bist du es doch,
Der mehr vermag' denn andere; o sieh
An meiner Liebe, wer du bist,
Und denke dein, und lebe!

EMPEDOKLES:
Du kennest mich und dich und Tod und Leben nicht.

they have known excess of joy and fortune, peculiar doom has been
allotted.

PAUSANIAS: Such words from you? I will not suffer it. You should not
trouble your soul and mine with such speeches. It seems a bad omen to
me when the ever-serene spirit of the mighty is thus beclouded.

EMPEDOCLES: You sense it, then? What it portends is that soon it must
come down to earth in a thunderstorm.

PAUSANIAS: Enough of this despondency, dear friend! You gods of
death, what did this pure one do to you to have called down such dark-
ness on his soul? Have mortals, then, no refuge of their own, not any-
where, and does the terrible power's scope extend into their very hearts?
And does it rule the feelings of the stronger even, eternal Fate? Control
this sorrow, and assert your strength. For it is you, you, who can do
more than others. See in my love the proof of what you are, remember
yourself, and live!

EMPEDOCLES: You do not know me, nor yourself, nor life, nor death.

PAUSANIAS: Den Tod, ich kenn' ihn wenig nur,
    Denn wenig dacht' ich sein.
EMPEDOKLES: Allein zu sein und ohne Götter, ist der Tod!
PAUSANIAS: Laß ihn, ich kenne *dich*, an deinen Taten
    Erkannt' ich dich, in seiner Macht
    Erfuhr ich deinen Geist und seine Welt,
    Wenn oft ein Wort von dir
    Im heil'gen Augenblick
    Das Leben vieler Jahre mir erschuf,
    Daß eine neue große Zeit von da
    Dem Jünglinge begann. Wie zahmen Hirschen,
    Wenn ferne rauscht der Wald und sie
    Der Heimat denken, schlug das Herz mir oft,
    Wenn du vom Glück der alten Urwelt sprachst,
    Der reinen Tage kundig, und dir lag
    Das ganze Schicksal offen; zeichnetest
    Du nicht der Zukunft große Linien
    Mir vor das Auge, sichern Blicks, wie Künstler
    Ein fehlend Glied zum ganzen Bilde reihn?
    Und kennst du nicht die Kräfte der Natur,
    Daß du vertraulich, wie kein Sterblicher,
    Sie, wie du willst, in stiller Herrschaft lenkst?

PAUSANIAS: Death I know little, for I have given it little thought.
EMPEDOCLES: To be alone and without gods is death!
PAUSANIAS: Forget about it. I know *you*, and by your deeds I recognized you, by its power experienced your spirit and its world, when often a word from you in one holy moment created the life of many years for me, so that at once a new great era began for the youth I was. Often my heart would pound like the hearts of tame stags when distantly the forest rustles and they recall their home, when of the old primeval world you spoke, versed in the lore of those pure days, and all of destiny lay open to your mind. Did you not draw the great lines of the future for me to scan, your vision sure, as artists add the one detail that will make the picture whole? Are you not intimate with the Powers of Nature, so that, more learned than ever mortal was, with silent power you rule them as you please?

EMPEDOKLES: Recht! Alles weiß ich, alles kann ich meistern;
Wie meiner Hände Werk, erkenn ich es
Durchaus und lenke, wie ich will,
Ein Herr der Geister, das Lebendige.
Mein ist die Welt und untertan und dienstbar
Sind alle Kräfte mir ...
... zur Magd ist mir
Die herrnbedürftige Natur geworden,
Und hat sie Ehre noch, so ist's von mir.
Was wäre denn der Himmel und das Meer
Und Inseln und Gestirn und was vor Augen
Den Menschen alles liegt, was wär es auch,
Dies tote Saitenspiel, gäb ich ihm Ton
Und Sprach und Seele nicht? was sind
Die Götter und ihr Geist, wenn ich sie nicht
Verkündige. Nun! Sage, wer bin ich?
PAUSANIAS: Verhöhne nur im Unmut dich und alles,
Was Menschen herrlich macht,
Ihr Wirken und ihr Wort, verleide mir
Den Mut im Busen, schröcke mich zurück,
O sprich es nur heraus! du hassest dich
Und was dich liebt und was dir gleichen möcht'.

EMPEDOCLES: Quite true! I know all things, can master all; like my own
handiwork I know them thoroughly, a lord of spirits, govern as I please
whatever lives. The world is mine, all Powers submissive and sub-
servient to my will, ... Nature herself, so much in need of masters, is
now my servant girl, and, if she has any dignity left, owes it to me alone.
And what, indeed, would Heaven be and the Ocean and the islands and
the stars and all that's set before the eyes of mortals, what would it be,
this dead stringed instrument, did I not lend it music and eloquence and
soul? What are the gods, and what their spirit, if I do not proclaim
them? Well? Now tell me: who am I?
PAUSANIAS: Go on then, out of mere ill-humour, scoff at all that makes
men glorious, their actions and their words, make me ashamed of my
own courage, cow me. Oh, say it all, and freely! You hate yourself, and
those that love you and those whose dearest wish is to be like you. Your

Ein anders willst du, denn du bist, genügst dir
In deiner Ehre nicht, du willst nicht bleiben, willst
Zugrunde gehen?
EMPEDOKLES: Unschuldiger!
PAUSANIAS: Und dich verklagst du?
EMPEDOKLES [*mit Ruhe*]: Wirken soll der Mensch,
    Der sinnende, soll entfaltend
    Das Leben um ihn fördern und heitern.
                              Denn hoher Bedeutung voll,
    Voll schweigender Kraft umfängt
    Den Ahnenden, daß er bilde,
    Die große Natur.
    Daß ihren Geist hervor er rufe, trägt
    Die Sorg' im Busen und die Hoffnung
    Der Mensch. Tiefwurzelnd strebt
    Das gewaltige Sehnen in ihm auf.
    Und viel vermag er; und herrlich ist
    Sein Wort, er wandelt die Welt
    Und unter den Händen ...
    .....

will is something other than what you are, your eminence does not
satisfy you, you do not wish to stay, but wish to perish?
EMPEDOCLES: You innocent!
PAUSANIAS: And you accuse yourself?
EMPEDOCLES [*calmly*]: The business of man, the pondering, is to work
upon what he finds, unfolding to promote and brighten the life around
him. For full of high significance, full of inarticulate power, great
Nature embraces foreknowing man, calling on him to impose order and
form. So that he will evoke her spirit, man bears grief and hope in his
heart. Deep-rooted, a mighty longing aspires within him. And there is
much he can do; and glorious is his word, he transforms the world, and
under his hands ...

## DER PRINZESSIN AUGUSTE VON HOMBURG
Den 28ten Nov. 1799

Noch freundlichzögernd scheidet vom Auge dir
  Das Jahr, und in hesperischer Milde glänzt
    Der Winterhimmel über deinen
      Gärten, den dichtrischen, immergrünen.

Und da ich deines Festes gedacht' und sann,
  Was ich dir dankend reichte, da weilten noch
    Am Pfade Blumen, daß sie dir zur
      Blühenden Krone, du Edle, würden.

Doch Andres beut dir, Größeres, hoher Geist!
  Die festlichere Zeit, denn es hallt hinab
    Am Berge das Gewitter, sieh! und
      Klar, wie die ruhigen Sterne, gehen

Aus langem Zweifel reine Gestalten auf;
  So dünkt es mir; und einsam, o Fürstin! ist
    Das Herz der Freigebornen wohl nicht
      Länger im eigenen Glück; denn würdig

## TO PRINCESS AUGUSTA OF HOMBURG
28 November 1799

Still kindly lingering, the year departs from your eyes, and in hesperian mildness the winter sky glimmers above your gardens, the poetic, the evergreen.

And as I remembered your birthday and wondered what token of thanks I might give you, still flowers remained on the wayside, to fashion a blossoming crown for you, noble one.

But other things, greater things does the more festive time offer you, lofty spirit, for on the mountain-side the thunderstorm rumbles down and, look! as clear as the tranquil stars

Out of long doubt pure apparitions arise; so it seems to me; and no longer, I think, Princess, shall the heart of the free-born be lonely in his own good fortune; for worthily

Gesellt im Lorbeer ihm der Heroe sich,
    Der schöngereifte, echte; die Weisen auch,
        Die Unsern sind es wert; sie blicken
           Still aus der Höhe des Lebens, die ernsten Alten.

Geringe dünkt der träumende Sänger sich,
    Und Kindern gleich am müßigen Saitenspiel,
        Wenn ihn der Edlen Glück, wenn ihn die
           Tat und der Ernst der Gewalt'gen aufweckt.

Doch herrlicht mir dein Name das Lied; dein Fest
    Augusta! durft' ich feiern; Beruf ist mirs,
        Zu rühmen Höhers, darum gab die
           Sprache der Gott und den Dank ins Herz mir.

O daß von diesem freudigen Tage mir
    Auch meine Zeit beginne, daß endlich auch
        Mir ein Gesang in deinen Hainen,
           Edle! gedeihe, der deiner wert sei.

Now he is joined by the hero wearing the laurel wreath, him who happily has matured, the true one; the sages, too, our sages are worthy; silently they gaze from the peak of life, the grave old men.

Very small the dreaming singer thinks himself, and child-like at his idle lyre, when the good fortune of the noble, the deeds and seriousness of the mighty rouse him.

Yet to me your name adds glory to my song; it was my right, Augusta, to celebrate your festive day. I consider it my vocation to praise what is higher than I; for that the God gave me speech and put gratitude in my heart.

Oh that from this joyful day my time too might begin, that at last a song of mine, noble one, too might thrive in your orchards, a song that is worthy of you.

Geh' unter, schöne Sonne, sie achteten
   Nur wenig dein, sie kannten dich, Heilge, nicht,
      Denn mühelos und stille bist du
         Über den mühsamen aufgegangen.

Mir gehst du freundlich unter und auf, o Licht!
   Und wohl erkennt mein Auge dich, herrliches!
      Denn göttlich stille ehren lernt' ich
         Da Diotima den Sinn mir heilte.

O du des Himmels Botin! wie lauscht ich dir!
   Dir, Diotima! Liebe! wie sah von dir
      Zum goldnen Tage dieses Auge
         Glänzend und dankend empor. Da rauschten

Lebendiger die Quellen, es atmeten
   Der dunkeln Erde Blüten mich liebend an,
      Und lächelnd über Silberwolken
         Neigte sich segnend herab der Äther.

Go down, then, lovely sun, for but little they regarded you, nor, holy one, knew your worth, since without toil you rose, in silence, over a people for ever toiling.

To me, however, kindly you rise and set, O glorious light, and brightly my eyes respond, for godlike, silent reverence I learned when Diotima soothed my frenzy.

Oh how I listened, Heaven's own messenger, to you, beloved one! How to the golden day these eyes looked up from gazing at you, so that more living

The brooks began to purl, so that lovingly the blossoms of dark Earth seemed to breathe on me, and through the silver clouds a smiling Aether bowed down to bestow his blessing.

## DER FRIEDEN

W ɪ ᴇ wenn die alten Wasser, die ...
... in andern Zorn,
 In schröcklichern verwandelt wieder
  Kämen, zu reinigen, da es not war,

So gählt und wuchs und wogte von Jahr zu Jahr
 Rastlos und überschwemmte das bange Land
  Die unerhörte Schlacht, daß weit hüllt
   Dunkel und Blässe das Haupt der Menschen.

Die Heldenkräfte flogen, wie Wellen, auf
 Und schwanden weg, du kürztest, o Rächerin!
  Den Dienern oft die Arbeit schnell und
   Brachtest in Ruhe sie heim, die Streiter.

O du, die unerbittlich und unbesiegt
 Den Feigen und den Übergewaltgen trifft,
  Daß bis ins letzte Glied hinab vom
   Schlage sein armes Geschlecht erzittert,

## PEACE

As though the ancient waters, ... changed into different, more terrible anger, now were returning to purify, since that was needed,
 So this unheard-of battle billowed and grew and swelled incessantly from year to year and flooded the awe-struck land, so that far and wide darkness and pallor shrouded the heads of men.
 The prowess of heroes surged up like waves and dwindled away; you, the avenging goddess, often cut short your servants' labour and quietly brought them back home, these warriors.
 O you who still inexorable and unvanquished strike both the coward and the too violent, so that to its last limb his poor lineage quivers with the blow,

Die du geheim den Stachel und Zügel hältst,
Zu hemmen und zu fördern, o Nemesis,
  Strafst du die Toten noch, es schliefen
    Unter Italiens Lorbeergärten

Sonst ungestört die alten Eroberer.
  Und schonst du auch des müßigen Hirten nicht,
    Und haben endlich wohl genug den
      Üppigen Schlummer gebüßt die Völker?

Wer hub es an? wer brachte den Fluch? von heut
Ists nicht und nicht von gestern, und die zuerst
  Das Maß verloren, unsre Väter
    Wußten es nicht, und es trieb ihr Geist sie.

Zu lang, zu lang schon treten die Sterblichen
  Sich gern aufs Haupt, und zanken um Herrschaft sich,
    Den Nachbar fürchtend, und es hat auf
      Eigenem Boden der Mann nicht Segen.

Und unstät wehn und irren, dem Chaos gleich,
  Dem gärenden Geschlechte die Wünsche noch
    Umher und wild ist und verzagt und kalt von
      Sorgen das Leben der Armen immer.

You who in secret hold both the goad and the rein, to hold back and drive on, O Nemesis, do you punish even the dead? Once undisturbed the old conquerors
Slept beneath Italy's laurel groves. And do you not spare the idle shepherd, and have the peoples at last done penance enough for their voluptuous slumber?
Who started it? Who brought us the curse? Neither today nor yesterday it arose, and those who first overstepped the bounds, our fathers, did not know it, driven to it by their spirit.
Too long, too long now mortals have delighted in treading on others' heads, and struggled for mastery, fearing their neighbours; and on his own soil a man can find no blessing.
And, chaos-like, inconstantly still the desires of this turbulent race whirl and stray about, and savage and disheartened and cold with cares the lives of these wretches remain.

Du aber wandelst ruhig die sichre Bahn,
   O Mutter Erd im Lichte. Dein Frühling blüht,
      Melodischwechselnd gehn dir hin die
         Wachsenden Zeiten, du Lebensreiche!

Komm du nun, du der heiligen Musen all,
   Und der Gestirne Liebling, verjüngender
      Ersehnter Friede, komm und gib ein
         Bleiben im Leben, ein Herz uns wieder.

Unschuldiger! sind klüger die Kinder doch
   Beinahe, denn wir Alten; es irrt der Zwist
      Den Guten nicht den Sinn, und klar und
         Freudig ist ihnen ihr Auge blieben.

Und wie mit andern Schauenden lächelnd ernst
   Der Richter auf der Jünglinge Rennbahn sieht,
      Wo glühender die Kämpfenden die
         Wagen in stäubende Wolken treiben,

So steht und lächelt Helios über uns
   Und einsam ist der Göttliche, Frohe nie,
      Denn ewig wohnen sie, des Äthers
         Blühende Sterne, die Heiligfreien.

---

But you, O Mother Earth, in the light calmly pursue your steady course. Your springtime flowers, melodiously changing your seasons grow and pass, you that are rich in life!

Now come, belovèd of all the Muses and of the constellations, long-sought rejuvenator, Peace, now come and give us back a firm foothold in life, a centre.

Innocent Peace! Almost the children are wiser than we, the old: conflict does not divide the minds of these dear ones, and clear and joyful their eyes have remained.

And as the umpire, smilingly serious, gazes with others upon the young men's race-course, where more fervently the combatants drive their chariots into clouds of dust,

So Helios stands and smiles above us, and never the divine, the glad one is lonely, for eternally they dwell, Aether's blossoming stars, in holy freedom.

71

## AN DIE DEUTSCHEN

Spottet nimmer des Kinds, wenn noch das alberne
   Auf dem Rosse von Holz herrlich und viel sich dünkt,
      O ihr Guten! auch wir sind
         Tatenarm und gedankenvoll!

Aber kommt, wie der Strahl aus dem Gewölke kommt,
   Aus Gedanken vielleicht, geistig und reif die Tat?
      Folgt die Frucht, wie des Haines
         Dunklem Blatte, der stillen Schrift?

Und das Schweigen im Volk, ist es die Feier schon
   Vor dem Feste? die Furcht, welche den Gott ansagt?
      O dann nimmt mich, ihr Lieben!
         Daß ich büße die Lästerung.

Schon zu lange, zu lang irr ich, dem Laien gleich,
   In des bildenden Geists werdender Werkstatt hier,
      Nur was blühet, erkenn ich,
         Was er sinnet, erkenn ich nicht.

## TO THE GERMANS

Never laugh at the child, when still the silly one on his wooden horse thinks himself glorious and great; O dear Germans, we too are poor in deeds and rich in fancies!

But, as the lighting ray from clouds, from fancies perhaps does action issue, lucid and mature? Does the fruit succeed the quiet script, as it does the orchard's dark leaf?

And the silence among the people, is it the festive mood before the celebration? The awe that announces the god? Oh then seize me, my dear ones, make me repent the blasphemy.

Too long already, too long like the layman I stray here in the imminent workshop of the shaping spirit; only what blossoms I recognize, what he ponders I cannot make out.

Und zu ahnen ist süß, aber ein Leiden auch,
    Und schon Jahre genug leb' ich in sterblicher
        Unverständiger Liebe
        Zweifelnd, immer bewegt vor ihm,

Der das stetige Werk immer aus liebender
    Seele näher mir bringt, lächelnd dem Sterblichen,
        Wo ich zage, des Lebens
        Reine Tiefe zu Reife bringt.

Schöpferischer, o wann, Genius unsers Volks,
    Wann erscheinest du ganz, Seele des Vaterlands,
        Daß ich tiefer mich beuge,
        Daß die leiseste Saite selbst

Mir verstumme vor dir, daß ich beschämt
    Eine Blume der Nacht, himmlischer Tag, vor dir
        Enden möge mit Freuden,
        Wenn sie alle, mit denen ich

Vormals trauerte, wenn unsere Städte nun
    Hell und offen und wach, reineren Feuers voll
        Und die Berge des deutschen
        Landes Berge der Musen sind,

And to divine is sweet, yet an affliction too, and for years enough I have
lived doubting in mortal, uncomprehending love, always moved in his
presence,
    Who in his loving soul ever more close to me brings the constant work,
and smiling at the mortal where I falter, brings to its ripeness the pure
depth of life.
    Creative one, oh when, genius of our people, when will you wholly
appear, soul of our fatherland, so that more deeply I shall bow, so that
even my most muted string
    Shall fall silent before you, so that ashamed, a flower of the night, in
your presence, heavenly day, I long to end in my joy, when all those in
whose midst
    Formerly I lamented, when our cities now are bright and open and
awake, full of purer fire, and the mountains of the German lands are moun-
tains of the Muses,

Wie die herrlichen einst, Pindos und Helikon,
  Und Parnassos, und rings unter des Vaterlands
    Goldnem Himmel die freie,
      Klare, geistige Freude glänzt.

Wohl ist enge begrenzt unsere Lebenszeit,
  Unserer Jahre Zahl sehen und zählen wir,
    Doch die Jahre der Völker,
      Sah ein sterbliches Auge sie?

Wenn die Seele dir auch über die eigne Zeit
  Sich die sehnende schwingt, trauernd verweilest du
    Dann am kalten Gestade
      Bei den Deinen und kennst sie nie,

Und die Künftigen auch, sie, die Verheißenen
  Wo, wo siehest du sie, daß du an Freundeshand
    Einmal wieder erwarmest,
      Einer Seele vernehmlich seist?

Klanglos, ... ists in der Halle längst,
  Armer Seher! bei dir, sehnend verlischt dein Aug
    Und du schlummerst hinunter
      Ohne Namen und unbeweint.


As those glorious ones before, Pindus and Helicon, and Parnassus, and round about under the fatherland's golden sky the free, the clear and lucid joy is gleaming.

True, our lives' duration is narrowly confined; we see and count the number of our years, but the years of the peoples, did mortal eye ever see them?

Though your soul, the yearning, soars beyond your own time, mourning then you linger on the cold shore with your own kin and never know them,

Nor yet those to come, the promised; where, where, can you see them, so that a friendly hand may warm you again, and one soul can hear what you say?

A long time now no resonance has stirred for you in the hall, poor seer; yearning, your eye extinguishes, and sleeping you fade away nameless and unwept.

## ROUSSEAU

WIE eng begrenzt ist unsere Tageszeit.
  Du warst und sahst und stauntest, schon Abend ists,
    Nun schlafe, wo unendlich ferne
      Ziehen vorüber der Völker Jahre.

Und mancher siehet über die eigne Zeit
  Ihm zeigt ein Gott ins Freie, doch sehnend stehst
    Am Ufer du, ein Ärgernis den
      Deinen, ein Schatten, und liebst sie nimmer,

Und jene, die du nennst, die Verheißenen,
  Wo sind die Neuen, daß du an Freundeshand
    Erwarmst, wo nahn sie, daß du einmal
      Einsame Rede, vernehmlich seiest?

Klanglos ists, armer Mann, in der Halle dir,
  Und gleich den Unbegrabenen, irrest du
    Unstet und suchest Ruh und niemand
      Weiß den beschiedenen Weg zu weisen.

## ROUSSEAU

How narrowly confined is our day's duration. You were and saw and marvelled, and already it's evening; now sleep, where infinitely distant the years of the peoples pass by.

And more than one there is who can see beyond his own time. A god shows him the way into the open, but yearning you stand on the shore, an offence to your own time, a shadow, and do not love them,

And those whom you name, the promised, where are those new ones, that a friendly hand may warm you; where do they approach, so that for once, lonely speech, you may be heard?

Not a resonance, poor man, stirs for you in the hall, and like a wraith you stray inconstantly seeking rest, and no one can show you the allotted way.

Sei denn zufrieden! ... der Baum entwächst
    Dem heimatlichen Boden, aber es sinken ihm
      Die liebenden, die jugendlichen
        Arme, und trauernd neigt er sein Haupt.

Des Lebens Überfluß, das Unendliche,
    Das um ihn ... und dämmert, er faßt es nie.
      Doch lebts in ihm und gegenwärtig,
        Wärmend und wirkend, die Frucht entquillt ihm.

Du hast gelebt! ... auch dir, auch dir
    Erfreuet die ferne Sonne dein Haupt,
      Und Strahlen aus der schönern Zeit. Es
        Haben die Boten dein Herz gefunden.

Vernommen hast du sie, verstanden die Sprache der Fremdlinge,
    Gedeutet ihre Seele! Dem Sehnenden war
      Der Wink genug, und Winke sind
        Von Alters her die Sprache der Götter.

Und wunderbar, als hätte von Anbeginn
    Des Menschen Geist das Werden und Wirken all,
      Des Lebens Weise schon erfahren
        . . . . .

Then be content! The tree outgrows its native soil, but his loving, his youthful arms droop, and mournfully he bows his head.

The superabundance of life, the infinite that ... and glimmers around him, he'll never grasp. Yet it lives in him and present, warming, and effective, the fruit flows out of him.

You have lived! your crest too, yours too, the distant sun rejoices, and beams of better days. The heralds have found your heart.

You heard them, understood the strangers' language, interpreted their soul! For the yearning a hint was enough, and hints have always been the language of the gods.

And marvellous, as though from the beginning the human mind had known all that grows and stirs, the very tune of life ...

Kennt er im ersten Zeichen Vollendetes schon,
Und fliegt, der kühne Geist, wie Adler den
Gewittern, weissagend seinen
Kommenden Göttern voraus, ...

WIE wenn am Feiertage, das Feld zu sehn,
Ein Landmann geht, des Morgens, wenn
Aus heißer Nacht die kühlenden Blitze fielen
Die ganze Zeit und fern noch tönet der Donner,
In sein Gestade wieder tritt der Strom,
Und frisch der Boden grünt
Und von des Himmels erfreuendem Regen
Der Weinstock trauft und glänzend
In stiller Sonne stehn die Bäume des Haines:

So stehn sie unter günstiger Witterung,
Sie, die kein Meister allein, die wunderbar
Allgegenwärtig erzieht in leichtem Umfangen
Die mächtige, die göttlichschöne Natur.
Drum wenn zu schlafen sie scheint zu Zeiten des Jahrs
Am Himmel oder unter den Pflanzen oder den Völkern,

In the first sign he reads the ultimate fruition and, the bold spirit, as eagles before thunderstorms, prophetically flies before his approaching gods.

As on a holiday to see the field a countryman goes out, at morning, when out of the hot night the cooling lightning rays had fallen for hours on end, and still in the distance the thunder sounds, the river enters its banks once more, and the ground is fresh with new verdure, and with the gladdening rain of heaven the grape-vine drips, and gleaming the trees of the orchard stand in the quiet sunlight:
So in favourable weather they stand whom no master alone, whom marvellously omnipresent in a light embrace, mighty, divinely beautiful Nature teaches. So when she seems to sleep at certain times of the year, in the sky or among the plants or the peoples, the poets' faces also will

So trauert der Dichter Angesicht auch,
Sie scheinen allein zu sein, doch ahnen sie immer.
Denn ahnend ruhet sie selbst auch.

Jetzt aber tagts! Ich harrt und sah es kommen,
Und was ich sah, das Heilige sei mein Wort,
Denn sie, sie selbst, die älter denn die Zeiten
Und über die Götter des Abends und Orients ist,
Die Natur ist jetzt mit Waffenklang erwacht,
Und hoch vom Äther bis zum Abgrund nieder
Nach festem Gesetze, wie einst, aus heiligem Chaos gezeugt,
Fühlt neu die Begeisterung sich,
Die Allerschaffende wieder.

Und wie im Aug ein Feuer dem Manne glänzt,
Wenn hohes er entwarf, so ist
Von neuem an den Zeichen, den Taten der Welt jetzt
Ein Feuer angezündet in Seelen der Dichter.
Und was zuvor geschah, doch kaum gefühlt,
Ist offenbar erst jetzt,
Und die uns lächelnd den Acker gebauet,
In Knechtsgestalt, sie sind erkannt,
Die Allebendigen, die Kräfte der Götter.

mourn; they seem to be alone, yet always they are foreknowing. For she herself foreknows as she rests.

But now day breaks! I waited and saw it come, and what I saw, it is holy, now be my word. For she, she herself, who is older than the ages and above the gods of Occident and Orient, Nature now has awoken with clamour of arms, and from the heights of Aether down to the lowest abyss, engendered out of holy Chaos, as once she was, according to rigid law, rapture, the all-creative, feels her own being anew.

And as a fire gleams in the eye of that man who has conceived a noble design; so now once again by the signs, the deeds of the world a fire has been kindled in the souls of the poets. And what came to pass before, though scarcely felt, only now is manifest, and they who smiling tended our fields for us, in the guise of labourers, now have been recognized, the all and ever living, the powers of the gods.

Erfrägst du sie? im Liede wehet ihr Geist,
Wenn es der Sonne des Tags und warmer Erd
Entwächst, und Wettern, die in der Luft, und andern,
Die vorbereiteter in Tiefen der Zeit
Und deutungsvoller, und vernehmlicher uns
Hinwandeln zwischen Himmel und Erd und unter den Völkern.
Des gemeinsamen Geistes Gedanken sind
Still endend in der Seele des Dichters,

Daß schnellbetroffen sie, Unendlichem
Bekannt seit langer Zeit, von Erinnerung
Erbebt, und ihr, von heilgem Strahl entzündet,
Die Frucht in Liebe geboren, der Götter und Menschen Werk,
Der Gesang, damit er beiden zeuge, glückt.
So fiel, wie Dichter sagen, da sie sichtbar
Den Gott zu sehen begehrte, sein Blitz auf Semeles Haus
Und die göttlichgetroffne gebar,
Die Frucht des Gewitters, den heiligen Bacchus.

Und daher trinken himmlisches Feuer jetzt
Die Erdensöhne ohne Gefahr.
Doch uns gebührt es, unter Gottes Gewittern,
Ihr Dichter! mit entblößtem Haupte zu stehen,

    Do you ask who they are? In song their spirit wafts when it grows from the sun of day and the warm soil, and storms high up in the air, and others that more prepared in the depths of time, and more full of meaning, and more perceptible to us, drift along between Heaven and Earth and amidst the peoples. The thoughts of the communal spirit they are, quietly ending in the poet's soul,
    So that swiftly visited, for a long time familiar to infinite powers, it quakes with recollection, and set on fire by the holy ray, the fruit conceived in love, the work of gods and men, the song, that it may bear witness to both, succeeds. Thus, poets tell, when she desired to see the god in person, visible, his lightning fell on Semele's house, and the divinely struck gave birth to the thunderstorm's fruit, to holy Bacchus.
    And hence it is that without danger now the sons of Earth drink heavenly fire. Yet us it behoves, you poets, to stand bare-headed beneath

Des Vaters Strahl, ihn selbst, mit eigner Hand
Zu fassen und dem Volk ins Lied
Gehüllt die himmlische Gabe zu reichen.
Denn sind nur reinen Herzens,
Wie Kinder, wir, sind schuldlos unsere Hände,

Des Vaters Strahl, der reine versengt es nicht
Und tieferschüttert, die Leiden des Stärkeren
Mitleidend, bleibt in den hochherstürzenden Stürmen
Des Gottes, wenn er nahet, das Herz doch fest.
Doch weh mir! wenn von
   [selbgeschlagener Wunde das Herz mir blutet, und tief-
verloren der Frieden ist, und freibescheidenes Genügen,
Und die Unruh, und der Mangel mich treibt zum
Überflusse des Göttertisches, wenn rings um mich] *
Weh mir!

God's thunderstorms, to grasp the Father's ray, itself, with our own hands, and to offer the heavenly gift to the people, wrapped in our song. For if only we are pure in heart, like children, and our hands are guiltless,
   Then the Father's ray, the pure, will not sear it, and, deeply shaken, sharing the sufferings of him who is stronger than we, in the storms, crashing down from the heights, of the god as he nears, yet the heart will stand fast. But woe is me! When with [a self-inflicted wound my heart is bleeding, and peace is deeply lost to me, and freely chosen modest self-contentment, and when unrest and lack drive me towards the luxury of the gods' banqueting table, when all around me ...] * Woe is me!

---

* The lines in brackets are taken from a prose draft (*Grosse Stuttgarter Ausgabe*, vol. II (2), pp. 669–70) and inserted here to explain the abrupt change of tone and the inconclusiveness of the poem.

Und sag ich gleich ...
Ich sei genaht, die Himmlischen zu schauen,
Sie selbst, sie werfen mich tief unter die Lebenden
Den falschen Priester, ins Dunkel, daß ich
Das warnende Lied den Gelehrigen singe.
Dort ...

## DER ARCHIPELAGUS

KEHREN die Kraniche wieder zu dir, und suchen zu deinen
Ufern wieder die Schiffe den Lauf? umatmen erwünschte
Lüfte dir die beruhigte Flut, und sonnet der Delphin,
Aus der Tiefe gelockt, am neuen Lichte den Rücken?
Blüht Ionien? ists die Zeit? denn immer im Frühling,
Wenn den Lebenden sich das Herz erneut und die erste
Liebe den Menschen erwacht und goldner Zeiten Erinnerung,
Komm' ich zu dir und grüß' in deiner Stille dich, Alter!

Immer, Gewaltiger! lebst du noch und ruhest im Schatten
Deiner Berge, wie sonst; mit Jünglingsarmen umfängst du
Noch dein liebliches Land, und deiner Töchter, o Vater!

And let me say at once ... that I approached to look upon the Heavenly,
and they themselves cast me down far below all the living, cast down the
false priest into the dark, that I may sing, for those eager to learn, my
warning song. There ...

## THE ARCHIPELAGO

ARE the cranes returning to you, and the vessels making again for your
shores? Are the winds you desire breathing around your calmed waters,
and does the dolphin, lured from the depths, sun his back in the new-born
light? Is Ionia in blossom? Is it blossoming time? For always in spring-
time, when the heart of the living is renewed, and men's first love is
awakened, and memories of the golden age, I come to you, ancient Sea-
God, and greet you in your stillness.

As ever, mighty one, you are living, and rest in the shade of your
mountains, as you did once; with youthful arms still embrace your lovely
land, and not one of your daughters, Father, not one of your islands, the

Deiner Inseln ist noch, der blühenden, keine verloren.
Kreta steht und Salamis grünt, umdämmert von Lorbeern,
Rings von Strahlen umblüht, erhebt zur Stunde des Aufgangs
Delos ihr begeistertes Haupt, und Tenos und Chios
Haben der purpurnen Früchte genug, von trunkenen Hügeln
Quillt der Cypriertrank, und von Kalauria fallen
Silberne Bäche, wie einst, in die alten Wasser des Vaters.
Alle leben sie noch, die Heroenmütter, die Inseln,
Blühend von Jahr zu Jahr, und wenn zu Zeiten, vom Abgrund
Losgelassen, die Flamme der Nacht, das untre Gewitter,
Eine der holden ergriff, und die Sterbende dir in den Schoß sank,
Göttlicher! du, du dauertest aus, denn über den dunklen
Tiefen ist manches schon dir auf und untergegangen.

Auch die Himmlischen, sie, die Kräfte der Höhe, die stillen,
Die den heiteren Tag und süßen Schlummer und Ahnung
Fernher bringen über das Haupt der fühlenden Menschen
Aus der Fülle der Macht, auch sie, die alten Gespielen,
Wohnen, wie einst, mit dir, und oft am dämmernden Abend,
Wenn von Asiens Bergen herein das heilige Mondlicht
Kömmt und die Sterne sich in deiner Woge begegnen,

flowering, is lost. Crete stands firm and Salamis grows green, girt round with the dark of laurels, and decked with a wreath of rays Delos lifts her inspired head at the hour of sunrise, and Tenos and Chios have no lack of purple fruit, the Cyprian liquor gushes from drunken hills, and from Kalauria the silver brooks fall, as ever, into the Father's ancient waters. All are living still, those mothers of heroes, the islands, flowering from year to year, and if at times, released from the abyss, the flame of night, the subterranean thunder seized one of those dear ones and, dying, she sank into your lap, yet you, divine one, endured, for you have seen many things rise, many go down, above your gloomy depths.

The Heavenly too, the powers of the height, the silent, who from afar bring the cloudless day and sweet slumber and premonitions upon the heads of feeling men, out of the fullness of power, these too, your old playmates, dwell with you as before, and often at glimmering nightfall, when from Asia's mountains the holy moonlight comes and the stars meet in

Leuchtest du von himmlischem Glanz, und so, wie sie wandeln,
Wechseln die Wasser dir, es tönt die Weise der Brüder
Droben, ihr Nachtgesang, im liebenden Busen dir wieder.
Wenn die allverklärende dann, die Sonne des Tages,
Sie, des Orients Kind, die Wundertätige, da ist,
Dann die Lebenden all' im goldenen Traume beginnen,
Den die Dichtende stets des Morgens ihnen bereitet,
Dir, dem trauernden Gott, dir sendet sie froheren Zauber,
Und ihr eigen freundliches Licht ist selber so schön nicht
Denn das Liebeszeichen, der Kranz, den immer, wie vormals,
Deiner gedenk, doch sie um die graue Locke dir windet.
Und umfängt der Äther dich nicht, und kehren die Wolken,
Deine Boten, von ihm mit dem Göttergeschenke, dem Strahle
Aus der Höhe dir nicht? dann sendest du über das Land sie,
Daß am heißen Gestad die gewittertrunkenen Wälder
Rauschen und wogen mit dir, daß bald, dem wandernden Sohn
    gleich,
Wenn der Vater ihn ruft, mit den tausend Bächen Mäander
Seinen Irren enteilt und aus der Ebne Kayster
Dir entgegenfrohlockt, und der Erstgeborne, der Alte,
Der zu lange sich barg, dein majestätischer Nil izt

your wave, you shine with heavenly radiance, and even as they change do
your waters change, and the tune of your brothers above, their nocturnal
song, finds its echo in your loving breast. Then, when the all-transfiguring,
the sun of day, the Orient's child, the miracle-worker, has come, when all
the living begin again in a golden dream which the poet sun grants them
anew every morning, then to you, the mourning god, she sends more
happy magic, and her own kindly light itself is not as beautiful as the love
token, the garland, which as ever mindful of you still she twines about
your grey locks. And does not Aether embrace you, and do not the clouds,
your messengers, return from him with the divine gift, the thunderbolt,
from above? Then you send them out over the country, so that on the hot
shores the storm-drunken forests roar and surge with you, so that soon,
like the errant son, when his father calls him, with his thousand streams
Meander hurries back from his wanderings and from the plain Kayster runs
exultant to meet you, and the first-born, the ancient one, he who hid him-
self too long, your majestic Nile now comes striding down victorious from

Hochherschreitend aus fernem Gebirg, wie im Klange der
    Waffen,
Siegreich kömmt, und die offenen Arme der sehnende reichet.

Dennoch einsam dünkest du dir; in schweigender Nacht hört
Deine Weheklage der Fels, und öfters entflieht dir
Zürnend von Sterblichen weg die geflügelte Woge zum Himmel.
Denn es leben mit dir die edlen Lieblinge nimmer,
Die dich geehrt, die einst mit den schönen Tempeln und
    Städten
Deine Gestade bekränzt, und immer suchen und missen,
Immer bedürfen ja, wie Heroen den Kranz, die geweihten
Elemente zum Ruhme das Herz der fühlenden Menschen.

Sage, wo ist Athen? ist über den Urnen der Meister
Deine Stadt, die geliebteste dir, an den heiligen Ufern,
Trauernder Gott! dir ganz in Asche zusammengesunken,
Oder ist noch ein Zeichen von ihr, daß etwa der Schiffer,
Wenn er vorüberkommt, sie nenn' und ihrer gedenke?
Stiegen dort die Säulen empor und leuchteten dort nicht
Sonst vom Dache der Burg herab die Göttergestalten?
Rauschte dort die Stimme des Volks, die stürmischbewegte,
Aus der Agora nicht her, und eilten aus freudigen Pforten
Dort die Gassen dir nicht zu gesegnetem Hafen herunter?

the heights of distant mountains, as though with the clang of weapons, and
extends his open arms to you in welcome.
    Yet you think yourself lonely; in the hushed night the rock hears your
lament and often your winged wave flees in anger from mortals up to the
sky. For no longer your noble beloved ones live with you, who honoured
you once, who crowned your shores with fine temples and cities, and yet
for ever they seek and miss, for ever need, as heroes need the wreath, for
ever the hallowed elements need the hearts of feeling men for their glory.
    Tell me, now, where is Athens? Over the urns of the masters has your
city, the dearest of all to you, mourning god, wholly crumbled to ashes on
the holy shores? Or is there a trace of her still, so that the sailor perhaps, as
he passes, may name her and think of her still? Did not the columns rise
here, and there did not the statues of gods gleam down from the citadel
roof? Did not the people's voice, the tempestuously impassioned, ring out
from the Agora, and there from joyful doors did not the streets hurry down
to your haven's blessing? Look, over there the distantly pondering mer-

Siehe! da löste sein Schiff der fernhinsinnende Kaufmann,
Froh, denn es wehet' auch ihm die beflügelnde Luft und die
    Götter
Liebten so, wie den Dichter, auch ihn, dieweil er die guten
Gaben der Erd' ausglich und Fernes Nahem vereinte.
Fern nach Cypros ziehet er hin und ferne nach Tyros,
Strebt nach Kolchis hinauf und hinab zum alten Ägyptos,
Daß er Purpur und Wein und Korn und Vließe gewinne
Für die eigene Stadt, und öfters über des kühnen
Herkules Säulen hinaus, zu neuen seligen Inseln
Tragen die Hoffnungen ihn und des Schiffes Flügel, indessen
Anders bewegt, am Gestade der Stadt ein einsamer Jüngling
Weilt und die Woge belauscht, und Großes ahndet der Ernste,
Wenn er zu Füßen so des erderschütternden Meisters
Lauschet und sitzt, und nicht umsonst erzog ihn der Meergott.

Denn des Genius Feind, der vielgebietende Perse,
Jahrlang zählt' er sie schon, der Waffen Menge, der Knechte,
Spottend des griechischen Lands und seiner wenigen Inseln,
Und sie deuchten dem Herrscher ein Spiel, und noch, wie ein
    Traum, war
Ihm das innige Volk, vom Göttergeiste gerüstet.

chant unmoored his ship, happy, because for him too the wing-giving
breezes blew, and the gods loved him too, as they loved the poet, because
he made fair division of the good gifts of Earth and joined the far to the
near. Far off to Cyprus he travels, and far off to Tyre, toils up to Colchis
and down to ancient Egypt, that he may acquire the purple dye and wine
and corn and fleeces for his own city, and often farther than the pillars of
bold Hercules, to new and blessed islands, his hopes and the ship's wings
will carry him, while, differently moved, on the city's shores a solitary
youth lingers and listens to the waves, and, serious, entertains presenti-
ments of greatness, as he sits listening at the feet of the earth-shaking
master; nor in vain did the Sea-God instruct him.

For the foe of all genius, the widely governing Persian, for years has
been counting his wealth of weapons and soldiers, mocking the Grecian
land and its few small islands, and they seemed a trifle to this ruler, and still
as in a dream he saw its fervent people armed with the spirit of gods.

Leicht aus spricht er das Wort und schnell, wie der flammende
    Bergquell,
Wenn er furchtbar umher vom gärenden Ätna gegossen,
Städte begräbt in der purpurnen Flut und blühende Gärten,
Bis der brennende Strom im heiligen Meere sich kühlet,
So mit dem Könige nun, versengend, städteverwüstend,
Stürzt von Ekbatana daher sein prächtig Getümmel;
Weh! und Athene, die herrliche, fällt; wohl schauen und ringen
Vom Gebirg, wo das Wild ihr Geschrei hört, fliehende Greise
Nach den Wohnungen dort zurück und den rauchenden
    Tempeln;
Aber es weckt der Söhne Gebet die heilige Asche
Nun nicht mehr, im Tal ist der Tod, und die Wolke des Brandes
Schwindet am Himmel dahin, und weiter im Lande zu ernten,
Zieht, vom Frevel erhitzt, mit der Beute der Perse vorüber.

Aber an Salamis Ufern, o Tag an Salamis Ufern!
Harrend des Endes stehn die Athenerinnen, die Jungfraun,
Stehn die Mütter, wiegend im Arm das gerettete Söhnlein,
Aber den Horchenden schallt von Tiefen die Stimme des
    Meergotts
Heilweissagend herauf, es schauen die Götter des Himmels

Lightly he speaks the word and swiftly, as the flaming mountain torrent,
horribly poured out of Etna in ferment and spread about, buries cities and
blossoming gardens in its crimson flood, till that burning stream is cooled
in the holy sea, so now the King, laying waste by fire and razing cities,
from Ekbatana drives down his splendid horde; and, woe! glorious Athens
falls; true, from the mountains, where the wild beast hears their outcry, old
men in flight look on and struggle to return to their houses there, and the
smoking temples; but no longer now can the prayers of their sons awaken
those holy ashes, death is in the valley, and the cloud of conflagration drifts
off in the sky, and to harvest further in that land, inflamed by his crime, the
Persian passes on with his booty.

    But on the shores of Salamis, O day on the shores of Salamis! Waiting
for the end the Athenian women stand, the virgins, the mothers rocking in
their arms the little sons they have saved from the massacre; but to these
attentively listening, from the depths the Sea-god's voice rises, prophesy-
ing salvation, and the gods of Heaven look down, weighing and judging,

Wägend und richtend herab, denn dort an den bebenden Ufern
Wankt seit Tagesbeginn, wie langsamwandelnd Gewitter,
Dort auf schäumenden Wassern die Schlacht, und es glühet der
    Mittag,
Unbemerket im Zorn, schon über dem Haupte den Kämpfern.
Aber die Männer des Volks, die Heroenenkel, sie walten
Helleren Auges jetzt, die Götterlieblinge denken
Des beschiedenen Glücks, es zähmen die Kinder Athenes
Ihren Genius, ihn, den todverachtenden, jetzt nicht.
Denn wie aus rauchendem Blut das Wild der Wüste noch
    einmal
Sich zuletzt verwandelt erhebt, der edleren Kraft gleich,
Und den Jäger erschröckt; kehrt jetzt im Glanze der Waffen,
Bei der Herrscher Gebot, furchtbargesammelt den Wilden,
Mitten im Untergang die ermattete Seele noch einmal.
Und entbrannter beginnts; wie Paare ringender Männer
Fassen die Schiffe sich an, in die Woge taumelt das Steuer,
Unter den Streitern bricht der Boden, und Schiffer und Schiff
    sinkt.

Aber in schwindelnden Traum vom Liede des Tages gesungen,
Rollt der König den Blick; irrlächelnd über den Ausgang

for there on the trembling shores, since daybreak, like a slowly gathering
thunderstorm the battle has swayed, there on the foaming waters, and al-
ready noon, unnoticed by them in their fury, glows above the combatants'
heads. But the men of that people, grandchildren of heroes, now strive with
clearer eyes; these beloved ones of gods think of the good fortune allotted
to them, and Athena's children no longer tame their genius that despises
death. For just as from its steaming blood the wild beast of the desert rises
once more transfigured, more like its noble self in strength, and frightens
the huntsman, so now in the flash of weapons, at their rulers' command, in
the midst of perdition their weary spirit returns to the fierce ones with a
terrible exertion of force. And the battle flares up; like pairs of wrestling
men the ships get to grips with each other, the rudder rides off on the
waves, the deck breaks under the combatants' feet, and both sailor and ship
go down.
    But lulled into dizzy dream by the song of that day, the King rolls his

Droht er, und fleht, und frohlockt, und sendet, wie Blitze, die
　　Boten.
Doch er sendet umsonst, es kehret keiner ihm wieder.
Blutige Boten, Erschlagne des Heers, und berstende Schiffe,
Wirft die Rächerin ihm zahllos, die donnernde Woge,
Vor den Thron, wo er sitzt am bebenden Ufer, der Arme,
Schauend die Flucht, und fort in die fliehende Menge gerissen,
Eilt er, ihn treibt der Gott, es treibt sein irrend Geschwader
Über die Fluten der Gott, der spottend sein eitel Geschmeid
　　ihm
Endlich zerschlug und den Schwachen erreicht' in der drohen-
　　den Rüstung.

Aber liebend zurück zum einsamharrenden Strome
Kommt der Athener Volk und von den Bergen der Heimat
Wogen, freudig gemischt, die glänzenden Scharen herunter
Ins verlassene Tal, ach! gleich der gealterten Mutter,
Wenn nach Jahren das Kind, das verlorengeachtete, wieder
Lebend ihr an die Brüste kehrt, ein erwachsener Jüngling,
Aber im Gram ist ihr die Seele gewelkt und die Freude
Kommt der hoffnungsmüden zu spät und mühsam vernimmt
　　sie,

eyes; deludely smiling at the outcome, he threatens, implores, and exults, and with lightning speed dispatches his messengers. But he dispatches them in vain, not one returns to him. Bleeding messengers, soldiers killed, and ships splitting asunder, these the avenger, the thundering wave, casts innumerable before his throne, where he sits on the trembling shore, the wretch; and sees his men in flight, and now, swept up by the fleeing crowd, he hurries on, driven by the god, his wandering fleet driven across the sea by the god, who at last mockingly smashed his vain finery and reached the weakling beneath his threatening armour.

But lovingly back to the river, lingering lonely, the Athenian people returns, and from the mountains of their homeland, joyfully mingled, the bright crowds come surging down to the forsaken valley; alas, like the agèd mother when after many years the child given up for lost returns alive to her breast, a full-grown youth, but her soul has withered with grief, and joy comes too late to her worn out with hoping, and with difficulty she

Was der liebende Sohn in seinem Danke geredet;
So erscheint den Kommenden dort der Boden der Heimat.
Denn es fragen umsonst nach ihren Hainen die Frommen,
Und die Sieger empfängt die freundliche Pforte nicht wieder,
Wie den Wanderer sonst sie empfing, wenn er froh von den
    Inseln
Wiederkehrt' und die selige Burg der Mutter Athene
Über sehnendem Haupt ihm fernherglänzend heraufging.
Aber wohl sind ihnen bekannt die verödeten Gassen
Und die trauernden Gärten umher und auf der Agora,
Wo des Portikus Säulen gestürzt und die göttlichen Bilder
Liegen, da reicht in der Seele bewegt, und der Treue sich
    freuend,
Jetzt das liebende Volk zum Bunde die Hände sich wieder.
Bald auch suchet und sieht den Ort des eigenen Hauses
Unter dem Schutt der Mann; ihm weint am Halse, der trauten
Schlummerstätte gedenk, sein Weib, es fragen die Kindlein
Nach dem Tische, wo sonst in lieblicher Reihe sie saßen,
Von den Vätern gesehn, den lächelnden Göttern des Hauses.
Aber Gezelte bauet das Volk, es schließen die alten
Nachbarn wieder sich an, und nach des Herzens Gewohnheit
Ordnen die luftigen Wohnungen sich umher an den Hügeln.

takes in what her loving son has uttered in his gratitude; so now the soil
of their homeland seems to those returning. For in vain the pious ask for
their groves, and the kindly gates do not receive the victors, as they re-
ceived the traveller once, when, glad, he returned from the islands and the
blessed fortress of Mother Athene, distantly gleaming, appeared to him
high above his yearning head. And yet all these deserted streets and
gardens in mourning are well known to them, and on the Agora, where the
portico's columns and statues of gods lie fallen now, moved in their souls,
and rejoicing in faith, the loving people clasp hands in token of commun-
ity. Soon too a man looks for and sees the site of his own house under the
rubble; his wife, recalling the familiar place where they once slept, weeps
with her arms about him, his young children ask where is the table at which
they used to sit in a charming row while ancestors looked on, and the
smiling gods of the household. But the people put up tents, neighbours are
reunited, and, according to the heart's habits, airy dwellings fall into place

So indessen wohnen sie nun, wie die Freien, die Alten,
Die, der Stärke gewiß und dem kommenden Tage vertrauend,
Wandernden Vögeln gleich, mit Gesange von Berge zu Berg'
    einst
Zogen, die Fürsten des Forsts und des weitumirrenden
    Stromes.
Doch umfängt noch, wie sonst, die Muttererde, die treue,
Wieder ihr edel Volk, und unter heiligem Himmel
Ruhen sie sanft, wenn milde, wie sonst, die Lüfte der Jugend
Um die Schlafenden wehn, und aus Platanen Ilissus
Ihnen herüberrauscht, und neue Tage verkündend,
Lockend zu neuen Taten, bei Nacht die Woge des Meergotts
Fernher tönt und fröhliche Träume den Lieblingen sendet.
Schon auch sprossen und blühn die Blumen mählich, die goldnen,
Auf zertretenem Feld, von frommen Händen gewartet,
Grünet der Ölbaum auf, und auf Kolonos Gefilden
Nähren friedlich, wie sonst, die Athenischen Rosse sich wieder.

Aber der Muttererd' und dem Gott der Woge zu Ehren
Blühet die Stadt izt auf, ein herrlich Gebild, dem Gestirn gleich
Sichergegründet, des Genius Werk, denn Fesseln der Liebe

once more all over the hills. So now they live like the free people, the
people they once were, who sure of their strength and trusting in the days
to come, like migrant birds, used to travel singing from mountain to moun-
tain, princes of the forest and the far-meandering river. Yet Mother Earth,
the faithful, still embraces anew her noble people, and under a holy heaven
they gently rest when mild, as before, the breezes of youth blow about
them asleep, and from plane-trees the purling of Ilissus reaches them and,
proclaiming new days, inciting them to new deeds, at night the Sea-God's
wave resounds from afar and sends happy dreams to his loved ones. And
already, too, the crops burgeon and flower in their season, the golden ones,
on the trampled fields, and, tended by pious hands, the olives grow green,
and on the plains of Colonus peacefully, as before, the Athenian horses are
grazing.

    But in honour of Mother Earth and the Sea-God, the city springs up and
blossoms, a glorious edifice, firmly founded as the stars, the work of their
genius, for he likes to forge fetters of love in this way, so that in mighty

Schafft er gerne sich so, so hält in großen Gestalten,
Die er selbst sich erbaut, der immerrege sich bleibend.
Sieh! und dem Schaffenden dienet der Wald, ihm reicht mit den
  andern
Bergen nahe zur Hand der Pentele Marmor und Erze;
Aber lebend, wie er, und froh und herrlich entquillt es
Seinen Händen, und leicht, wie der Sonne, gedeiht das Geschäft
  ihm.
Brunnen steigen empor und über die Hügel in reinen
Bahnen gelenkt, ereilt der Quell das glänzende Becken;
Und umher an ihnen erglänzt, gleich festlichen Helden
Am gemeinsamen Kelch, die Reihe der Wohnungen, hoch ragt
Der Prytanen Gemach, es stehn Gymnasien offen,
Göttertempel entstehn, ein heiligkühner Gedanke
Steigt, Unsterblichen nah, das Olympion auf in den Äther
Aus dem seligen Hain; noch manche der himmlischen Hallen!
Mutter Athene, dir auch, dir wuchs dein herrlicher Hügel
Stolzer aus der Trauer empor und blühte noch lange,
Gott der Wogen und dir, und deine Lieblinge sangen
Frohversammelt noch oft am Vorgebirge den Dank dir.

O die Kinder des Glücks, die frommen! wandeln sie fern nun
Bei den Vätern daheim, und der Schicksalstage vergessen,

shapes, which he has raised for himself, he, the ever-active, may stay his flight and subsist. And, look! the forest serves this creator, Pentelicus and the other mountains close by offer him marble and ores; but alive, as he is, and glad and splendid it wells from his hands, and easily as the sun he succeeds in his labour. Fountains rise up and, conducted over the hills in pure channels, the stream speeds to the gleaming basin; and, clustered around them, like festive heroes around the communal cup, the houses gleam in rows; high towers the Prytanean hall, the gymnasia are open, temples are built to the gods, and, a thought both holy and bold, near to immortals, that of Olympian Zeus rises to Aether from the sacred grove; and many another heavenly hall, Mother Athene, for your sake, for you also your glorious hill more proudly rose from affliction and long remained in flower for you and the God of the Waves, and your beloved ones, happily fore-gathered, still often sang their thanks to you on the lower mountains.
  Oh those children of joy, the godly! do they now wander far away, with

Drüben am Lethestrom, und bringt kein Sehnen sie wieder?
Sieht mein Auge sie nie? ach! findet über den tausend
Pfaden der grünenden Erd', ihr göttergleichen Gestalten!
Euch das Suchende nie, und vernahm ich darum die Sprache,
Darum die Sage von euch, daß immertrauernd die Seele
Vor der Zeit mir hinab zu euern Schatten entfliehe?
Aber näher zu euch, wo eure Haine noch wachsen,
Wo sein einsames Haupt in Wolken der heilige Berg hüllt,
Zum Parnassos will ich, und wenn im Dunkel der Eiche
Schimmernd, mir Irrenden dort Kastalias Quelle begegnet,
Will ich, mit Tränen gemischt, aus blütenumdufteter Schale
Dort, auf keimendes Grün, das Wasser gießen, damit doch,
O ihr Schlafenden all! ein Totenopfer euch werde.
Dort im schweigenden Tal, an Tempes hangenden Felsen,
Will ich wohnen mit euch, dort oft, ihr herrlichen Namen!
Her euch rufen bei Nacht, und wenn ihr zürnend erscheinet,
Weil der Pflug die Gräber entweiht, mit der Stimme des Herzens
Will ich mit frommem Gesang euch sühnen, heilige Schatten!
Bis zu leben mit euch, sich ganz die Seele gewöhnet.
Fragen wird der Geweihtere dann euch manches, ihr Toten!

their fathers at home, oblivious of fateful days on the yonder side of Lethe, and shall no yearning make them return? Shall my eye never see them? Alas, on all the thousand paths of the verdant earth shall the seeker never find you, O god-like beings? And was it for this I heard your language, for this the legend about you, that for ever in mourning my soul should flee from me to your shades before it is time? But closer to you, where your groves are still growing, where the holy mountain still veils its lovely head in the clouds above, to Parnassus I'll go, and when glistening out of the oak-trees to me, the straying, Castalia's spring appears, from the cup surrounded with fragrance of blossoms on the sprouting verdure I'll pour the water, mingled with tears, so that, you sleeping ones all, one funeral libation at least shall be offered to you still. There, in the silent valley, by Tempe's overhanging rocks, I will live with you still; and often, you glorious names, will invoke you by night; and, when angry you then appear, because the plough desecrates your graves, with the voice of the heart, with pious song I'll appease you, holy shades, till my soul grows entirely accustomed to living with you. Then the more hallowed, O you dead, will put many a question to you, and to you living ones also, exalted powers of

Euch, ihr Lebenden auch, ihr hohen Kräfte des Himmels,
Wenn ihr über dem Schutt mit euren Jahren vorbeigeht,
Ihr in der sicheren Bahn! denn oft ergreifet das Irrsal
Unter den Sternen mir, wie schaurige Lüfte, den Busen,
Daß ich spähe nach Rat, und lang schon reden sie nimmer
Trost den Bedürftigen zu, die prophetischen Haine Dodonas,
Stumm ist der delphische Gott, und einsam liegen und öde
Längst die Pfade, wo einst, von Hoffnungen leise geleitet,
Fragend der Mann zur Stadt des redlichen Sehers heraufstieg.
Aber droben das Licht, es spricht noch heute zu Menschen,
Schöner Deutungen voll und des großen Donnerers Stimme
Ruft es: denket ihr mein? und die trauernde Woge des Meer-
        gotts
Hallt es wieder: gedenkt ihr nimmer meiner, wie vormals?
Denn es ruhn die Himmlischen gern am fühlenden Herzen;
Immer, wie sonst, geleiten sie noch, die begeisternden Kräfte,
Gerne den strebenden Mann und über Bergen der Heimat
Ruht und waltet und lebt allgegenwärtig der Äther,
Daß ein liebendes Volk in des Vaters Armen gesammelt,
Menschlich freudig, wie sonst, und Ein Geist allen gemein sei.
Aber weh! es wandelt in Nacht, es wohnt, wie im Orkus,

Heaven, when you pass by with your years over the rubble, you of the
certain course! For often beneath the stars, like gruesome breezes, con-
fusion takes hold of my heart, so that I look about me for counsel; and not
for a long time now have they granted comforting speech to me in my
need, the prophetic groves of Dodona; but silent is the Delphic god, and
lonely and waste long these paths have lain by which once, quietly guided
by hopes, a questioning man climbed up to the town of the truthful seer.
Yet the light above even today speaks to mortals; full of fine significance
and the mighty thunderer's voice, it calls out: do you think of me still? and
the roaring wave of the Sea-God echoes it back: do you never think of me
now, as once you did? For the heavenly like to repose on a feeling heart;
as ever, enrapturing powers, they like to escort the aspiring man, and
above his homeland's mountains still ubiquitous Aether reposes and rules
and lives, so that a loving people, conjoined in the Father's arms, may be
humanly joyful as ever, and one spirit be common to all. But, woe, it
wanders about in night, and dwells as in Orcus, without the divine, our

Ohne Göttliches unser Geschlecht. Ans eigene Treiben
Sind sie geschmiedet allein, und sich in der tosenden Werkstatt
Höret jeglicher nur und viel arbeiten die Wilden
Mit gewaltigem Arm, rastlos, doch immer und immer
Unfruchtbar, wie die Furien, bleibt die Mühe der Armen.
Bis, erwacht vom ängstigen Traum, die Seele den Menschen
Aufgeht, jugendlich froh, und der Liebe segnender Odem
Wieder, wie vormals oft, bei Hellas blühenden Kindern,
Wehet in neuer Zeit und über freierer Stirne
Uns der Geist der Natur, der fernherwandelnde, wieder
Stilleweilend der Gott in goldnen Wolken erscheinet.
Ach! und säumest du noch? und jene, die göttlichgebornen,
Wohnen immer, o Tag! noch als in Tiefen der Erde
Einsam unten, indes ein immerlebender Frühling
Unbesungen über dem Haupt den Schlafenden dämmert?
Aber länger nicht mehr! schon hör' ich ferne des Festtags
Chorgesang auf grünem Gebirg' und das Echo der Haine,
Wo der Jünglinge Brust sich hebt, wo die Seele des Volks sich
Stillvereint im freieren Lied, zur Ehre des Gottes,
Dem die Höhe gebührt, doch auch die Tale sind heilig;
Denn, wo fröhlich der Strom in wachsender Jugend hinauseilt,

kind. Each man to his labour riveted, only his own, in the workshop's deaf-ening din he hears only himself; and greatly these savages toil, with power-ful arms, unceasing, yet ever and ever infertile, like the Furies, the wretches' exertions remain. Till, roused from their oppressive dream, men grow aware of their soul once more, youthfully glad as it used to be, and the blessing breath of love, as once with Hellas' blossoming children, blows again in these latter times and, above brows not so burdened, the spirit of Nature, that comes from afar, and, calmly abiding, the god appears to us once more in golden clouds. What, do you hesitate still? And, O day, those divinely born continue to live lonely below, as though in the depths of earth, while an ever-living Spring fades unsung above the heads of those sleepers? But no longer now! Already in the distance I hear the feast-day's choral song on the green mountains, and its echo in the groves, where the young men's chests dilate and the soul of the people quietly joins in freer song in praise of the god to whom the heights are sacred; but the valleys too are holy, for where the river hurries out in the exuberance of growth

Unter Blumen des Lands, und wo auf sonnigen Ebnen
Edles Korn und der Obstwald reift, da kränzen am Feste
Gerne die Frommen sich auch, und auf dem Hügel der Stadt
    glänzt,
Menschlicher Wohnung gleich, die himmlische Halle der
    Freude.
Denn voll göttlichen Sinns ist alles Leben geworden,
Und vollendend, wie sonst, erscheinst du wieder den Kindern
Überall, o Natur! und, wie vom Quellengebirg, rinnt
Segen von da und dort in die keimende Seele dem Volke.
Dann, dann, o ihr Freuden Athens! ihr Taten in Sparta!
Köstliche Frühlingszeit im Griechenlande! wenn unser
Herbst kömmt, wenn ihr gereift, ihr Geister alle der Vorwelt!
Wiederkehret und siehe! des Jahrs Vollendung ist nahe!
Dann erhalte das Fest auch euch, vergangene Tage!
Hin nach Hellas schaue das Volk, und weinend und dankend
Sänftige sich in Erinnerungen der stolze Triumphtag!

Aber blühet indes, bis unsre Früchte beginnen,
Blüht, ihr Gärten Ioniens! nur, und die an Athens Schutt
Grünen, ihr Holden! verbergt dem schauenden Tage die Trauer!
Kränzt mit ewigem Laub, ihr Lorbeerwälder! die Hügel

and youth, amidst the country's flowers, and where on sunny plains noble
corn and the orchard ripen, there, too, the pious like to adorn themselves
for the festival, and on the city's hill there gleams, like human dwellings,
the heavenly hall of joy. For life has now been filled with divine meaning,
and, perfecting as ever, you, Nature, appear again everywhere to your chil-
dren; and, as down from the stream-threaded mountains, blessings well
from this place and that into the burgeoning soul of the people. Then, oh,
then, you joys of Athens, you deeds in Sparta, delicious spring-time in the
Grecian lands, when our autumn comes, when matured, you spirits all of
the ancient world, you return and behold! the year's consummation is
near – then may the feast-day preserve you too, days that are gone, may
the people look to Hellas and, offering tears and thanks, make gentle the
proud day of triumph with memories.
    Yet meanwhile bloom on, till our fruit begin, bloom on, you gardens of
Ionia, and you that grow verdant by Athens' rubble, dear ones, conceal her
sorrow from onlooking day! You laurel woods, with perennial foliage

Eurer Toten umher, bei Marathon dort, wo die Knaben
Siegend starben, ach! dort auf Chäroneas Gefilden,
Wo mit den Waffen ins Blut die letzten Athener enteilten,
Fliehend vor dem Tage der Schmach, dort, dort von den Bergen
Klagt ins Schlachttal täglich herab, dort singet von Oetas
Gipfeln das Schicksalslied, ihr wandelnden Wasser, herunter!
Aber du, unsterblich, wenn auch der Griechengesang schon
Dich nicht feiert, wie sonst, aus deinen Wogen, o Meergott!
Töne mir in die Seele noch oft, daß über den Wassern
Furchtlosrege der Geist, dem Schwimmer gleich, in der Starken
Frischem Glücke sich üb', und die Göttersprache, das Wechseln
Und das Werden versteh', und wenn die reißende Zeit mir
Zu gewaltig das Haupt ergreift und die Not und das Irrsal
Unter Sterblichen mir mein sterblich Leben erschüttert,
Laß der Stille mich dann in deiner Tiefe gedenken.

wreathe the hills of your dead all around, over there by Marathon where
boys died conquering, oh, and there on Charonea's plains, where the last
Athenians rushed with their arms into blood, fleeing the day of disgrace,
and there, you wandering waters, from the mountains down to the valley
of battle, daily lament, from the peaks of Oetas sing the song of fate! But
you, immortal, even though now not celebrated by Greek song, as once
you were, O Sea-God, still often out of your waves with music infuse my
soul, that over your waters fearlessly active my mind, like the swimmer,
may practise the quickening joy of the strong, and learn the divine
language of Change and Becoming; and if Time tearing on too mightily
seizes my head, and need and wandering astray among mortals shatter
my mortal life, let my mind dwell on the stillness in your deeps.

## MENONS KLAGEN UM DIOTIMA

### I

TÄGLICH geh' ich heraus, und such' ein Anderes immer,
  Habe längst sie befragt alle die Pfade des Lands;
Droben die kühlenden Höhn, die Schatten alle besuch' ich,
  Und die Quellen; hinauf irret der Geist und hinab,
Ruh' erbittend; so flieht das getroffene Wild in die Wälder,
  Wo es um Mittag sonst sicher im Dunkel geruht;
Aber nimmer erquickt sein grünes Lager das Herz ihm,
  Jammernd und schlummerlos treibt es der Stachel umher.
Nicht die Wärme des Lichts, und nicht die Kühle der Nacht hilft,
  Und in Wogen des Stroms taucht es die Wunden umsonst.
Und wie ihm vergebens die Erd' ihr fröhliches Heilkraut
  Reicht, und das gährende Blut keiner der Zephyre stillt,
So, ihr Lieben! auch mir, so will es scheinen, und niemand
  Kann von der Stirne mir nehmen den traurigen Traum?

## MENON'S LAMENT FOR DIOTIMA

### I

DAILY I go out, for ever seeking another, though I have long since questioned them all, every path of the land; those cooling heights above, all the shaded places I visit, and the sources; up my spirit strays, and down again, begging for rest; thus a stricken deer will flee to the forests, where safely before in the dark it had rested at noon; but now its green lair no longer refreshes its heart, but wailing and sleepless the thorn drives it about. Neither the warmth of light nor the coolness of night helps, and in vain it dips its wounds into the river's wavelets. And just as Earth in vain offers her cheering remedial herbs, and none of the zephyrs stills its fermenting blood, so, it seems, my dear ones, it is with me, and no one can lift the weight of this doleful dream from my brow?

97

2

Ja! es frommet auch nicht, ihr Todesgötter! wenn einmal
   Ihr ihn haltet, und fest habt den bezwungenen Mann,
Wenn ihr Bösen hinab in die schaurige Nacht ihn genommen,
   Dann zu suchen, zu flehn, oder zu zürnen mit euch,
Oder geduldig auch wohl im furchtsamen Banne zu wohnen,
   Und mit Lächeln von euch hören das nüchterne Lied.
Soll es sein, so vergiß dein Heil, und schlummere klanglos!
   Aber doch quillt ein Laut hoffend im Busen dir auf,
Immer kannst du noch nicht, o meine Seele! noch kannst du's
   Nicht gewohnen, und träumst mitten im eisernen Schlaf!
Festzeit hab' ich nicht, doch möcht' ich die Locke bekränzen;
   Bin ich allein denn nicht? aber ein Freundliches muß
Fernher nahe mir sein, und lächeln muß ich und staunen,
   Wie so selig doch auch mitten im Leide mir ist.

3

Licht der Liebe! scheinest du denn auch Toten, du goldnes!
   Bilder aus hellerer Zeit leuchtet ihr mir in die Nacht?
Liebliche Gärten seid, ihr abendrötlichen Berge,
   Seid willkommen und ihr, schweigende Pfade des Hains,

2

And indeed, you gods of death, it is of no avail, when once you hold and bind fast the defeated man, when you evil ones down into horrible night have conveyed him, then to plead, to implore or to be angry with you, nor yet in patience to dwell in that fearful constraint, and with a smile to hear you chanting the sober song. If it must be, forget your welfare and mutely slumber. But even now a sound hopefully wells from your breast; still you cannot, my soul, even now you cannot accept it, and still out of habit you dream in the midst of your iron sleep! Festal time it is not for me, yet I long to put on a garland; am I not wholly alone? But something kind must be near to me from afar, and now I must smile and marvel to think how blissful too I feel in the midst of grief.

3

Golden light of love, do you then shine even for the dead? Visions of brighter days, do you illumine my night? Lovely gardens and mountains tinged with the sundown's red, welcome, and you, silent paths of the

Zeugen himmlischen Glücks, und ihr, hochschauende Sterne,
  Die mir damals so oft segnende Blicke gegönnt!
Euch, ihr Liebenden auch, ihr schönen Kinder des Maitags,
  Stille Rosen und euch, Lilien, nenn' ich noch oft!
Wohl gehn Frühlinge fort, ein Jahr verdränget das andre,
  Wechselnd und streitend, so tost droben vorüber die Zeit
Über sterblichem Haupt, doch nicht vor seligen Augen,
  Und den Liebenden ist anderes Leben geschenkt.
Denn sie alle die Tag' und Jahre der Sterne, sie waren
  Diotima! um uns innig und ewig vereint;

4

Aber wir, zufrieden gesellt, wie die liebenden Schwäne,
  Wenn sie ruhen am See, oder, auf Wellen gewiegt,
Niedersehn in die Wasser, wo silberne Wolken sich spiegeln,
  Und ätherisches Blau unter den Schiffenden wallt,
So auf Erden wandelten wir. Und drohte der Nord auch,
  Er, der Liebenden Feind, klagenbereitend, und fiel
Von den Ästen das Laub, und flog im Winde der Regen,
  Ruhig lächelten wir, fühlten den eigenen Gott

orchard, you that witnessed heavenly bliss; and you, high-gazing stars that so often granted me blessing glances. And you lovers too, the May day's beautiful children, tranquil roses, and you, lilies, still often I name. Springs, it is true, go by, one year supplants the other, changing and warring Time roars on up above, beyond the heads of us mortals, yet not to the eyes of the blessed; and to lovers too a different life has been given. For all these, Diotima, the days and years of the stars, were at one with us then, closely, eternally;

4

But we, content in our union like loving swans when they rest by the lake or, cradled on the wavelets, gaze down at the waters where silvery clouds are reflected and aetherial azure ripples among the voyagers in their boats, travelled over this earth. And though Boreas threatened, he, the enemy of lovers, scattering lamentations, and though the leaves came down from the branches and rain flew about in the wind, calmly we smiled, feeling our own god's presence within our intimate converse, in a single song of our

Unter trautem Gespräch; in Einem Seelengesange,
 Ganz in Frieden mit uns kindlich und freudig allein.
Aber das Haus ist öde mir nun, und sie haben mein Auge
 Mir genommen, auch mich hab' ich verloren mit ihr.
Darum irr' ich umher, und wohl, wie die Schatten, so muß ich
 Leben, und sinnlos dünkt lange das Übrige mir.

5

Feiern möcht' ich; aber wofür? und singen mit Andern,
 Aber so einsam fehlt jegliches Göttliche mir.
Dies ist's, dies mein Gebrechen, ich weiß, es lähmet ein Fluch mir
 Darum die Sehnen, und wirft, wo ich beginne, mich hin,
Daß ich fühllos sitze den Tag, und stumm wie die Kinder,
 Nur vom Auge mir kalt öfters die Träne noch schleicht,
Und die Pflanze des Felds, und der Vögel Singen mich trüb
 macht,
 Weil mit Freuden auch sie Boten des Himmlischen sind,
Aber mir in schaudernder Brust die beseelende Sonne,
 Kühl und fruchtlos mir dämmert, wie Strahlen der Nacht,
Ach! und nichtig und leer, wie Gefängniswände, der Himmel
 Eine beugende Last über dem Haupte mir hängt!

souls, wholly at peace with ourselves, childlike and joyful alone. But my house is desolate now, and they have taken away my eyes, and together with her I have lost my own self. That is why I stray about, and I fear that now I must live like the shades of the dead, and all else has long seemed senseless to me.

5

To celebrate is my will; but what? And to sing with others, but in this utter solitude I lack all that's divine. This is it, this is my failing, I know, this is why a curse maims my sinews and, where I begin, hurls me down, so that unfeeling I sit all day and dumb as small children, only from time to time still a tear coldly creeps out of my eyes, and the plant of the field and the singing of birds make me sad, because, bearing joys, these too are heralds of the divine, but to me in my shuddering emptiness the inspiring sun coolly and fruitlessly dawns, like rays of the night, oh, and futile and dreary like prison walls now the heavens, a burden that bows me down, hang over my head.

6

Sonst mir anders bekannt! o Jugend, und bringen Gebete
    Dich nicht wieder, dich nie? führet kein Pfad mich zurück?
Soll es werden auch mir, wie den Götterlosen, die vormals
    Glänzenden Auges doch auch saßen an seligem Tisch',
Aber übersättiget bald, die schwärmenden Gäste,
    Nun verstummet, und nun, unter der Lüfte Gesang,
Unter blühender Erd' entschlafen sind, bis dereinst sie
    Eines Wunders Gewalt sie, die Versunkenen, zwingt,
Wiederzukehren, und neu auf grünendem Boden zu wandeln. –
    Heiliger Odem durchströmt göttlich die lichte Gestalt,
Wenn das Fest sich beseelt, und Fluten der Liebe sich regen,
    Und vom Himmel getränkt, rauscht der lebendige Strom,
Wenn es drunten ertönt, und ihre Schätze die Nacht zollt,
    Und aus Bächen herauf glänzt das begrabene Gold. –

7

Aber o du, die schon am Scheidewege mir damals,
    Da ich versank vor dir, tröstend ein Schöneres wies,

6

Once known to me in a different guise, O youth! Will no prayers make you return, never again? Does no path lead me back? Shall it be with me as with the godless who also once sat with shining eyes at the heavenly banqueting table, but soon cloyed with the food, these fantastical guests now are silenced, and now, under the song of the breezes, under the blossoming earth are asleep, till one day a miracle's power shall compel them, the deeply engulfed, to return and to walk anew on ground all sprouting and green. – Holy breath divinely transfuses the radiant shape when a soul inspires the feasting, and the currents of love are released, and watered by Heaven the living river roars, when down below there's a rumbling, and night contributes her treasures, and up from the beds of streams comes the glitter of buried gold. –

7

But you that already then, at the crossroads of parting, when I fell at your feet, comforting pointed to better things yet to be sought, you that taught

Du, die Großes zu sehn, und froher die Götter zu singen,
 Schweigend, wie sie, mich einst stille begeisternd gelehrt;
Götterkind! erscheinest du mir, und grüßest, wie einst, mich,
 Redest wieder, wie einst, höhere Dinge mir zu?
Siehe! weinen vor dir, und klagen muß ich, wenn schon noch,
 Denkend edlerer Zeit, dessen die Seele sich schämt.
Denn so lange, so lang auf matten Pfaden der Erde
 Hab' ich, deiner gewohnt, dich in der Irre gesucht,
Freudiger Schutzgeist! aber umsonst, und Jahre zerrannen,
 Seit wir ahnend um uns glänzen die Abende sahn.

8

Dich nur, dich erhält dein Licht, o Heldin! im Lichte,
 Und dein Dulden erhält liebend, o Gütige, dich;
Und nicht einmal bist du allein; Gespielen genug sind,
 Wo du blühest und ruhst unter den Rosen des Jahrs;
Und der Vater, er selbst, durch sanftumatmende Musen
 Sendet die zärtlichen Wiegengesänge dir zu.
Ja! noch ist sie es ganz! noch schwebt vom Haupte zur Sohle,
 Stillherwandelnd, wie sonst, mir die Athenerin vor.

me to see what is great and more blithely to sing the gods, silent, as they
are, quietly filled me with rapture; child of the gods, once more will you
appear to me and greet me as once you did, speaking to me once again of
exalted things? Look, I am forced to weep and lament in your presence,
though remembering nobler times my soul is ashamed. For so long, so
long now on weary paths of the earth, accustomed to you, I have looked for
you in the wilds, joyous guardian spirit! But in vain, and years have dis-
solved into nothing since, foreboding, around us we saw those evenings
gleam.

8

You alone, O heroine, your own light sustains in the light, and your
patience, kind one, sustains you in love; nor, even, are you alone, there are
playmates enough where you flower and rest amidst the roses of the year;
and the Father Himself, by the Muses that exhale gentleness, sends those
tender lullabies to you. Yes, still she is quite the same! Still from head to
heel the Athenian, silently walking towards me, hovers in front of my gaze!

Und wie, freundlicher Geist! von heitersinnender Stirne
  Segnend und sicher dein Strahl unter die Sterblichen fällt;
So bezeugest du mir's, und sagst mir's, daß ich es andern
  Wiedersage, denn auch Andere glauben es nicht,
Daß unsterblicher doch, denn Sorg' und Zürnen, die Freude
  Und ein goldener Tag täglich am Ende noch ist.

9

So will ich, ihr Himmlischen! denn auch danken, und endlich
  Atmet aus leichter Brust wieder des Sängers Gebet.
Und wie, wenn ich mit ihr, auf sonniger Höhe mit ihr stand,
  Spricht belebend ein Gott innen vom Tempel mich an.
Leben will ich denn auch! schon grünt's! wie von heiliger Leier
  Ruft es von silbernen Bergen Apollons voran!
Komm! es war wie ein Traum! Die blutenden Fittige sind ja
  Schon genesen, verjüngt leben die Hoffnungen all.
Großes zu finden, ist viel, ist viel noch übrig, und wer so
  Liebte, gehet, er muß, gehet zu Göttern die Bahn.
Und geleitet ihr uns, ihr Weihestunden! ihr ernsten,
  Jugendlichen! o bleibt, heilige Ahnungen, ihr

And, kindly spirit, when blessing and sure your radiance falls among mortals from your serenely pensive brow, then you prove it to me, and tell me, so that to others I can repeat it, for there are others too who do not believe it, that joy after all outlasts both care and anger, and a golden day daily still shines in the end.

9

Therefore, you Heavenly powers, I will thank you too, and at last the singer's prayer freely can issue once more from an unburdened breast. And, as once when with her I stood on the sunlit hilltop, life-giving, now a god speaks to me again from the temple within. Let me live again, then! Already all grows green! And from a holy lyre 'forward' rings out from Apollo's silvery peaks. Come, then! It was like a dream! already your blood-stained pinions are healed, and all your hopes live renewed. To find what is great is much, but much remains, and who thus has loved will follow, must follow the way that leads up to gods. Then accompany us, O sacred Hours, you solemn, youthful ones! Stay with us always, holy

Fromme Bitten! und ihr Begeisterungen und all ihr
    Guten Genien, die gerne bei Liebenden sind;
Bleibt so lange mit uns, bis wir auf gemeinsamem Boden
    Dort, wo die Seligen all niederzukehren bereit,
Dort, wo die Adler sind, die Gestirne, die Boten des Vaters,
    Dort, wo die Musen, woher Helden und Liebende sind,
Dort uns, oder auch hier, auf tauender Insel begegnen,
    Wo die Unsrigen erst, blühend in Gärten gesellt,
Wo die Gesänge wahr und länger die Frühlinge schön sind,
    Und von neuem ein Jahr unserer Seele beginnt.

## BROT UND WEIN

### AN HEINZE

#### I

Rings um ruhet die Stadt; still wird die erleuchtete Gasse,
    Und, mit Fackeln geschmückt, rauschen die Wagen hinweg.
Satt gehn heim von Freuden des Tags zu ruhen die Menschen,
    Und Gewinn und Verlust wäget ein sinniges Haupt

Presentiments, pious Entreaties, and you, Inspirations, and all you benevolent spirits that like to consort with lovers. Stay with us two until on communal ground, where all the blessèd prepare to descend again, where the eagles are, the constellations, the Father's heralds, where the Muses are and whence heroes and lovers have come, until there, or here perhaps, we meet on a dewy island, where gathered together in gardens, blossoming jointly at last, our songs will be true and Springs remain beautiful longer, and another year of our souls will begin.

## BREAD AND WINE

### TO HEINSE

#### I

All around the city rests; the lighted street falls silent, and, adorned with torches, the carriages rumble off. Sated with the day's pleasures, men go home to rest, and a pensive head weighs up gain and loss contentedly in the house; bare of its grapes and flowers and of its hand-made goods, the

Wohlzufrieden zu Haus; leer steht von Trauben und Blumen,
  Und von Werken der Hand ruht der geschäftige Markt.
Aber das Saitenspiel tönt fern aus Gärten; vielleicht, daß
  Dort ein Liebendes spielt oder ein einsamer Mann
Ferner Freunde gedenkt und der Jugendzeit; und die Brunnen
  Immerquillend und frisch rauschen an duftendem Beet.
Still in dämmriger Luft ertönen geläutete Glocken,
  Und der Stunden gedenk rufet ein Wächter die Zahl.
Jetzt auch kommet ein Wehn und regt die Gipfel des Hains auf,
  Sieh! und das Schattenbild unserer Erde, der Mond,
Kommet geheim nun auch; die Schwärmerische, die Nacht
  kommt,
  Voll mit Sternen und wohl wenig bekümmert um uns,
Glänzt die Erstaunende dort, die Fremdlingin unter den
  Menschen,
  Über Gebirgeshöhn traurig und prächtig herauf.

2

Wunderbar ist die Gunst der Hocherhabnen und niemand
  Weiß von wannen und was einem geschiehet von ihr.
So bewegt sie die Welt und die hoffende Seele der Menschen,
  Selbst kein Weiser versteht, was sie bereitet, denn so

busy market rests. But music of strings distantly drifts from gardens; it may be that a lover plays there or that a lonely man is recalling distant friends and the days of his youth; and the fountains, ever flowing and cool, plash beside the fragrant flower beds. Quiet in the glimmering air the ringing of bells resounds, and, recording the hours, a watchman calls out the number. Now a breeze rises also and ruffles the crests of the orchard; look, and our Earth's shadowy image, the moon, comes mysterious too; Night, the fantastical, comes; full of stars and not greatly concerned about us, there the astonishing comes, the stranger amidst us mortals, up over mountain-tops sadly and splendidly gleams.

2

Marvellous is the favour of Night, the greatly exalted, and no one can tell whence and what it is she bestows on one. So she moves the world and the hopeful souls of us mortals, even no sage understands what she prepares,

Will es der oberste Gott, der sehr dich liebet, und darum
   Ist noch lieber, wie sie, dir der besonnene Tag.
Aber zuweilen liebt auch klares Auge den Schatten
   Und versuchet zu Lust, eh' es die Not ist, den Schlaf,
Oder es blickt auch gern ein treuer Mann in die Nacht hin,
   Ja, es ziemet sich, ihr Kränze zu weihn und Gesang,
Weil den Irrenden sie geheiliget ist und den Toten,
   Selber aber besteht, ewig, in freiestem Geist.
Aber sie muß uns auch, daß in der zaudernden Weile,
   Daß im Finstern für uns einiges Haltbare sei,
Uns die Vergessenheit und das Heiligtrunkene gönnen,
   Gönnen das strömende Wort, das, wie die Liebenden, sei,
Schlummerlos und vollern Pokal und kühneres Leben,
   Heilig Gedächtnis auch, wachend zu bleiben bei Nacht.

for such is the will of the Highest God, who loves you greatly, and there-
fore reasoning day is still dearer to you than Night. But even the clear eye
at times loves her shadows and, for pleasure's sake, before there is need,
tastes of sleep; or even a true man will gladly gaze into Night and, indeed,
it is fitting to consecrate garlands to her, and song, because she is sacred to
those astray and to the dead, though herself she subsists, everlasting, most
free in spirit. But to us in return, so that in the wavering moment, in the
dark we may find something at least that endures, she must grant oblivion
and grant the sacredly drunken, grant us the onrushing word which will be
sleepless like lovers, grant us the fuller cup and more reckless life, holy
remembrance, too, to remain wakeful by night.

3

Auch verbergen umsonst das Herz im Busen, umsonst nur
   Halten den Mut noch wir, Meister und Knaben, denn wer
Möcht' es hindern und wer möcht' uns die Freude verbieten?
   Göttliches Feuer auch treibet, bei Tag und bei Nacht,
Aufzubrechen. So komm! daß wir das Offene schauen,
   Daß ein Eigenes wir suchen, so weit es auch ist.
Fest bleibt Eins; es sei um Mittag oder es gehe
   Bis in die Mitternacht, immer bestehet ein Maß,
Allen gemein, doch jeglichem auch ist eignes beschieden,
   Dahin gehet und kommt jeder, wohin er es kann.
Drum! und spotten des Spotts mag gern frohlockender Wahn-
   sinn,
   Wenn er in heiliger Nacht plötzlich die Sänger ergreift.
Drum an den Isthmos komm! dorthin, wo das offene Meer
   rauscht
Am Parnaß und der Schnee delphische Felsen umglänzt,
Dort ins Land des Olymps, dort auf die Höhe Cithärons,
   Unter die Fichten dort, unter die Trauben, von wo
Thebe drunten und Ismenos rauscht im Lande des Kadmos,
   Dorther kommt und zurück deutet der kommende Gott.

3

And in vain it is that we hide our hearts within us, in vain that we hold back
our courage still, both masters and novices; for who would prevent it, and
who would forbid us rejoicing? And divine fire also by day and by night
impels us to set out. Then, come! That we may see open spaces, that we
may seek what is proper to us, distant as it may be. One thing remains
sure; whether it be towards noon or late, towards midnight, always a
measure persists, common to all, though also to each his own is allotted,
and each of us goes and comes where he can. Jubilant madness, therefore,
well may deride derision, when in holy night it suddenly takes possession
of the singers. Come to the Isthmus, then! There, where the green sea roars
by Parnassus, and snow gleams on the Delphian rocks, there to the land of
Olympus, there to the peak of Cithaeron, amidst the pine-trees there,
amidst the grapes, from where Thebe below and Ismenos roar in the coun-
try of Cadmus; thence has come and back to them points the approaching
god.

4

Seliges Griechenland! du Haus der Himmlischen alle,
    Also ist wahr, was einst wir in der Jugend gehört?
Festlicher Saal! der Boden ist Meer! und Tische die Berge,
    Wahrlich zu einzigem Brauche vor alters gebaut!
Aber die Thronen, wo? die Tempel, und wo die Gefäße,
    Wo mit Nektar gefüllt, Göttern zu Lust der Gesang?
Wo, wo leuchten sie denn, die fernhintreffenden Sprüche?
    Delphi schlummert und wo tönet das große Geschick?
Wo ist das schnelle? wo brichts, allgegenwärtigen Glücks voll
    Donnernd aus heiterer Luft über die Augen herein?
Vater Äther! so riefs und flog von Zunge zu Zunge,
    Tausendfach, es ertrug keiner das Leben allein;
Ausgeteilet erfreut solch Gut und getauschet, mit Fremden,
    Wirds ein Jubel, es wächst schlafend des Wortes Gewalt:
Vater! heiter! und hallt, so weit es gehet, das uralt
    Zeichen, von Eltern geerbt, treffend und schaffend hinab.
Denn so kehren die Himmlischen ein, tiefschütternd gelangt so
    Aus den Schatten herab unter die Menschen ihr Tag.

4

Blessèd land of the Greeks, you house of all the Heavenly, so it is true, what once in our youth we heard? Festive hall! The floor is ocean! Its tables are mountains, truly built for a single use in times out of mind! But the thrones, where are they? Where the temples, and where the vessels, where, filled with nectar, fit to please gods, is song? Where, oh where do they shine, then, the far-striking oracles? Delphi slumbers, and where does the great destiny sound? Where is the swift one? Where, full of ubiquitous joy does it break thundering out of clear skies upon mortal eyes? Father Aether! they cried, and from tongue to tongue it flew on a thousandfold, not one endured life alone; shared out, such wealth delights and, bartered with strangers, it swells into exultation, asleep the word's power increases, Father! Aether serene! and far as it can travel, the ancient sign handed down from forbears, striking, creating, resounds. For it is thus that the Heavenly enter, deeply convulsing thus that down from the darkness their Day reaches men.

5

Unempfunden kommen sie erst, es streben entgegen
    Ihnen die Kinder, zu hell kommet, zu blendend das Glück,
Und es scheut sich der Mensch, kaum weiß zu sagen ein Halb-
        gott
    Wer mit Namen sie sind, die mit den Gaben ihm nahn.
Aber der Mut von ihnen ist groß, es füllen das Herz ihm
    Ihre Freuden und kaum weiß er zu brauchen das Gut,
Schafft, verschwendet und fast ward ihm Unheiliges heilig,
    Das er mit segnender Hand törig und gütig berührt.
Möglichst dulden die Himmlischen dies; dann aber in Wahrheit
    Kommen sie selbst, und gewohnt werden die Menschen des
        Glücks
Und des Tags und zu schaun die Offenbaren, das Antlitz
    Derer, welche, schon längst Eines und Alles genannt,
Tief die verschwiegene Brust mit freier Genüge gefüllet,
    Und zuerst und allein alles Verlangen beglückt;
So ist der Mensch; wenn da ist das Gut, und es sorget mit Gaben
    Selber ein Gott für ihn, kennet und sieht er es nicht.
Tragen muß er, zuvor; nun aber nennt er sein Liebstes,
    Nun, nun müssen dafür Worte, wie Blumen entstehn.

5

Unperceived at first they come, the children surge forward to meet them;
too bright, too dazzling this good fortune comes, and men avoid them, a
demi-god even can hardly say who they are by name that approach him
with gifts. But their courage is great, and their joys fill his heart, and he
scarcely knows to what use he should put his wealth, bustles, squanders it,
and almost regarded as holy things profane which his blessing hand fool-
ishly, kindly has touched. This the Heavenly tolerate as far as they can;
but then they appear in truth, in person, and men grow used to good for-
tune, to Day, and to the sight of these now manifest, the countenances of
those who, long ago called the One and All, deeply had filled the taciturn
heart with free self-content, and were the first and only to satisfy every
longing. Such is man; when the wealth is at hand, and a god in person
provides him with gifts, he neither knows nor sees it. First he must suffer;
but now he names his most cherished, now words for it, like flowers, must
spring to life.

6

Und nun denkt er zu ehren in Ernst die seligen Götter,
  Wirklich und wahrhaft muß alles verkünden ihr Lob.
Nichts darf schauen das Licht, was nicht den Hohen gefället,
  Vor den Äther gebührt Müßigversuchendes nicht.
Drum in der Gegenwart der Himmlischen würdig zu stehen,
  Richten in herrlichen Ordnungen Völker sich auf
Untereinander und baun die schönen Tempel und Städte
  Fest und edel, sie gehn über Gestaden empor –
Aber wo sind sie? wo blühn die Bekannten, die Kronen des
    Festes?
  Thebe welkt und Athen; rauschen die Waffen nicht mehr
In Olympia, nicht die goldnen Wagen des Kampfspiels,
  Und bekränzen sich denn nimmer die Schiffe Korinths?
Warum schweigen auch sie, die alten heilgen Theater?
  Warum freuet sich denn nicht der geweihete Tanz?
Warum zeichnet, wie sonst, die Stirne des Mannes ein Gott
    nicht,
  Drückt den Stempel, wie sonst, nicht dem Getroffenen auf?
Oder er kam auch selbst und nahm des Menschen Gestalt an
  Und vollendet' und schloß tröstend das himmlische Fest.

6

And now in earnest he means to honour the blessèd gods, truly, effectively
all must redound to their praises. Nothing must see the light that does not
please the Exalted, for that which idly endeavours is unworthy of Aether's
sight. Therefore, to stand unashamed in the presence of the Heavenly,
ranged in glorious hierarchies peoples arise, rivals for glory, and build
those beautiful temples and cities; firm and noble they tower above river
and sea – But where are they? Where do the well-known thrive, the festi-
val's crowns? Thebes wilts, and Athens; do, then, the weapons no longer
sound at Olympia, nor the golden chariots of the games, and are the ships
of Corinth no longer, then, wreathed with flowers? Why are they silent
too, the ancient and sacred theatres? Why does the hallowed dance not re-
joice? Why no more does a god mark the brow of a man, imprinting the
stamp, as before, on him he has struck? Or he would come in person,
assuming the shape of a mortal, and completed and, comforting, ended the
divine festivity.

7

Aber Freund! wir kommen zu spät. Zwar leben die Götter,
  Aber über dem Haupt droben in anderer Welt.
Endlos wirken sie da und scheinens wenig zu achten,
  Ob wir leben, so sehr schonen die Himmlischen uns.
Denn nicht immer vermag ein schwaches Gefäß sie zu fassen,
  Nur zu Zeiten erträgt göttliche Fülle der Mensch.
Traum von ihnen ist drauf das Leben. Aber das Irrsal
  Hilft, wie Schlummer, und stark machet die Not und die
    Nacht,
Bis daß Helden genug in der ehernen Wiege gewachsen,
  Herzen an Kraft, wie sonst, ähnlich den Himmlischen sind.
Donnernd kommen sie drauf. Indessen dünket mir öfters
  Besser zu schlafen, wie so ohne Genossen zu sein,
So zu harren, und was zu tun indes und zu sagen,
  Weiß ich nicht, und wozu Dichter in dürftiger Zeit?
Aber sie sind, sagst du, wie des Weingotts heilige Priester,
  Welche von Lande zu Land zogen in heiliger Nacht.

7

But, my friend, we have come too late. True, the gods are living, but
above our heads, up there in a different world. Endlessly there they are
active and – so much do the Heavenly spare us – little they seem to care
whether we live or not. For not always a fragile vessel can hold them, only
at times can men bear the plenitude of the divine. Henceforth our life is a
dream about them. But to wander astray helps, like sleep, and need and
Night make us strong, until heroes enough have grown in the iron cradle,
and hearts, as before, resemble the Heavenly in strength. Thundering then
they come. Meanwhile it sometimes seems better to me to sleep than to be
utterly without companions as we are, to be always waiting like this, and
what's to be done or said in the meantime, I do not know, and what is the
use of poets at a time of dearth? But they are, you say, like those holy
priests of the wine-god who travelled from country to country in holy
Night.

8

Nämlich, als vor einiger Zeit, uns dünket sie lange,
    Aufwärts stiegen sie all, welche das Leben beglückt,
Als der Vater gewandt sein Angesicht von den Menschen,
    Und das Trauern mit Recht über der Erde begann,
Als erschienen zuletzt ein stiller Genius, himmlisch
    Tröstend, welcher des Tags End verkündet' und schwand,
Ließ zum Zeichen, daß einst er da gewesen und wieder
    Käme, der himmlische Chor einige Gaben zurück,
Derer menschlich, wie sonst, wir uns zu freuen vermöchten,
    Denn zur Freude, mit Geist, wurde das Größre zu groß
Unter den Menschen und noch, noch fehlen die Starken zu
    höchsten
    Freuden, aber es lebt stille noch einiger Dank.
Brot ist der Erde Frucht, doch ists vom Lichte gesegnet,
    Und vom donnernden Gott kommet die Freude des Weins.
Darum denken wir auch dabei der Himmlischen, die sonst
    Da gewesen und die kehren in richtiger Zeit,
Darum singen sie auch mit Ernst, die Sänger, den Weingott
    Und nicht eitel erdacht tönet dem Alten das Lob.

8

For when some time ago, to us it seems long, they all ascended by whom life had been granted with joy, when the Father averted His face from mankind and all over the earth mourning, rightly, began, when last of all a quiet spirit had appeared, divinely comforting, who proclaimed the end of Day and withdrew, as a sign that they had once been here and would come again, the heavenly choir left a few gifts behind in which humanly, as before, we could take pleasure, since for joy of the spirit what is great became too great among men and still, even now we lack those strong enough for supreme joy though some gratitude still lives on in silence. Bread is the fruit of Earth, but is blessed by the light, and from the thundering god comes the gladness of wine. That is why through these we think of the Heavenly, who once were here and who will return at the proper time; that is why in earnest too the singers hymn the wine-god and not vainly devised the ancient one's praises are sung.

9

Ja! sie sagen mit Recht, er söhne den Tag mit der Nacht aus,
  Führe des Himmels Gestirn ewig hinunter, hinauf,
Allzeit froh, wie das Laub der immergrünenden Fichte,
  Das er liebt, und der Kranz, den er von Efeu gewählt,
Weil er bleibet und selbst die Spur der entflohenen Götter
  Götterlosen hinab unter das Finstere bringt.
Was der Alten Gesang von Kindern Gottes geweissagt,
  Siehe! wir sind es, wir; Frucht von Hesperien ists!
Wunderbar und genau ists als an Menschen erfüllet,
  Glaube, wer es geprüft! aber so vieles geschieht,
Keines wirket, denn wir sind herzlos, Schatten, bis unser
  Vater Äther erkannt jeden und allen gehört.
Aber indessen kommt als Fackelschwinger des Höchsten
  Sohn, der Syrier, unter die Schatten herab.
Selige Weise sehns; ein Lächeln aus der gefangnen
  Seele leuchtet, dem Licht tauet ihr Auge noch auf.
Sanfter träumet und schläft in Armen der Erde der Titan,
  Selbst der neidische, selbst Cerberus trinket und schläft.

9

Yes, and rightly they say that he reconciles Night and Day, eternally
moves the planets and stars of Heaven, now down, now up, joyous at all
times like the evergreen pine-tree branches, which he loves, and the wreath,
of ivy wound by his choice, because it lasts and conveys the trace of the
vanished gods themselves to the godless who live in darkness below. What
the ancient's song foretold of the children of God, look, we are it, of us it
is true; the fruit of Hesperia it is! Marvellously and strictly it has been ful-
filled in men, let him who has proved it believe! But so much happens,
nothing takes effect, for we are heartless, mere shadows, until our Father
Aether, acclaimed, belongs to each and to all. But meanwhile as torch-
bearer the Son of the Highest, the Syrian, comes down among the shadows.
Blissful wise men see it; a smile is kindled from the imprisoned soul, and
their eyes yet shall thaw to the light. In the arms of Earth more gently the
Titan lies dreaming, even the jealous one, Cerberus, drinks and sleeps.

## DER NECKAR

In deinen Tälern wachte mein Herz mir auf
Zum Leben, deine Wellen umspielten mich,
   Und all der holden Hügel, die dich,
      Wanderer! kennen, ist keiner fremd mir.

Auf ihren Gipfeln löste des Himmels Luft
Mir oft der Knechtschaft Schmerzen; und aus dem Tal,
   Wie Leben aus dem Freudebecher,
      Glänzte die bläuliche Silberwelle.

Der Berge Quellen eilten hinab zu dir,
Mit ihnen auch mein Herz, und du nahmst uns mit
   Zum stillerhabnen Rhein, zu seinen
      Städten hinunter und lustgen Inseln.

Noch dünkt die Welt mir schön, und das Aug entflieht
Verlangend nach den Reizen der Erde mir
   Zum goldenen Paktol, zu Smyrnas
      Ufer, zu Ilions Wald. Auch möcht ich

## THE NECKAR

In your valleys my heart awoke to life, your wavelets played about me, and of all the dear hills that know you, wanderer, none is unknown to me.

On their summits often the air of heaven rid me of servitude's pains; and from the valley, as life does from the cup of joy, the bluish silver wavelet gleamed.

The mountain streams hurried down to you, and with them my heart as well, and you took us with you to calmly dignified Rhine, down to his cities and cheerful islets.

Still the world seems lovely to me, and my eyes flee from me, longing for the allurements of Earth, to golden Pactolus, to Smyrna's shore, to the woods of Ilion. Also I often

Bei Sunium oft landen, den stummen Pfad
Nach deinen Säulen fragen, Olympion!
Noch eh der Sturmwind und das Alter
Hin in den Schutt der Athenertempel

Und ihrer Gottesbilder auch dich begräbt,
Denn lang schon einsam stehst du, o Stolz der Welt,
Die nicht mehr ist. Und o ihr schönen
Inseln Ioniens! wo die Meerluft

Die heißen Ufer kühlt und den Lorbeerwald
Durchsäuselt, wenn die Sonne den Weinstock wärmt,
Ach! wo ein goldner Herbst dem armen
Volk in Gesänge die Seufzer wandelt,

Wenn sein Granatbaum reift, wenn aus grüner Nacht
Die Pomeranze blinkt, und der Mastixbaum
Von Harze träuft, und Pauk und Cymbel
Zum labyrinthischen Tanze klingen.

Zu euch, ihr Inseln! bringt mich vielleicht, zu euch,
Mein Schutzgott einst; doch weicht mir aus treuem Sinn
Auch da mein Neckar nicht mit seinen
Lieblichen Wiesen und Uferweiden.

Wish I could land near Sunium, inquire of the silent path for your columns, Olympion, before tempest and time bury you too in the rubble of Athens' temples
And their statues of gods; for long now you have stood lonely, O pride of the world that is no more. And O you beautiful isles of Ionia, where the sea breeze
Cools the hot shores and rustles through the laurel wood, when the sun warms the vine and, oh, where a golden autumn transforms a poor people's sighs into songs,
When their pomegranate tree ripens, when out of a green night the orange glints, and the mastic tree drips with resin, and cymbal and kettle drum sound for the labyrinthine dance.
To you, O islands, one day perhaps my tutelar god will take me; but even then my faithful mind will not cease to dwell on my Neckar with its charming meadows and waterside willows.

## DIE HEIMAT

Froh kehrt der Schiffer heim an den stillen Strom,
  Von Inseln fernher, wenn er geerntet hat;
    So käm' auch ich zur Heimat, hätt' ich
      Güter so viele, wie Leid, geerntet.

Ihr teuern Ufer, die mich erzogen einst,
  Stillt ihr der Liebe Leiden, versprecht ihr mir,
    Ihr Wälder meiner Jugend, wenn ich
      Komme, die Ruhe noch einmal wieder?

Am kühlen Bache, wo ich der Wellen Spiel,
  Am Strome, wo ich gleiten die Schiffe sah,
    Dort bin ich bald; euch traute Berge,
      Die mich behüteten einst, der Heimat

Verehrte sichre Grenzen, der Mutter Haus
  Und liebender Geschwister Umarmungen
    Begrüß' ich bald und ihr umschließt mich,
      Daß, wie in Banden, das Herz mir heile,

## HOME

Happy the boatman returns home to the quiet river from distant islands where he has harvested; so I too should now come home, had I reaped as much wealth as suffering.

Dear river banks, you that once brought me up, do you soothe the sufferings of love? You woods of my childhood, when I return, do you promise me peace once more?

By that cool stream where I saw the ripples play, the river where I watched many boats glide past, there soon I'll be; you long-loved mountains, once my protectors, my native region's

Revered and certain boundaries, my mother's house and the embraces of loving brother and sister I'll welcome soon; and you'll enclose me, so that, as though bandaged, my heart shall heal,

Ihr treugebliebnen! aber ich weiß, ich weiß,
  Der Liebe Leid, dies heilet so bald mir nicht,
    Dies singt kein Wiegensang, den tröstend
      Sterbliche singen, mir aus dem Busen.

Denn sie, die uns das himmlische Feuer leihn,
  Die Götter schenken heiliges Leid uns auch,
    Drum bleibe dies. Ein Sohn der Erde
      Schein ich; zu lieben gemacht, zu leiden.

## DIE LIEBE

WENN ihr Freunde vergeßt, wenn ihr die Euern all,
  O ihr Dankbaren, sie, euere Dichter schmäht,
    Gott vergeb' es, doch ehret
      Nur die Seele der Liebenden.

Denn o saget, wo lebt menschliches Leben sonst,
  Da die knechtische jetzt alles, die Sorge zwingt?
    Darum wandelt der Gott auch
      Sorglos über dem Haupt uns längst.

---

You that are faithful still! Yet I know, I know, the grief of love, this will not easily heal, of this no lullaby which mortals sing to console can rid my heart.

For they who lend us the heavenly fire, the gods, with holy sorrow endow us too; so be it, then. A son of Earth I seem; one intended to love, to suffer.

## LOVE

IF you forget your friends, if you abuse them all, O you grateful ones, abuse all the poets, your own, may God forgive you; but always respect the soul of lovers.

For, tell me, where else does human life live still, now that the slavish one, Care, rules and compels all things? That too is why the god has long moved uncaring above our heads.

Doch, wie immer das Jahr kalt und gesanglos ist
  Zur beschiedenen Zeit, aber aus weißem Feld
    Grüne Halme doch sprossen,
      Oft ein einsamer Vogel singt,

Wenn sich mählich der Wald dehnet, der Strom sich regt,
  Schon die mildere Luft leise von Mittag weht
    Zur erlesenen Stunde,
      So ein Zeichen der schönern Zeit,

Die wir glauben, erwächst einziggenügsam noch,
  Einzig edel und fromm über dem ehernen,
    Wilden Boden die Liebe,
      Gottes Tochter, von ihm allein.

Sei gesegnet, o sei, himmlische Pflanze, mir
  Mit Gesange gepflegt, wenn des ätherischen
    Nektars Kräfte dich nähren,
      Und der schöpfrische Strahl dich reift.

Wachs und werde zum Wald! eine beseeltere,
  Vollentblühende Welt! Sprache der Liebenden
    Sei die Sprache des Landes,
      Ihre Seele der Laut des Volks!

Yet, however cold and songless the year at the allotted season, still from the white field green blades will shoot, often a solitary bird will sing,
  When the wood gradually stretches, the river stirs, and already the milder breeze softly blows from the south at the elected hour, when, a sign of the better age,
  In which we believe, uniquely self-sufficient, uniquely noble and pious, over the brazen desolate soil, Love, the daughter of God, springs up from Him alone.
  Let me bless you, then, O heavenly plant, let me tend you with song, when the powers of aetherial nectar nourish you, and you are ripened by the creative ray.
  Grow and become a wood! A world more soulful, more copiously blossoming! Language of lovers be the language of the land! Their soul the people's lilt!

## LEBENSLAUF

Gröbers wolltest auch du, aber die Liebe zwingt
   All uns nieder, das Leid beuget gewaltiger,
     Doch es kehret umsonst nicht
      Unser Bogen, woher er kommt!

Aufwärts oder hinab! herrschet in heil'ger Nacht,
   Wo die stumme Natur werdende Tage sinnt,
     Herrscht im schiefesten Orkus
      Nicht ein Grades, ein Recht noch auch?

Dies erfuhr ich. Denn nie, sterblichen Meistern gleich,
   Habt ihr Himmlischen, ihr Alleserhaltenden,
     Daß ich wüßte, mit Vorsicht
      Mich des ebenen Pfads geführt.

Alles prüfe der Mensch, sagen die Himmlischen,
   Daß er, kräftig genährt, danken für Alles lern',
     Und verstehe die Freiheit,
      Aufzubrechen, wohin er will.

## THE COURSE OF LIFE

Higher you too aspired, but love forces all of us down, suffering bows us down more mightily still, though not in vain our arc returns to where it began.

Upwards or downwards! In holy night, where silent Nature thinks out the days to come, even in most crooked Orcus does not a straightness, a rightness prevail?

This I discovered. For never, as far as I know, like mortal masters did you Heavenly ones, you the all-preservers, lead me cautiously along a level path.

All things let man try out, the Heavenly say, so that strongly nourished he may learn to be thankful for all things, and grasp the freedom to set out for wherever he wills.

## DER ABSCHIED
*Zweite Fassung*

TRENNEN wollten wir uns? wähnten es gut und klug?
   Da wirs taten, warum schröckte, wie Mord, die Tat?
     Ach! wir kennen uns wenig,
       Denn es waltet ein Gott in uns.

Den verraten? ach ihn, welcher uns alles erst,
   Sinn und Leben erschuf, ihn, den beseelenden
     Schutzgott unserer Liebe,
       Dies, dies Eine vermag ich nicht.

Aber anderen Fehl denket der Weltsinn sich,
   Andern ehernen Dienst übt er und anders Recht,
     Und es listet die Seele
       Tag für Tag der Gebrauch uns ab.

Wohl! ich wußt' es zuvor. Seit die gewurzelte
   Ungestalte die Furcht Götter und Menschen trennt,
     Muß, mit Blut sie zu sühnen,
       Muß der Liebenden Herz vergehn.

## THE FAREWELL
*Second version*

So we wanted to part? Thought it both good and wise? When we did so, why did the deed appal us like murder? Ah, little we know ourselves, for within us a god commands.

Betray him? O him, who created our all, gave us meaning and life, him, the inspiring tutelary god of our love – this, this only, I cannot do.

But the worldly mind invents other wrongs, imposes other inflexible duties and other laws, and day by day usage wears down our souls.

Well, I knew it before. Ever since the deep-rooted, misshapen Fear, divided gods and men, to appease it with blood, the hearts of lovers must perish.

Laß mich schweigen! o laß nimmer von nun an mich
Dieses Tödliche sehn, daß ich im Frieden doch
Hin ins Einsame ziehe,
Und noch unser der Abschied sei!

Reich die Schale mir selbst, daß ich des rettenden
Heilgen Giftes genug, daß ich des Lethetranks
Mit dir trinke, daß alles
Haß und Liebe vergessen sei!

Hingehn will ich. Vielleicht seh' ich in langer Zeit
Diotima! dich hier. Aber verblutet ist
Dann das Wünschen und friedlich
Gleich den Seligen, fremde gehn

Wir umher, ein Gespräch führet uns ab und auf,
Sinnend, zögernd, doch izt mahnt die Vergessenen
Hier die Stelle des Abschieds,
Es erwarmet ein Herz in uns,

Staunend seh' ich dich an, Stimmen, und süßen Sang,
Wie aus voriger Zeit' hör' ich und Saitenspiel,
Und die Lilie duftet
Golden über dem Bach uns auf.

---

Let me keep silent! Oh, never from now on let me look again upon this deadly thing, so that at least in peace I may go off into solitude and the parting at least may be ours!

Pass me the cup yourself, so that I may drink enough of the holy and saving poison, so that with you I may drink of Lethe's water, so that all, both hatred and love, may be forgotten!

To go is my will. Perhaps long after, Diotima, I shall see you here. But then desire will have bled away, and peacefully as the blessèd spirits, and estranged we shall

Walk about, calm converse leading us to and fro, pensive, hesitant; but now the oblivious are recalled, here, by the place of our parting, and a heart grows warm in us,

Wondering I look at you, voices and lovely song as from former times I hear, and the music of strings, and the lily unfurls her fragrance, golden above the brook.

## RÜCKKEHR IN DIE HEIMAT

Ihr milden Lüfte! Boten Italiens!
    Und du mit deinen Pappeln, geliebter Strom!
      Ihr wogenden Gebirg! o all ihr
        Sonnigen Gipfel, so seid ihr's wieder?

Du stiller Ort! in Träumen erschienst du fern
    Nach hoffnungslosem Tage dem Sehnenden,
      Und du mein Haus, und ihr Gespielen,
        Bäume des Hügels, ihr wohlbekannten!

Wie lang ists, o wie lange! des Kindes Ruh
    Ist hin, und hin ist Jugend und Lieb' und Lust;
      Doch du, mein Vaterland! du heilig –
        Duldendes! siehe, du bist geblieben.

Und darum, daß sie dulden mit dir, mit dir
    Sich freun, erziehst du, teures! die Deinen auch
      Und mahnst in Träumen, wenn sie ferne
        Schweifen und irren, die Ungetreuen.

## RETURN TO THE HOMELAND

You gentle breezes! Heralds of Italy! And you with all your poplars, beloved river! You billowing mountain ranges! O all you sunny peaks, so it is you again?

You quiet place, in dreams you appeared to the homesick man, distant after a hopeless day; and you, my house, and you, my playmates, trees of the hillside, the long familiar!

How long it is, oh, how long! The quietude of the child is gone, and gone are youth and love and delight; but you, my homeland, the holy and patient, look, you are still the same.

And because they are patient when you are, and rejoice when you rejoice, dear one, you rear your children and remind them in dreams, even when far away they wander and stray, the disloyal.

Und wenn im heißen Busen dem Jünglinge
   Die eigenmächt'gen Wünsche besänftiget
     Und stille vor dem Schicksal sind, dann
      Gibt der Geläuterte dir sich lieber.

Lebt wohl dann, Jugendtage, du Rosenpfad
   Der Lieb', und all' ihr Pfade des Wanderers,
     Lebt wohl! und nimm und segne du mein
      Leben, o Himmel der Heimat, wieder!

## ERMUNTERUNG
### Zweite Fassung

Echo des Himmels! heiliges Herz! warum,
   Warum verstummst du unter den Lebenden?
     Schläfst, Freies! von den Götterlosen
      Ewig hinab in die Nacht verwiesen?

Wacht denn, wie vormals, nimmer des Äthers Licht?
   Und blüht die alte Mutter, die Erde, nicht?
     Und übt der Geist nicht da und dort, nicht
      Lächelnd die Liebe das Recht noch immer?

---

And when in his fervid heart the self-willed desires of the youth have been stilled, and fall silent before fate, then the mellowed one more gladly submits to you.

Then farewell, days of youth, you rose-lined path of love, and all the paths of the wanderer, farewell! And you, O heaven of my homeland, take back my life and bless it once more!

## EXHORTATION
### Second Version

Echo of Heaven, heart that is hallowed, why, why now do you fall silent among the living, and sleep, you free one, by the godless banished for ever to the depths of night?

Is not the light of Aether awake, as before? And is not the ancient mother, Earth, in blossom? And, here and there, does not the spirit, Love, with a smile wield her rights as ever?

Nur du nicht mehr! doch mahnen die Himmlischen,
   Und stillebildend weht, wie ein kahl Gefild,
      Der Odem der Natur dich an, der
         Alleserheiternde, seelenvolle.

O Hoffnung! bald, bald singen die Haine nicht
   Des Lebens Lob allein, denn es ist die Zeit,
      Daß aus der Menschen Munde sie, die
         Schönere Seele, sich neuverkündet,

Dann liebender, im Bunde mit Sterblichen,
   Das Element sich bildet, und dann erst reich,
      Bei frommer Kinder Dank, der Erde
         Brust, die unendliche, sich entfaltet,

Und unsre Tage wieder, wie Blumen, sind,
   Wo sie, des Himmels Sonne, sich ausgeteilt
      Im stillen Wechsel sieht und wieder
         Froh in den Frohen das Licht sich findet,

Und er, der sprachlos waltet und unbekannt
   Zukünftiges bereitet, der Gott, der Geist
      Im Menschenwort, am schönen Tage
         Kommenden Jahren, wie einst, sich ausspricht.

You only cease! Yet the Heavenly exhort you, and silently creative, like a stubble field, the breath of Nature blows upon you, that breath full of soul which brightens all.

O hope! Quite soon, quite soon not the groves alone shall sing in praise of life, for the time has come when out of the mouths of mortals this, the loftier soul shall proclaim herself anew,

When, more lovingly allied with human kind, the element shall take shape, and only then grown rich by the thanks of pious children, the breast of Earth, the infinite shall unfold,

And our days once more shall be like flowers where he, the sun of Heaven, sees himself shared all around in quiet alternation, and once again glad light meets itself in human gladness,

And He who speechless governs and unbeknown prepares what is to come, the god, the spirit within the human word, on a fine day once more shall speak to future ages.

## NATUR UND KUNST

### ODER

## SATURN UND JUPITER

Du waltest hoch am Tag' und es blühet dein
　　Gesetz, du hältst die Wage, Saturnus Sohn!
　　　Und teilst die Los' und ruhest froh im
　　　　Ruhm der unsterblichen Herrscherkünste.

Doch in den Abgrund, sagen die Sänger sich,
　　Habst du den heil'gen Vater, den eignen, einst
　　　Verwiesen und es jammre drunten,
　　　　Da, wo die Wilden vor dir mit Recht sind,

Schuldlos der Gott der goldenen Zeit schon längst:
　　Einst mühelos, und größer, wie du, wenn schon
　　　Er kein Gebot aussprach und ihn der
　　　　Sterblichen keiner mit Namen nannte.

## NATURE AND ART

### OR

## SATURN AND JUPITER

High up in day you govern, and your laws are thriving. You, son of Saturn, hold the scales, apportion lots and well-contented rest on the fame of the immortal arts of ruling.

Yet down to the abyss, the singers tell themselves, you banished the holy father, your own, and long he has lain lamenting there, where the wild ones before you rightly languish,

Though guiltless he, the god of the golden age; once effortless and greater than you, although he uttered no commandment and no mortal called him by his name.

Herab denn! oder schäme des Danks dich nicht!
Und willst du bleiben, diene dem Älteren,
Und gönn' es ihm, daß ihn vor Allen,
  Göttern und Menschen, der Sänger nenne!

Denn, wie aus dem Gewölke dein Blitz, so kömmt
Von ihm, was dein ist, siehe! so zeugt von ihm,
Was du gebeutst, und aus Saturnus
  Frieden ist jegliche Macht erwachsen.

Und hab' ich erst am Herzen Lebendiges
Gefühlt und dämmert, was du gestaltetest,
Und war in ihrer Wiege mir in
  Wonne die wechselnde Zeit entschlummert:

Dann kenn' ich dich, Kronion!* dann hör' ich dich,
Den weisen Meister, welcher, wie wir, ein Sohn
Der Zeit, Gesetze gibt und, was die
  Heilige Dämmerung birgt, verkündet.

Then down with you! Or don't be ashamed to give thanks! And if you wish to stay, serve the more ancient one, and grant him that before all others, both gods and men, the singer name him!

For, as from clouds your lightning, so from him all that is yours has come and, look, what you command bears witness to him thus, and from Saturn's peace every power has evolved.

And once in my own heart I have learnt to feel that which is living, and what you have shaped grows dim as dusk, and for me in his cradle mutable Time has lulled himself to blissful sleep,

I'll know you then, Kronion,* and listen to you, the one wise master who, like ourselves a son of Time, dispenses laws and makes known to us all that lies hidden in holy twilight.

---

* Kronion is Jupiter, the son of Kronos or Saturn. Jupiter is 'a son of Time' because Hölderlin identifies Kronos with Chronos, Time.

## UNTER DEN ALPEN GESUNGEN

Heilige Unschuld, du der Menschen und der
Götter liebste vertrauteste! du magst im
Hause oder draußen ihnen zu Füßen
             Sitzen, den Alten,

Immerzufriedner Weisheit voll; denn manches
Gute kennet der Mann, doch staunet er, dem
Wild gleich, oft zum Himmel, aber wie rein ist
             Reine, dir alles!

Siehe! das rauhe Tier des Feldes, gerne
Dient und trauet es dir, der stumme Wald spricht
Wie vor alters, seine Sprüche zu dir, es
             Lehren die Berge

Heil'ge Gesetze dich, und was noch jetzt uns
Vielerfahrenen offenbar der große
Vater werden heißt, du darfst es allein uns
             Helle verkünden.

## SUNG BENEATH THE ALPS

Holy Innocence, you to gods and men alike most dear and most near! In the house or outside you may sit at the feet of these ancient ones,

    Full of ever-contented wisdom, for a man knows much that is good, yet like the wild beast often amazed he looks up to heaven; but, pure one, how pure are all things to you!

    Look! the rough animal of the field is glad to serve and to trust you, the silent wood, as of old, addresses his maxims to you, the mountains teach you

    Holy laws, and what even now the great Father ordains to be made manifest to us, the widely experienced, you alone may clearly proclaim to us.

So mit den Himmlischen allein zu sein, und
Geht vorüber das Licht, und Strom und Wind, und
Zeit eilt hin zum Ort, vor ihnen ein stetes
                    Auge zu haben,

Seliger weiß und wünsch' ich nichts, so lange
Nicht auch mich, wie die Weide, fort die Flut nimmt,
Daß wohl aufgehoben, schlafend dahin ich
                    Muß in den Wogen;

Aber es bleibt daheim gern, wer in treuem
Busen Göttliches hält, und frei will ich, so
Lang ich darf, euch all', ihr Sprachen des Himmels!
                    Deuten und singen.

## HEIMKUNFT

### AN DIE VERWANDTEN

#### I

Drin in den Alpen ists noch helle Nacht und die Wolke,
Freudiges dichtend, sie deckt drinnen das gähnende Tal.

To be thus alone with the Heavenly and when the light passes by, and current and wind and Time hurry on to the place, to have a steady eye in their presence –

Nothing more blessed I know or desire, as long as the flood does not bear me away, as it does the willow, so that, well taken care of, sleeping I must travel on with the waves;

Yet gladly he stays at home who in a loyal heart harbours the divine, and freely, as long as I may, all you languages of heaven! you I'll interpret and sing.

## HOMECOMING

### TO HIS RELATIONS

#### I

Still in the Alps it is shining night and the cloud, composing a joyful work, covers the yawning valley within. Hither, yonder the teasing moun-

Dahin, dorthin toset und stürzt die scherzende Bergluft,
   Schroff durch Tannen herab glänzet und schwindet ein Strahl.
Langsam eilt und kämpft das freudigschauernde Chaos,
   Jung an Gestalt, doch stark, feiert es liebenden Streit
Unter den Felsen, es gährt und wankt in den ewigen Schranken,
   Denn bacchantischer zieht drinnen der Morgen herauf.
Denn es wächst unendlicher dort das Jahr und die heilgen
   Stunden, die Tage, sie sind kühner geordnet, gemischt.
Dennoch merket die Zeit der Gewittervogel und zwischen
   Bergen, hoch in der Luft weilt er und rufet den Tag.
Jetzt auch wachet und schaut in der Tiefe drinnen das Dörflein
   Furchtlos, Hohem vertraut, unter den Gipfeln hinauf.
Wachstum ahnend, denn schon, wie Blitze, fallen die alten
   Wasserquellen, der Grund unter den Stürzenden dampft,
Echo tönet umher, und die unermeßliche Werkstatt
   Reget bei Tag und Nacht, Gaben versendend, den Arm.

tain wind roars and tumbles, sheer through the fir-trees a shaft of light
gleams and is lost. Slowly it hurries and wars, this chaos that trembles with
joy; young in appearance, yet strong, it celebrates loving conflict amidst
the rocks, seethes and reels in its eternal bounds, for more bacchantically
morning rises within. For there more endlessly does the year grow, and the
holy hours, the days, are more boldly marshalled and mixed. Yet the bird
of thunderstorms knows the time, and between mountains high in the air,
he hovers and calls out that it's day. And now, deep down within, the little
village awakens and, fearless, familiar with what is high, looks up from
under the peaks. Divining growth, for already, like lightning, the ancient
torrents fall, the ground steams beneath them as they crash down, echo
sounds round about, and the immeasurable workshop, dispensing gifts,
both by day and by night is astir.

2

Ruhig glänzen indes die silbernen Höhen darüber,
    Voll mit Rosen ist schon droben der leuchtende Schnee.
Und noch höher hinauf wohnt über dem Lichte der reine
    Selige Gott vom Spiel heiliger Strahlen erfreut.
Stille wohnt er allein und hell erscheinet sein Antlitz,
    Der ätherische scheint Leben zu geben geneigt,
Freude zu schaffen, mit uns, wie oft, wenn, kundig des Maßes,
    Kundig der Atmenden auch zögernd und schonend der Gott
Wohlgediegenes Glück den Städten und Häusern und milde
    Regen, zu öffnen das Land, brütende Wolken, und euch,
Trauteste Lüfte dann, euch, sanfte Frühlinge, sendet,
    Und mit langsamer Hand Traurige wieder erfreut,
Wenn er die Zeiten erneut, der Schöpferische, die stillen
    Herzen der alternden Menschen erfrischt und ergreift,
Und hinab in die Tiefe wirkt, und öffnet und aufhellt,
    Wie ers liebt, und jetzt wieder ein Leben beginnt,
Anmut blühet, wie einst, und gegenwärtiger Geist kömmt,
    Und ein freudiger Mut wieder die Fittige schwellt.

2

Calmly meanwhile the silver heights gleam above, and the shining snow up there is full of roses already. And still higher up, above the light, dwells the pure and blissful God, gladdened by the play of holy beams. In silence he dwells alone, and bright his countenance appears; the aetherial one seems inclined to grant life, to offer joy; still with us, as often before, though, knowing the right measure, knowing those who breathe, hesitant and sparing the God sends well-apportioned fortune to the cities and houses, sends mild showers to open the land, brooding clouds and then you, most dearly beloved breezes, and you, gentle springs, and with a slow hand he gladdens again those grown sad, when he renews the seasons, the creative one, quickens and moves the hearts of ageing men, works upon the depths and opens and brightens all, as he loves to do; and now once again life begins, grace is in flower, as before, and present spirit comes, and a glad courage once more makes pinions beat and swell.

### 3

Vieles sprach ich zu ihm, denn, was auch Dichtende sinnen
    Oder singen, es gilt meistens den Engeln und ihm;
Vieles bat ich, zu lieb dem Vaterlande, damit nicht
    Ungebeten uns einst plötzlich befiele der Geist;
Vieles für euch auch, die im Vaterlande besorgt sind,
    Denen der heilige Dank lächelnd die Flüchtlinge bringt,
Landesleute! für euch, indessen wiegte der See mich,
    Und der Ruderer saß ruhig und lobte die Fahrt.
Weit in des Sees Ebene wars Ein freudiges Wallen
    Unter den Segeln und jetzt blühet und hellet die Stadt
Dort in der Frühe sich auf, wohl her von schattigen Alpen
    Kommt geleitet und ruht nun in dem Hafen das Schiff.
Warm ist das Ufer hier und freundlich offene Tale,
    Schön von Pfaden erhellt grünen und schimmern mich an.
Gärten stehen gesellt und die glänzende Knospe beginnt schon,
    Und des Vogels Gesang ladet den Wanderer ein.
Alles scheinet vertraut, der vorübereilende Gruß auch
    Scheint von Freunden, es scheint jegliche Miene verwandt.

### 3

Much I said to him; for, whatever poets may ponder or sing, mostly it is addressed to the angels and him; much I begged for, on my country's behalf, lest unbidden one day the spirit should suddenly seize upon us; and much for your sake, too, who are troubled in our country, and for you, compatriots to whom holy gratitude will bring back the fugitives with a smile; meanwhile the lake rocked me, and the oarsman sat calmly, praising the voyage. Far over the lake's level there was *one* joyous motion among the sails; and now the city bursts and flares into view in the early morning light, and safely guided there from the shadowy Alps, the boat arrives, and now it rests in the harbour. Here the shore is warm, and valleys open in welcome, beautifully lit up by paths, they beckon to me green and glistening. Gardens lie there conjoined, and the gleaming bud is beginning, and birds' song invites the traveller. All seems familiar, even the casual greeting seems that of friends, and every face looks like a kinsman's face.

## 4

Freilich wohl! das Geburtsland ists, der Boden der Heimat,
    Was du suchest, es ist nahe, begegnet dir schon.
Und umsonst nicht steht, wie ein Sohn, am wellenumrauschten
    Tor' und siehet und sucht liebende Namen für dich,
Mit Gesang ein wandernder Mann, glückseliges Lindau!
    Eine der gastlichen Pforten des Landes ist dies,
Reizend hinauszugehn in die vielversprechende Ferne,
    Dort, wo die Wunder sind, dort, wo das göttliche Wild
Hoch in die Ebnen herab der Rhein die verwegene Bahn bricht,
    Und aus Felsen hervor ziehet das jauchzende Tal,
Dort hinein, durchs helle Gebirg, nach Como zu wandern,
    Oder hinab, wie der Tag wandelt, den offenen See;
Aber reizender mir bist du, geweihete Pforte!
    Heimzugehn, wo bekannt blühende Wege mir sind,
Dort zu besuchen das Land und die schönen Tale des Neckars,
    Und die Wälder, das Grün heiliger Bäume, wo gern
Sich die Eiche gesellt mit stillen Birken und Buchen,
    Und in Bergen ein Ort freundlich gefangen mich nimmt.

## 4

And, indeed, it's the land of your birth, the soil of your homeland; what you seek is near, and you'll find it in the end. And not for nothing at the gates surrounded with music of wavelets stands the wandering man, like a son, looking at you and seeking names for you, most blessèd Lindau! For this is one of the country's hospitable portals, inviting us to sally out from there into the distance that promises much, where the marvels are, high up where the godlike wild beast, the Rhine, blasts his reckless course into the plains, and draws forth the jubilant valley out of the rocks, to wander in there, through shining mountain ranges, to Como or, as the day proceeds, down the open lake; yet me, sanctified portals, still more you invite to go home by flowering paths that are known to me, there to visit the country and the Neckar's beautiful valleys, and the woods, the verdure of holy trees, where the oak loves to consort with quiet birches and beeches, and within mountains a place will kindly imprison me.

5

Dort empfangen sie mich. O Stimme der Stadt, der Mutter!
     O du triffest, du regst Langegelerntes mir auf!
Dennoch sind sie es noch! noch blühet die Sonn' und die
     Freud' euch,
     O ihr Liebsten! und fast heller im Auge, wie sonst.
Ja! das Alte noch ists! Es gedeihet und reifet, doch keines
     Was da lebet und liebt, lässet die Treue zurück.
Aber das Beste, der Fund, der unter des heiligen Friedens
     Bogen lieget, er ist Jungen und Alten gespart.
Törig red ich. Es ist die Freude. Doch morgen und künftig
     Wenn wir gehen und schaun draußen das lebende Feld
Unter den Blüten des Baums, in den Feiertagen des Frühlings
     Red' und hoff' ich mit euch vieles, ihr Lieben! davon.
Vieles hab' ich gehört vom großen Vater und habe
     Lange geschwiegen von ihm, welcher die wandernde Zeit
Droben in Höhen erfrischt, und waltet über Gebirgen
     Der gewähret uns bald himmlische Gaben und ruft
Hellern Gesang und schickt viel gute Geister. O säumt nicht,
     Kommt, Erhaltenden ihr! Engel des Jahres! und ihr,

5

There they welcome me. O voice of the town, my mother! It is you that strike, that stir up things I learnt long ago! And yet they are still what they were! Still the sun and joy flower for you, my most dearly beloved, and almost more brightly meet your eyes than before! Truly, the old things are still the same. They thrive and they ripen, but nothing that lives and loves abandons faith. But the best of all, the find that lies under the rainbow of holy peace has been saved up for the young and old. I speak like a fool. Joy it is. But tomorrow, and later, when we go out and look at the living field beneath the trees in blossom, in the festive days of spring, I shall speak with you and hope with you at length about it. Much I have heard about the Great Father and have long kept silent about him, who up there in the heights refreshes wandering Time, and reigns over the mountain ranges, who soon will vouchsafe us heavenly gifts and will call for brighter song and send many beautiful spirits. O do not tarry, but come, you preservers, angels of the year, and you,

6

Engel des Hauses, kommt! in die Adern alle des Lebens,
　　Alle freuend zugleich, teile das Himmlische sich!
Adle! verjünge! damit nichts Menschlichgutes, damit nicht
　　Eine Stunde des Tags ohne die Frohen und auch
Solche Freude, wie jetzt, wenn Liebende wieder sich finden,
　　Wie es gehört für sie, schicklich geheiliget sei.
Wenn wir segnen das Mahl, wen darf ich nennen und wenn wir
　　Ruhn vom Leben des Tags, saget, wie bring' ich den Dank?
Nenn' ich den Hohen dabei? Unschickliches liebet ein Gott
　　nicht,
　　Ihn zu fassen, ist fast unsere Freude zu klein.
Schweigen müssen wir oft; es fehlen heilige Namen,
　　Herzen schlagen und doch bleibet die Rede zurück?
Aber ein Saitenspiel leiht jeder Stunde die Töne,
　　Und erfreuet vielleicht Himmlische, welche sich nahn.
Das bereitet und so ist auch beinahe die Sorge
　　Schon befriediget, die unter das Freudige kam.
Sorgen, wie diese, muß, gern oder nicht, in der Seele
　　Tragen ein Sänger und oft, aber die anderen nicht.

6

Angel of our house, come soon! Into all the veins of life, rejoicing them all
at once, may the heavenly divide! Ennoble! Rejuvenate! So that nothing
that's humanly good, not one hour of the day shall pass without those glad
ones, and that joy experienced now when lovers are reunited shall be
worthily consecrated, as it is fitting for them. When we bless the meal,
whom may I name, and when we rest from the day's exertions, tell me, how
shall I offer thanks? Should I name the Exalted One then? A God does not
like what's unseemly; to grasp him, our joy is almost too small. Often we
must be silent; there is a lack of holy names; hearts beat high, and yet
speech holds back? But there's a lyre that lends the right notes to every
hour, and perhaps gives pleasure to Heavenly ones who are now approach-
ing. This make ready; and at once the care that troubled my joy is almost
laid at rest. Cares of this kind, whether he likes it or not, a singer must bear
in his soul, and often; but not those of a different kind.

## DICHTERBERUF

Des Ganges Ufer hörten des Freudengotts
Triumph, als alleroberd vom Indus her
    Der junge Bacchus kam, mit heilgem
        Weine vom Schlafe die Völker weckend.

Und du, des Tages Engel! erweckst sie nicht,
Die jetzt noch schlafen? gib die Gesetze, gib
    Uns Leben, siege, Meister, du nur
        Hast der Eroberung Recht, wie Bacchus.

Nicht, was wohl sonst des Menschen Geschick und Sorg'
Im Haus und unter offenem Himmel ist,
    Wenn edler, denn das Wild, der Mann sich
        Wehret und nährt! denn es gilt ein anders,

Zu Sorg' und Dienst den Dichtenden anvertraut!
Der Höchste, der ists, dem wir geeignet sind,
    Daß näher, immerneu besungen
        Ihn die befreundete Brust vernehme.

## THE POET'S VOCATION

THE banks of Ganges heard the triumph of the God of Joy, when all-conquering from Indus young Bacchus came, rousing the peoples from sleep with holy wine.

And you, angel of the day, do not rouse them, those who are still asleep? Give us the laws, give us life, be victorious, Master, for you alone have the right to conquer like Bacchus.

Not of that which otherwise is the business and çare of mankind in the house and under the open sky, when nobler than the wild beast, a man labours and earns his living, I speak – for a different task is in question here,

Entrusted to the poet's care and service! The Highest it is to whom we are dedicated, so that nearer, ever newly sung, the well-disposed heart may perceive Him.

Und dennoch, o ihr Himmlischen all, und all
  Ihr Quellen und ihr Ufer und Hain' und Höhn,
    Wo wunderbar zuerst, als du die
      Locken ergriffen, und unvergeßlich

Der unverhoffte Genius über uns
  Der schöpferische, göttliche kam, daß stumm
    Der Sinn uns ward und, wie vom
      Strahle gerührt das Gebein erbebte,

Ihr ruhelosen Taten in weiter Welt!
  Ihr Schicksalstag', ihr reißenden, wenn der Gott
    Stillsinnend lenkt, wohin zorntrunken
      Ihn die gigantischen Rosse bringen,

Euch sollten wir verschweigen, und wenn in uns
  Vom stetigstillen Jahre der Wohllaut tönt,
    So sollt' es klingen, gleich als hätte
      Mutig und müßig ein Kind des Meisters

Geweihte, reine Saiten im Scherz gerührt?
  Und darum hast du, Dichter! des Orients
    Propheten und den Griechengesang und
      Neulich die Donner gehört, damit du

And yet, O you Heavenly all, and all you sources and banks and groves
and summits, where marvellous at first, when you seized us by the hair and
unforgettable
  The never yet hoped for Genius, the creative, divine, took possession of
us, so that our minds fell silent and, as though touched by the ray, our
bones trembled,
  You restless deeds the wide world over! You fateful days, you sweeping
ones, when the God, quietly pondering, drives to where drunken with
wrath, the gigantic horses take him –
  Should we keep silent about you, and when the euphony of the calmly
constant year is pealing within us, should it sound, then, as though,
capricious and idle,
  A child had plucked the Master's sacred, pure strings in jest? And, poet,
was it for that you heard the Orient's prophets and Grecian song, and
lately the thunder, to make

Den Geist zu Diensten brauchst und die Gegenwart
   Des Guten übereilest, in Spott, und den Albernen
     Verleugnest, herzlos, und zum Spiele
       Feil, wie gefangenes Wild, ihn treibest?

Bis aufgereizt vom Stachel im Grimme der
   Des Ursprungs sich erinnert und ruft, daß selbst
     Der Meister kommt, dann unter heißen
       Todesgeschossen entseelt dich lässet.

Zu lang ist alles Göttliche dienstbar schon
   Und alle Himmelskräfte verscherzt, verbraucht
     Die Gütigen, zur Lust, danklos, ein
       Schlaues Geschlecht und zu kennen wähnt es,

Wenn ihnen der Erhabne den Acker baut,
   Das Tagslicht und den Donnerer, und es späht
     Das Sehrohr wohl sie alle und zählt und
       Nennet mit Namen des Himmels Sterne.

Der Vater aber decket mit heilger Nacht,
   Damit wir bleiben mögen, die Augen zu.
     Nicht liebt er Wildes! Doch es zwinget
       Nimmer die weite Gewalt den Himmel.

A trade of the Spirit and anticipate its beneficent presence, in mockery, and, heartless, deny the simple-minded and drive it about, like a captured beast exhibited to the vulgar for a fee?

Till, stung by that thorn, in anger it remembers its origin and calls out, so that the Master himself arrives, to leave you lifeless amidst hot lethal missiles.

Too long now all that's divine has been exploited for gain, and all the powers of Heaven trifled away, and a cunning generation ungratefully have used up the Benign ones for their pleasure.

And when the Exalted tills their fields for them, they think they know the daylight and the Thunderer, and truly the telescope finds and counts and calls by name all the stars of the sky,

But the Father with holy darkness covers our eyes, so that we may remain. He does not like what is savage! But never will Heaven be coerced by far-flung violence.

Noch ists auch gut, zu weise zu sein. Ihn kennt
   Der Dank. Doch nicht behält er es leicht allein,
     Und gern gesellt, damit verstehn sie
       Helfen, zu anderen sich ein Dichter.

Furchtlos bleibt, aber, so er es muß, der Mann
   Einsam vor Gott, es schützet die Einfalt ihn,
     Und keiner Waffen brauchts und keiner
       Listen, so lange, bis Gottes Fehl hilft.

## STIMME DES VOLKS
### Zweite Fassung

Du seiest Gottes Stimme, so glaubt ich sonst
   In heil'ger Jugend; ja, und ich sag es noch!
     Um unsre Weisheit unbekümmert
       Rauschen die Ströme doch auch, und dennoch,

Wer liebt sie nicht? und immer bewegen sie
   Das Herz mir, hör' ich ferne die Schwindenden,
     Die Ahnungsvollen meine Bahn nicht,
       Aber gewisser ins Meer hin eilen.

Nor is it good to be too wise. Thankfulness too knows Heaven. But the poet does not easily keep it to himself, and likes to seek the company of others, so that they will help him to understand.

Yet, if it must be, fearlessly the man remains alone before God, ingenuousness protects him, and he needs no weapons and no wiles till God's absence comes to his aid.

## VOICE OF THE PEOPLE
### Second Version

THAT you are God's own voice, so once I believed in holy youth; and indeed I say so still! Untroubled by our wisdom, the rivers roar all the same, and yet

Who does not love them? And always they move my heart when far away I hear these vanishing, foreknowing ones hasten towards the sea, not by my course, but more surely,

Denn selbstvergessen, allzubereit, den Wunsch
Der Götter zu erfüllen, ergreift zu gern,
    Was sterblich ist, wenn offnen Augs auf
        Eigenen Pfaden es einmal wandelt,

Ins All zurück die kürzeste Bahn; so stürzt
Der Strom hinab, er suchet die Ruh, es reißt,
    Es ziehet wider Willen ihn, von
        Klippe zu Klippe, den Steuerlosen

Das wunderbare Sehnen dem Abgrund zu;
Das Ungebundne reizet und Völker auch
    Ergreift die Todeslust und kühne
        Städte, nachdem sie versucht das Beste,

Von Jahr zu Jahr forttreibend das Werk, sie hat
Ein heilig Ende troffen; die Erde grünt
    Und stille vor den Sternen liegt, den
        Betenden gleich, in den Sand geworfen

Freiwillig überwunden die lange Kunst
Vor jenen Unnachahmbaren da; er selbst,
    Der Mensch, mit eigner Hand zerbrach, die
        Hohen, zu ehren, sein Werk, der Künstler.

For, self-oblivious, all too ready to fulfil the wishes of the gods, who-
ever is mortal, when open-eyed he travels along his own paths, too gladly
takes
    The shortest way back into the All; so does the river plunge, seeking
rest; against his will the rudderless is swept on, from boulder to boulder,
    By the mysterious yearning towards the abyss; the unbound attracts,
and peoples too are seized by desire for death, and valiant cities, when they
have done their utmost,
    Adding to their endeavours year after year, have been visited with a
holy end; the earth grows green, and silent before the stars, like men in
prayer, flung down into the sand,
    Outgrown, discarded voluntarily, there lies long art prostrate before the
inimitable powers; he himself, the mortal, with his own hand, in homage to
the Exalted, the artist has broken his own work.

Doch minder nicht sind jene den Menschen hold,
　Sie lieben wieder, so wie geliebt sie sind,
　　Und hemmen öfters, daß er lang im
　　　Lichte sich freue, die Bahn des Menschen.

Und, nicht des Adlers Jungen allein, sie wirft
　Der Vater aus dem Neste, damit sie nicht
　　Zu lang' ihm bleiben, uns auch treibt mit
　　　Richtigem Stachel hinaus der Herrscher.

Wohl jenen, die zur Ruhe gegangen sind,
　Und vor der Zeit gefallen, auch die, auch die
　　Geopfert, gleich den Erstlingen der
　　　Ernte, sie haben ein Teil gefunden.

Am Xanthos lag, in griechischer Zeit, die Stadt,
　Jetzt aber, gleich den größeren die dort ruhn
　　Ist durch ein Schicksal sie dem heilgen
　　　Lichte des Tages hinweggekommen.

Sie kamen aber nicht in der offnen Schlacht
　Durch eigne Hand um. Fürchterlich ist davon,
　　Was dort geschehn, die wunderbare
　　　Sage von Osten zu uns gelanget.

---

Yet these are no less well-disposed towards men; as they are loved, so they return that love, and frequently, so that long he shall enjoy the light, they will impede a man's passage.

And not the eagle's fledglings alone does their father push out of the eyrie, so that they will not stay there too long, but us too the Ruler drives out with a proper goad.

Happy are those who have gone to their rest and have fallen before their time, and those, those too who were sacrificed like the first fruits of the harvest – they have been granted their lot.

By Xanthos, at the time of the Greeks, there stood a city, but now, like the greater ones now at rest in those regions, by a destiny it was parted from holy daylight.

But not in open battle they perished, by their own hands. Terrible the marvellous legend of what happened there has come down to us from the East.

Es reizte sie die Güte von Brutus. Denn
　　Als Feuer ausgegangen, so bot er sich
　　　　Zu helfen ihnen, ob er gleich, als Feldherr,
　　　　　　Stand in Belagerung vor den Toren.

Doch von den Mauern warfen die Diener sie
　　Die er gesandt. Lebendiger ward darauf
　　　　Das Feuer und sie freuten sich und ihnen
　　　　　　Strecket' entgegen die Hände Brutus

Und alle waren außer sich selbst. Geschrei
　　Entstand und Jauchzen. Drauf in die Flamme warf
　　　　Sich Mann und Weib, von Knaben stürzt' auch
　　　　　　Der von den Dach, in der Väter Schwert der.

Nicht rätlich ist es, Helden zu trotzen. Längst
　　Wars aber vorbereitet. Die Väter auch
　　　　Da sie ergriffen waren, einst, und
　　　　　　Heftig die persischen Feinde drängten,

Entzündeten, ergreifend des Stromes Rohr,
　　Daß sie das Freie fänden, die Stadt. Und Haus
　　　　Und Tempel nahm, zum heilgen Äther
　　　　　　Fliegend, und Menschen hinweg die Flamme.

---

It was the kindness of Brutus that provoked them. For, when fire had broken out, he offered them his help, although as general he stood at their gates to lay siege to their city.

Yet from the walls they threw down the servants whom he had sent. Livelier then grew the blaze, and they were glad, and Brutus extended his hands towards them,

And all were beside themselves. A great outcry arose, and jubilation. Then into the flames both men and women hurled themselves, and, of the boys also, some threw themselves down from the roof, others on to the swords of their elders.

It is not prudent to defy heroes. But it had been prepared long before. Their ancestors too, when they had been encircled, once, and strongly their Persian enemies pressed them,

Took rushes from the river and, so that these would find mere wasteland there, set fire to their own city. And house and temple, flying up to holy Aether, and men did the flame take away.

So hatten es die Kinder gehört, und wohl
Sind gut die Sagen, denn ein Gedächtnis sind
Dem Höchsten sie, doch auch bedarf es
Eines, die heiligen auszulegen.

## DER BLINDE SÄNGER

Ελυσεν αινον αχος απ' ομματων Αρης – Sophokles

Wo bist du, Jugendliches! das immer mich
Zur Stunde weckt des Morgens, wo bist du, Licht!
Das Herz ist wach, doch bannt und hält in
Heiligem Zauber die Nacht mich immer.

Sonst lauscht' ich um die Dämmerung gern, sonst harrt'
Ich gerne dein am Hügel, und nie umsonst!
Nie täuschten mich, du Holdes, deine
Boten, die Lüfte, denn immer kamst du,

Kamst allbeseligend den gewohnten Pfad
Herein in deiner Schöne, wo bist du, Licht!
Das Herz ist wieder wach, doch bannt und
Hemmt die unendliche Nacht mich immer.

Such was the tale their descendants had heard; and legends are good, for they commemorate what is noblest, yet someone to interpret such holy lore is also needed.

## THE BLIND SINGER

'Cruel woe has Ares lifted from our eyes'
– (Sophocles, *Ajax*, l. 706)

WHERE are you, the youthful that always at the due hour at morning wakes me, where are you, light? The heart's awake, but always now Night constricts and binds me by holy magic.

Once towards dawn I liked to listen, to wait for you on the hillside, and never in vain! Never, belovèd, your heralds the breezes deceived me, for always you came,

Infusing all with your soul, entered by the accustomed path in your beauty – where are you, light? The heart's awake once more, yet always infinite Night constricts me and hems me in.

Mir grünten sonst die Lauben; es leuchteten
  Die Blumen, wie die eigenen Augen, mir;
    Nicht ferne war das Angesicht der
      Meinen und leuchtete mir und droben

Und um die Wälder sah ich die Fittige
  Des Himmels wandern, da ich ein Jüngling war;
    Nun sitz ich still allein, von einer
      Stunde zur anderen und Gestalten

Aus Lieb und Leid der helleren Tage schafft
  Zur eignen Freude nun mein Gedanke sich,
    Und ferne lausch' ich hin, ob nicht ein
      Freundlicher Retter vielleicht mir komme.

Dann hör' ich oft die Stimme des Donnerers
  Am Mittag, wenn der eherne nahe kommt,
    Wenn ihm das Haus bebt und der Boden
      Unter ihm dröhnt und der Berg es nachhallt.

Den Retter hör' ich dann in der Nacht, ich hör'
  Ihn tötend, den Befreier, belebend ihn,
    Den Donnerer vom Untergang zum
      Orient eilen und ihm nach tönt ihr,

---

Once the bowers grew green for me; the flowers shone for me like my own eyes; not far from me were the faces of those I love, and they shone for me, and above

And around the forests I saw the pinions of Heaven travel, when I was a youth; now I sit alone in silence, from one hour to the next, and my thought devises

Shapes for itself out of the love and grief of brighter days, for its own delight, and far into the distance I listen, wondering whether perhaps a kindly redeemer is coming to me.

Then often I hear the Thunderer's voice at noon, when the brazen one draws near, when his house is trembling, and the ground booms beneath him, and the mountain echoes the noise.

Then in the night I hear the Deliverer, hear him killing, the Liberator, and giving life, hear him, the Thunderer, hurry from Sundown to Orient, and you, my strings,

Ihm nach, ihr meine Saiten! es lebt mit ihm
  Mein Lied und wie die Quelle dem Strome folgt,
    Wohin er denkt, so muß ich fort und
      Folge dem Sicheren auf der Irrbahn.

Wohin? wohin? ich höre dich da und dort
  Du Herrlicher! und rings um die Erde tönts.
    Wo endest du? und was, was ist es
      Über den Wolken und o wie wird mir?

Tag! Tag! du über stürzenden Wolken! sei
  Willkommen mir! es blühet mein Auge dir.
    O Jugendlicht! o Glück! das alte
      Wieder! doch geistiger rinnst du nieder

Du goldner Quell aus heiligem Kelch! und du,
  Du grüner Boden, friedliche Wieg'! und du,
    Haus meiner Väter! und ihr Lieben,
      Die mir begegneten einst, o nahet,

O kommt, daß euer, euer die Freude sei,
  Ihr alle, daß euch segne der Sehende!
    O nimmt, daß ichs ertrage, mir das
      Leben, das Göttliche mir vom Herzen.

Resound to his passing! My song lives with him, and as the source makes for the river, where his thoughts go I must away and follow the sure one on the erratic course.

Whither? Whither? I hear you now here, now there, most glorious one! And all round the earth there is music. Where do you end? And what, what is it above the clouds and, oh, what is happening to me?

Day! Day! You above tottering clouds, let me welcome you! My vision breaks into blossom for you. O light of youth! O bliss, the old bliss again! But more spiritually you flow down

You golden stream from the holy chalice! And you, verdant ground, peaceful cradle, and you, house of my fathers! And you dear ones whom I encountered once, O draw near,

Oh, come, that the joy may be yours, all of you, that the seeing one may bless you! Oh take it, so that I may bear it; of this life, the divine, unburden my heart.

## AM QUELL DER DONAU

. . . . .

DENN, wie wenn hoch von der herrlichgestimmten, der Orgel
Im heiligen Saal,
Reinquillend aus den unerschöpflichen Röhren,
Das Vorspiel, weckend, des Morgens beginnt
Und weitumher, von Halle zu Halle,
Der erfrischende nun, der melodische Strom rinnt,
Bis in den kalten Schatten das Haus
Von Begeisterungen erfüllt,
Nun aber erwacht ist, nun, aufsteigend ihr,
Der Sonne des Fests, antwortet
Der Chor der Gemeinde; so kam
Das Wort aus Osten zu uns,
Und an Parnassos Felsen und am Kithäron hör' ich
O Asia, das Echo von dir und es bricht sich
Am Kapitol und jählings herab von den Alpen

   Kommt eine Fremdlingin sie
Zu uns, die Erweckerin,
Die menschenbildende Stimme.


## AT THE SOURCE OF THE DANUBE

. . . . .

FOR, as when from the gloriously tuned, the organ, in the sanctified hall,
welling up pure from the inexhaustible pipes, the prelude, awakening men,
begins in the morning and far around, from court to court, now the re-
freshing, melodious current flows, until in the chilly shade of the house,
filled with inspirations, now it is awake, now, ascending to it, to the sun of
the festive day, the community's chorus responds; so did the word come
to us from the East, and by the rocks of Parnassus and by Cithaeron I hear
the echo of you, O Asia, and it breaks itself against the capitol and sudden
down from the Alps,
   A stranger, it comes to us, the arousing, the voice that gives shape to

Da faßt' ein Staunen die Seele
Der Betroffenen all und Nacht
War über den Augen der Besten.
Denn vieles vermag
Und die Flut und den Fels und Feuersgewalt auch
Bezwinget mit Kunst der Mensch
Und achtet, der Hochgesinnte, das Schwert
Nicht, aber es steht
Vor Göttlichen der Starke niedergeschlagen,

    Und gleichet dem Wild fast; das,
Von süßer Jugend getrieben,
Schweift rastlos über die Berg'
Und fühlet die eigene Kraft
In der Mittagshitze. Wenn aber
Herabgeführt, in spielenden Lüften,
Das heilige Licht, und mit dem kühleren Strahl
Der freudige Geist kommt zu
Der seligen Erde, dann erliegt es, ungewohnt
Des Schönsten und schlummert wachenden Schlaf,
Noch ehe Gestirn naht. So auch wir. Denn manchen erlosch
Das Augenlicht schon vor den göttlichgesendeten Gaben,

men. Then amazement seized the souls of all those who were struck, and night covered the eyes of the best. For much mankind can accomplish, and the flood and the rock and the might of fire by their art they subdue, and, lofty in mind, do not heed the sword, but before the divine downcast the strong will stand,

And almost is like the wild beast; which, driven by sweet youth, restlessly rambles over the mountains and feels its own power in the heat of noon. But when holy light has been moved down, in frolicking breezes, and with the cooler beam the joyous spirit descends to blissful Earth, then it succumbs, unaccustomed to utmost beauty, and drowses in waking sleep, even before the stars appear. So too with us. For many's the man whose vision has failed, extinguished, in face of those god-sent gifts,

Den freundlichen, die aus Ionien uns,
Auch aus Arabia kamen, und froh ward
Der teuern Lehr' und auch der holden Gesänge
Die Seele jener Entschlafenen nie,
Doch einige wachten. Und sie wandelten oft
Zufrieden unter euch, ihr Bürger schöner Städte,
Beim Kampfspiel, wo sonst unsichtbar der Heros
Geheim bei Dichtern saß, die Ringer schaut' und lächelnd
Pries, der gepriesene, die müßigernsten Kinder.
Ein unaufhörlich Lieben wars und ists.
Und wohlgeschieden, aber darum denken
Wir aneinander doch, ihr Fröhlichen am Isthmos,
Und am Cephyß und am Taygetos,
Auch eurer denken wir, ihr Tale des Kaukasos,
So alt ihr seid, ihr Paradiese dort
Und deiner Patriarchen und deiner Propheten,

O Asia, deiner Starken, o Mutter!
Die furchtlos vor den Zeichen der Welt,
Und den Himmel auf Schultern und alles Schicksal,
Taglang auf Bergen gewurzelt,
Zuerst es verstanden,

The kindly, which from Ionia to us, and from Arabia, have come, and never the souls of these now gone to their rest were glad of the precious doctrine, nor yet of the lovely songs; yet some were awake. And often they walked in your midst contented, you citizens of beautiful towns, at the Games, where once invisible the hero in secret sat with poets, watched the wrestlers and smiling praised – he, the object of praise – those idly serious children. An interminable loving it was, and is. And well divided; but nonetheless we think of one another, you happy ones at the Isthmus, and by Cephissus and by Taygetus, and of you we think, you valleys of the Caucasus, ancient as you are, your paradises there, and of your patriarchs and your prophets,

O Asia, of your strong ones, O Mother, who fearless in face of the signs of the world, and the heavens heaped on shoulders and all manner of fate, for days rooted in mountains, were the first who knew how to speak alone

Allein zu reden
Zu Gott. Die ruhn nun. Aber wenn ihr
Und dies ist zu sagen,
Ihr Alten all, nicht sagtet, woher?
Wir nennen dich, heiliggenötiget, nennen,
Natur! dich wir, und neu, wie dem Bad entsteigt
Dir alles Göttlichgeborne.

    Zwar gehn wir fast, wie die Waisen;
Wohl ists, wie sonst, nur jene Pflege nicht wieder;
Doch Jünglinge, der Kindheit gedenk,
Im Hause sind auch diese nicht fremde.
Sie leben dreifach, eben wie auch
Die ersten Söhne des Himmels.
Und nicht umsonst ward uns
In die Seele die Treue gegeben.
Nicht uns, auch Eures bewahrt sie,
Und bei den Heiligtümern, den Waffen des Worts
Die scheidend ihr den Ungeschickteren uns
Ihr Schicksalssöhne, zurückgelassen

    Ihr guten Geister, da seid ihr auch,
Oftmals, wenn einen dann die heilige Wolk umschwebt,
Da staunen wir und wissens nicht zu deuten.

to God. These are now at rest. But if, and this has to be said, you ancients all did not tell us whence it is that we name you, then, sacredly compelled, we call you Nature, and new, as from a bath, all that's divinely born steps out of you.

    True, almost like orphans we go about; all is still as it was, only this tutelage lacking; but youths who recall their childhood, these too are not strangers in the house. Threefold they live, even as did the first sons of Heaven. And not for nothing was faithfulness implanted in our souls. Not us, but what is yours too it preserves, and in those sacred relics, the weapons of the word, which, parting, you left behind for us, you sons of Fate, for us the more awkward, more fateless,

    In them you also are present, beneficent spirits; often, when the holy cloud hovers around a man, we marvel and cannot tell what it means. But

Ihr aber würzt mit Nektar uns den Odem
Und dann frohlocken wir oft oder es befällt uns
Ein Sinnen, wenn ihr aber einen zu sehr liebt
Er ruht nicht, bis er euer einer geworden.
Darum, ihr Gütigen! umgebet mich leicht,
Damit ich bleiben möge, denn noch ist manches zu singen,
Jetzt aber endiget, seligweinend,
Wie eine Sage der Liebe,
Mir der Gesang, und so auch ist er
Mir, mit Erröten, Erblassen,
Von Anfang her gegangen. Doch Alles geht so.


## DIE WANDERUNG

Gᴌᴜ̈ᴄᴋsᴇᴌɪɢ Suevien, meine Mutter,
Auch du, der glänzenderen, der Schwester
Lombarda drüben gleich,
Von hundert Bächen durchflossen!
Und Bäume genug, weißblühend und rötlich,
Und dunklere, wild, tiefgrünenden Laubs voll,
Und Alpengebirg der Schweiz auch überschattet,
Benachbartes, dich; denn nah dem Herde des Hauses

you with nectar spice our breath, and often then we exult or a pondering befalls us; but if you love a man too much, he will have no peace till he has become one of you. Therefore, kind ones, lightly surround me, so that I may remain, for still there is much to be sung; but now my song, blissfully weeping, like a legend of love, comes to an end, and so too, amidst blushing and blanching, it has gone for me since it began. But that is how all things go.


## THE JOURNEY

Mosᴛ happy Swabia, my mother, and like the more luminous your sister Lombarda on the other side, veined with a hundred books! And trees enough, white-flowering and reddish, and darker ones, wild, full of deep-green leaves, and the Alpine ranges of Switzerland shade you, the neighbouring, too; for near to the hearth of the house you dwell, and hear how

Wohnst du, und hörst, wie drinnen
Aus silbernen Opferschalen
Der Quell rauscht, ausgeschüttet
Von reinen Händen, wenn berührt

Von warmen Strahlen
Kristallenes Eis und umgestürzt
Vom leichtanregenden Lichte
Der schneeige Gipfel übergießt die Erde
Mit reinestem Wasser. Darum ist
Dir angeboren die Treue. Schwer verläßt,
Was nahe dem Ursprung wohnet, den Ort.
Und deine Kinder, die Städte,
Am weithindämmernden See,
An Neckars Weiden, am Rheine,
Sie alle meinen, es wäre
Sonst nirgend besser zu wohnen.

Ich aber will dem Kaukasos zu!
Denn sagen hört' ich
Noch heut in den Lüften:
Frei sei'n, wie Schwalben, die Dichter.
Auch hat mir ohnedies
In jüngeren Tagen Eines vertraut,
Es seien vor alter Zeit
Die Eltern einst, das deutsche Geschlecht,

within, from silver vessels of sacrifice the source purls up, poured out by pure hands, when, touched

By the warm rays, crystalline ice and, overturned by gently quickening light, the snowy summit drenches the earth with purest water. Therefore faithfulness is inborn in you. For that which dwells near to its origin is reluctant to leave the place. And your children, the towns, by the widely glimmering lake, by the Neckar's willows and by the Rhine, all these affirm that no dwelling-place could be better.

But I am bound for the Caucasus! For only today I heard it said in the breezes that the poets are free as swallows. And, besides, when I was younger someone confided to me that in olden times our parents, the Ger-

Still fortgezogen von Wellen der Donau,
Dort mit der Sonne Kindern
Am Sommertage, da diese
Sich Schatten suchten, zusammen
Mit Kindern der Sonn'
Am schwarzen Meere gekommen;
Und nicht umsonst sei dies
Das gastfreundliche genennet.

Denn, als sie erst sich angesehen,
Da nahten die Andern zuerst; dann satzten auch
Die Unseren sich neugierig unter den Ölbaum.
Doch als sich ihre Gewande berührt,
Und keiner vernehmen konnte
Die eigene Rede des andern, wäre wohl
Entstanden ein Zwist, wenn nicht aus Zweigen herunter
Gekommen wäre die Kühlung,
Die Lächeln über das Angesicht
Der Streitenden öfters breitet; und eine Weile
Sahn still sie auf, dann reichten sie sich
Die Hände liebend einander. Und bald

Vertauschten sie Waffen und all
Die lieben Güter des Hauses,
Vertauschten das Wort auch und es wünschten

man people, had quietly left the Danube's waves on a summer day and, when those were looking for shade, by the Black Sea had met with children of the Sun; and not for nothing this sea was called the hospitable.

For, when first they looked at one another, it was the others who first approached; then our people, too, sat down inquisitive under the olive-tree. But when their garments had touched, and none could understand the peculiar speech of the others, a quarrel would probably have arisen, had not coolness descended upon them from the branches, coolness that often spreads a smile over the faces of quarrelling men, and for a while they looked up in silence, then lovingly they clasped hands. And soon

They exchanged weapons and all the precious goods of the house, ex-changed the word as well, and not in vain did kindly fathers wish their

Die freundlichen Väter umsonst nichts
Beim Hochzeitjubel den Kindern.
Denn aus den heiligvermählten
Wuchs schöner, denn Alles,
Was vor und nach
Von Menschen sich nannt', ein Geschlecht auf. Wo,
Wo aber wohnt ihr, liebe Verwandten,
Daß wir das Bündnis wiederbegehn
Und der teuern Ahnen gedenken?

Dort an den Ufern, unter den Bäumen
Ionias, in Ebenen des Kaysters,
Wo Kraniche, des Äthers froh,
Umschlossen sind von fernhindämmernden Bergen,
Dort wart auch ihr, ihr Schönsten! oder pflegtet
Der Inseln, die mit Wein bekränzt
Voll tönten von Gesang; noch andere wohnten
Am Tayget, am vielgepriesnen Hymettos,
Die blühten zuletzt; doch von
Parnassos Quell bis zu des Tmolos
Goldglänzenden Bächen erklang
Ein ewiges Lied; so rauschten damals
Die heiligen Wälder und all
Die Saitenspiele zusamt
Von himmlischer Milde gerühret.

children anything at the jubilant nuptials that followed. For from the
sacredly married a people grew up, more beautiful than any other named
among mortals before or since. Where, but where do you dwell, dear rela-
tives, that we may celebrate the pact once more and remember our dear
forefathers?

There, on the shores, under the trees of Ionia, on the Cayster's plains,
where delighting in Aether, cranes are surrounded by far-glimmering
mountains; there you were also, most beautiful of all! Or haunted the
islands which garlanded with vines, resounded full of song; and others
dwelled by Taygetus, by widely praised Himettus, and were the last to
thrive; yet from the source of Parnassus to the brooks of Tmolus gleaming
with gold an eternal song rang out; so did the woods murmur then and all
the harps in unison plucked by heavenly mildness.

O Land des Homer!
Am purpurnen Kirschbaum, oder wenn
Von dir gesandt, im Weinberg mir
Die jungen Pfirsiche grünen,
Und die Schwalbe fernher kommt und vieleserzählend
An meinen Wänden ihr Haus baut, in
Den Tagen des Mais, auch unter den Sternen
Gedenk' ich, o, Ionia, dein! Drum bin ich
Gekommen, euch, ihr Inseln, zu sehn, und euch,
Ihr Mündungen der Ströme, Hallen der Thetis,
Ihr Wälder, euch, und euch, ihr Wolken des Ida!

Doch nicht zu bleiben gedenk ich.
Unfreundlich ist, und schwer zu gewinnen,
Die Verschlossene, der ich entkommen, die Mutter.
Von ihren Söhnen einer, der Rhein,
Mit Gewalt wollt' er ans Herz ihr stürzen und schwand,
Der Zurückgestoßene, niemand weiß, wohin in die Ferne,
Doch so nicht wünscht' ich gegangen zu sein
Von ihr und nur, euch einzuladen,
Bin ich zu euch, ihr Grazien Griechenlands,
Ihr Himmelstöchter, gegangen,
Daß, wenn die Reise zu weit nicht ist,
Zu uns ihr kommet, ihr Holden!

O land of Homer! By the crimson cherry-tree or when, sent by you, in the vineyard, I see the young peaches hang green, and the swallow comes from afar, and, telling me much, builds its house on my walls, in May-time, and under the stars, Ionia, I think of you! But to men what is present is dear. That is why I have come, you islands, to see you, and you, mouths of the rivers, and you, O halls of Thetis, you woods and you, O clouds over Ida!

Yet not to stay I am minded. Ungracious and intractable is the taciturn one whom I fled from, my mother. One of her sons, the Rhine, by force tried to rush to her heart, and vanished, repulsed, no one knows where, in the distance. Yet not thus would I wish to have left her, and only to invite you I went to you, you Graces of Greece, you daughters of Heaven, so that, if the journey is not too long, you will come to us, beloved ones!

Wenn milder atmen die Lüfte,
Und liebende Pfeile der Morgen
Uns Allzugedultigen schickt,
Und leichte Gewölke blühn
Uns über den schüchternen Augen,
Dann werden wir sagen, wie kommt,
Ihr' Charitinnen, zu Wilden?
Die Dienerinnen des Himmels
Sind aber wunderbar,
Wie alles Göttlichgeborne.
Zum Traume wirds ihm, will es Einer
Beschleichen und straft den, der
Ihm gleichen will mit Gewalt;
Oft überrascht es einen,
Der eben kaum es gedacht hat.

## GERMANIEN

Nicht sie, die Seligen, die erschienen sind,
Die Götterbilder in dem alten Lande,
Sie darf ich ja nicht rufen mehr, wenn aber
Ihr heimatlichen Wasser! jetzt mit euch
Des Herzens Liebe klagt, was will es anders,
Das Heiligtrauernde? Denn voll Erwartung liegt

When more mildly the soft winds breathe, and morning sends loving arrows to us all too patient ones, and the light clouds bloom over our diffident eyes, then we shall say: how did you Charites come to barbarians? But the serving-maids of Heaven are miraculous, like all that is born of gods. He who would grasp it by stealth holds a dream in his hand; and it punishes him who seeks to grow like it by force; often it takes by surprise him who has hardly begun to give it a thought.

## GERMANIA

NOT them, the blessèd, who once appeared, the images of gods in the ancient land, these, it is true, I may no more invoke, but if, you waters of my homeland, now with you the love of my heart laments, what else does

Das Land und als in heißen Tagen
Herabgesenkt, umschattet heut,
Ihr Sehnenden! uns ahnungsvoll ein Himmel.
Voll ist er von Verheißungen und scheint
Mir drohend auch, doch will ich bei ihm bleiben,
Und rückwärts soll die Seele mir nicht fliehn
Zu euch, Vergangene! die zu lieb mir sind.
Denn euer schönes Angesicht zu sehn,
Als wärs, wie sonst, ich fürcht' es, tödlich ists
Und kaum erlaubt, Gestorbene zu wecken.

Entflohene Götter! auch ihr, ihr gegenwärtigen, damals
Wahrhaftiger, ihr hattet eure Zeiten!
Nichts leugnen will ich hier und nichts erbitten.
Denn wenn es aus ist, und der Tag erloschen,
Wohl trifft den Priester erst, doch liebend folgt
Der Tempel und das Bild ihm auch und seine Sitte
Zum dunkeln Land und keines mag noch scheinen.
Nur als von Grabesflammen, ziehet dann,
Ein goldner Rauch, die Sage drob hinüber,
Und dämmert jetzt uns Zweifelnden um das Haupt,
Und keiner weiß, wie ihm geschieht. Er fühlt

it desire in its hallowed sadness? For full of expectation lies the land and, as if lowered in sultry days, today a heaven, you yearning ones, envelops us in its foreboding shade. It is fraught with promises and seems to me threatening too, yet I will stay with it, and backwards my soul shall not flee to you that are past, too dear to me. For to look upon your lovely presences, as if they were still the same, I am afraid: deadly it is, and scarcely permitted, to waken those that have died.

Gods that are fled! And you, still present, yet more real at that time, you had your span of ages! Nothing here I'll deny and ask for nothing. For when it's over and Day extinguished, true, the priest is the first to be struck, but lovingly the temple and the image follow him too, and their rite, to the land of darkness, and none of them now may shine. Only as from a funeral pyre henceforth a golden smoke, the legend of it, drifts above it still, and now grows dim about the heads of us doubting ones, and

Die Schatten derer, so gewesen sind,
Die Alten, so die Erde neubesuchen.
Denn die da kommen sollen, drängen uns,
Und länger säumt von Göttermenschen
Die heilige Schar nicht mehr im blauen Himmel.

Schon grünet ja, im Vorspiel rauherer Zeit
Für sie erzogen, das Feld, bereitet ist die Gabe
Zum Opfermahl und Tal und Ströme sind
Weitoffen um prophetische Berge,
Daß schauen mag bis in den Orient
Der Mann und ihn von dort der Wandlungen viele bewegen.
Vom Äther aber fällt
Das treue Bild und Göttersprüche regnen
Unzählbare von ihm, und es tönt im innersten Haine.
Und der Adler, der vom Indus kömmt,
Und über des Parnassos
Beschneite Gipfel fliegt, hoch über den Opferhügeln
Italias, und frohe Beute sucht
Dem Vater, nicht wie sonst, geübter im Fluge
Der Alte, jauchzend überschwingt er
Zuletzt die Alpen und sieht die vielgearteten Länder.

no one knows what is happening to him. He feels the shades of those that once were here, the ancients, newly visiting the earth. For those who are to come are pressing us, and longer the holy host of human gods, god-men will not delay in an azure heaven.

Already, reared for them in the prelude of a ruder age, the field grows green, the offering is prepared for the sacrificial feast and valley and rivers are wide open around prophetic mountains, so that a man may gaze as far as the Orient, and many transformations move him, conveyed to him from those parts. But down from Aether falls the faithful image, and utterance of gods rain down from it innumerable, and the innermost grove resounds. And the eagle that comes from the Indus and flies over the snow-covered peaks of Parnassus, high above the sacrificial hills of Italy, and seeks glad prey for the Father, not as before, more practised in flight that ancient one, crying for joy last of all he swoops over the Alps and sees the variously fashioned countries.

Die Priesterin, die stillste Tochter Gottes,
Sie, die zu gern in tiefer Einfalt schweigt,
Sie suchet er, die offnen Auges schaute,
Als wüßte sie es nicht, jüngst da ein Sturm
Toddrohend über ihrem Haupt ertönte;
Es ahnete das Kind ein Besseres,
Und endlich ward ein Staunen weit im Himmel,
Weil Eines groß an Glauben, wie sie selbst,
Die segnende, die Macht der Höhe sei;
Drum sandten sie den Boten, der, sie schnell erkennend,
Denkt lächelnd so: Dich, unzerbrechliche, muß
Ein ander Wort erprüfen, und ruft es laut,
Der Jugendliche, nach Germania schauend:
«Du bist es, auserwählt
Alliebend und ein schweres Glück
Bist du zu tragen stark geworden.

Seit damals, da im Walde versteckt und blühendem Mohn
Voll süßen Schlummers, trunkene, meiner du
Nicht achtetest, lang, ehe noch auch Geringere fühlten
Der Jungfrau Stolz, und staunten, wes du wärst und woher,
Doch du es selbst nicht wußtest. Ich mißkannte dich nicht,
Und heimlich, da du träumtest, ließ ich

The priestess, her, the quietest daughter of God, too fond of keeping
silent in deep ingenuousness, her now he seeks, who open-eyed looked up,
as if she did not know it, lately, when a storm, threatening death, was
rumbling over her head; a better destiny that child divined, and far and
wide at last amazement spread in Heaven because one being was as great in
faith as is that blessing power itself, the power on high; therefore they sent
the messenger who, quick to recognize her, smilingly thus reflects: You the
unbreakable a different word must try, and cries aloud, the youthful, gazing
towards Germania: 'Yes, it is you, elected, all-loving and to bear a burden-
some good fortune have grown strong,
    Since then, when hidden in the forest and in flowering poppies full of
sweet drowsiness, O drunken one, you did not heed me, long, and still be-
fore lesser ones even felt the virgin's pride and marvelled whose you were,
and whence, yet you yourself did not know it. But I did not misjudge you,
and, while you dreamed, at noon in secret left a token of friendship for you

Am Mittag scheidend dir ein Freundeszeichen,
Die Blume des Mundes, zurück und du redetest einsam.
Doch Fülle der goldenen Worte sandtest du auch,
Glückselige! mit den Strömen und sie quillen unerschöpflich
In die Gegenden all. Denn fast, wie der heiligen,
Die Mutter ist von allem, und den Abgrund trägt,
Die Verborgene sonst genannt von Menschen,
So ist von Lieben und Leiden
Und voll von Ahnungen dir
Und voll von Frieden der Busen.

O trinke Morgenlüfte,
Bis daß du offen bist,
Und nenne, was vor Augen dir ist,
Nicht länger darf Geheimnis mehr
Das Ungesprochene bleiben,
Nachdem es lange verhüllt ist;
Denn Sterblichen geziemet die Scham,
Und so zu reden die meiste Zeit,
Ist weise auch von Göttern.
Wo aber überflüssiger, denn lautere Quellen
Das Gold und ernst geworden ist der Zorn an dem Himmel,
Muß zwischen Tag und Nacht

as I departed, the flower of the mouth, and you spoke in your solitude. Yet an abundance of golden words also you sent, most happy one, with the rivers, and inexhaustible they flow into every region. For almost as is the holy one's, who is the Mother of us all, otherwise called the concealed by men, full of loves and sorrows, and full of presentiments, and full of peace is your bosom.

Oh drink the morning breezes until you are opened up, and name what is in front of your eyes, no longer now the unspoken must remain a mystery, after long being veiled; shame is fitting for mortals, and most of the time to speak thus, even of gods, is wise. But where more superabundant than limpid sources gold has become, and the anger in Heaven grown

Einsmals ein Wahres erscheinen.
Dreifach umschreibe du es,
Doch ungesprochen auch, wie es da ist,
Unschuldige, muß es bleiben.

O nenne, Tochter du der heiligen Erd',
Einmal die Mutter. Es rauschen die Wasser am Fels
Und Wetter im Wald und bei dem Namen derselben
Tönt auf aus alter Zeit Vergangengöttliches wieder.
Wie anders ists! und rechthin glänzt und spricht
Zukünftiges auch erfreulich aus den Fernen.
Doch in der Mitte der Zeit
Lebt ruhig mit geweihter
Jungfräulicher Erde der Äther
Und gerne, zur Erinnerung, sind
Die unbedürftigen sie
Gastfreundlich bei den unbedürftgen,
Bei deinen Feiertagen,
Germania, wo du Priesterin bist
Und wehrlos Rat gibst rings
Den Königen und den Völkern.»

earnest, for once between day and night a truth must appear. Threefold circumscribe it, but unspoken too, as it is, guileless one, it must remain.

Oh once, you daughter of holy Earth, call your mother by name. The waters roar by the rock and thunderstorms in the woods, and at their name, out of ancient ages, perished divinity sounds once more. How different it is! And, to the right as well, things yet to come, joy-giving, shine and speak from afar. Yet at the middle of Time Aether dwells in peace with hallowed, virginal Earth and gladly, in commemoration, the unrequiring hospitably dwell with the unrequiring, with your holidays, Germania, where you are priestess, and weaponless proffer advice to the kings and peoples around you.'

## DER RHEIN

### AN ISAAK VON SINCLAIR

Iᴍ dunklen Efeu saß ich, an der Pforte
Des Waldes, eben, da der goldene Mittag,.
Den Quell besuchend, herunterkam
Von Treppen des Alpengebirgs,
Das mir die göttlichgebaute,
Die Burg der Himmlischen heißt
Nach alter Meinung, wo aber
Geheim noch manches entschieden
Zu Menschen gelanget; so
Vernahm ich ohne Vermuten
Ein Schicksal, denn noch kaum
War mir im warmen Schatten
Sich manches beredend, die Seele
Italia zu geschweift
Und fernhin an die Küsten Moreas.

Jetzt aber, drin im Gebirg,
Tief unter den silbernen Gipfeln,
Und unter fröhlichem Grün,
Wo die Wälder schauernd zu ihm
Und der Felsen Häupter übereinander
Hinabschaun, taglang, dort

## THE RHINE

### TO ISAAK VON SINCLAIR

I sᴀᴛ in the dark ivy, at the forest's gate, just as golden noon, to visit the
source, came down from steps of the Alpine ranges, which I call the
divinely-built, the stronghold of the Heavenly, following old opinion, but
where determined in secret something still reaches men; thence without
surmise I heard a fate, for debating diverse things in that warm shade, my
soul had hardly begun to wander towards Italy and far away to Morea's
shores.

But now, amidst the mountains, deep down below the snowy summits
and surrounded with cheerful green, where shuddering the forests and the
heads of rocks overlapping look down upon him, day after day there in the

Im kältesten Abgrund hört'
Ich um Erlösung jammern
Den Jüngling, es hörten ihn, wie er tobt',
Und die Mutter Erd' anklagt'
Und den Donnerer, der ihn gezeuget,
Erbarmend die Eltern, doch
Die Sterblichen flohn von dem Ort,
Denn furchtbar war, da lichtlos er
In den Fesseln sich wälzte,
Das Rasen des Halbgotts.

Die Stimme wars des edelsten der Ströme,
Des freigeborenen Rheins,
Und anderes hoffte der, als droben von den Brüdern,
Dem Teßin und dem Rhodanus,
Er schied und wandern wollt', und ungeduldig ihn
Nach Asia trieb die königliche Seele.
Doch unverständig ist
Das Wünschen vor dem Schicksal.
Die Blindesten aber
Sind Göttersöhne. Denn es kennet der Mensch
Sein Haus und dem Tier ward, wo
Es bauen solle, doch jenen ist
Der Fehl, daß sie nicht wissen wohin,
In die unerfahrne Seele gegeben.

coldest abyss I heard the youth wail for release; pitying him, as he raged and accused Mother Earth and the Thunderer who begot him, his parents heard him, but mortals fled from the place, for as he writhed without light in his fetters, terrible was the demi-god's raving.

It was the voice of the noblest of rivers, of free-born Rhine, and different was his hope when up above, from his brothers Ticino and Rhône he parted and wanted to ramble, and his kingly soul impatiently drove him towards Asia. Yet in the face of Fate wishing is senseless. But the blindest of all are the sons of gods. For a man knows his own house and in the animal's soul where it must build was implanted, but in their inexperienced souls the defect that they do not know whither.

Ein Rätsel ist Reinentsprungenes. Auch
Der Gesang kaum darf es enthüllen. Denn
Wie du anfingst, wirst du bleiben,
So viel auch wirket die Not
Und die Zucht, das meiste nämlich
Vermag die Geburt,
Und der Lichtstrahl, der
Dem Neugebornen begegnet.
Wo aber ist einer,
Um frei zu bleiben
Sein Leben lang, und des Herzens Wunsch
Allein zu erfüllen, so
Aus günstigen Höhn, wie der Rhein,
Und so aus heiligem Schoße
Glücklich geboren, wie jener?

Drum ist ein Jauchzen sein Wort.
Nicht liebt er, wie andere Kinder,
In Wickelbanden zu weinen;
Denn wo die Ufer zuerst
An die Seit ihm schleichen, die krummen,
Und durstig umwindend ihn,
Den Unbedachten, zu ziehn

An enigma are things of pure origin. Even song may hardly disclose it.
For as you began, so you will remain, much as need can accomplish, and
breeding, for birth can accomplish most, and the ray of light that meets the
new-born infant. But where is one as happily born as the Rhine from
propitious heights and, like him, from a holy womb, to remain free his
whole life long and by his own efforts fulfil his heart's desire?
Therefore his word is exultation. Nor, like other children, does he like
to weep in swaddling bands; for where at first the banks slink to his side,
the crooked, and thirstily entwining the still imprudent one, long to train
him and carefully guard him within their teeth, laughing he tears up the

Und wohl zu behüten begehren
Im eigenen Zahne, lachend
Zerreißt er die Schlangen und stürzt
Mit der Beut und wenn in der Eil'
Ein Größerer ihn nicht zähmt,
Ihn wachsen läßt, wie der Blitz, muß er
Die Erde spalten, und wie Bezauberte fliehn
Die Wälder ihm nach und zusammensinkend die Berge.

Ein Gott will aber sparen den Söhnen
Das eilende Leben und lächelt,
Wenn unenthaltsam, aber gehemmt
Von heiligen Alpen, ihm
In der Tiefe, wie jener, zürnen die Ströme.
In solcher Esse wird dann
Auch alles Lautre geschmiedet,
Und schön ists, wie er drauf,
Nachdem er die Berge verlassen,
Stillwandelnd sich im deutschen Lande
Begnüget und das Sehnen stillt
Im guten Geschäfte, wenn er das Land baut,
Der Vater Rhein, und liebe Kinder nährt
In Städten, die er gegründet.

snakes and rushes off with his prey, and if a greater one does not tame him, but allows him to grow, like lightning he will split the earth and, as though bewitched the forests follow his flight and, collapsing, the mountains.

But a God would spare his sons fleeting life, and smiles when incontinent, but hindered by holy Alps, the rivers, like this one, rage at him in the deeps. Then, upon such a forge, even all that's pure is shaped, and it is lovely to see how henceforth, after leaving the mountains, quietly moving through German country he is content, and stills his yearning in useful industry, when he cultivates land, now Father Rhine, and nourishes loving children in cities which he has founded.

Doch nimmer, nimmer vergißt ers.
Denn eher muß die Wohnung vergehn,
Und die Satzung, und zum Unbild werden
Der Tag der Menschen, ehe vergessen
Ein solcher dürfte den Ursprung
Und die reine Stimme der Jugend.
Wer war es, der zuerst
Die Liebesbande verderbt
Und Stricke von ihnen gemacht hat?
Dann haben des eigenen Rechts
Und gewiß des himmlischen Feuers
Gespottet die Trotzigen, dann erst
Die sterblichen Pfade verachtend
Verwegnes erwählt
Und den Göttern gleich zu werden getrachtet.

Es haben aber an eigner
Unsterblichkeit die Götter genug, und bedürfen
Die Himmlischen eines Dings,
So sinds Heroen und Menschen
Und Sterbliche sonst. Denn weil
Die Seligsten nichts fühlen von selbst,
Muß wohl, wenn solches zu sagen
Erlaubt ist, in der Götter Namen
Teilnehmend fühlen ein Andrer,

Yet never, never does he forget it. For sooner the dwelling shall perish, and the laws, and the day of men become an iniquity, than such as he forget his origin and the pure voice of youth. Who was it that first corrupted the bonds of love and made ropes out of them? Then the defiant scoffed at their own rights, and certain of the heavenly fire, only then despising mortal paths, chose foolhardy arrogance and strove to become the equals of gods.

But their own immortality suffices the gods; and if the Heavenly need one thing it is heroes and human beings and other mortals. For, because the most Blessed in themselves feel nothing, another, if to say such a thing is permitted, must, I suppose, sympathetically feel on the gods' behalf;

Den brauchen sie; jedoch ihr Gericht
Ist, daß sein eigenes Haus
Zerbreche der und das Liebste
Wie den Feind schelt' und sich Vater und Kind
Begrabe unter den Trümmern,
Wenn einer, wie sie, sein will und nicht
Ungleiches dulden, der Schwärmer.

Drum wohl ihm, welcher fand
Ein wohlbeschiedenes Schicksal,
Wo noch der Wanderungen
Und süß der Leiden Erinnerung
Aufrauscht am sichern Gestade,
Daß da und dorthin gern
Er sehn mag bis an die Grenzen,
Die bei der Geburt ihm Gott
Zum Aufenthalte gezeichnet.
Dann ruht er, seligbescheiden,
Denn alles, was er gewollt,
Das Himmlische, von selber umfängt
Es unbezwungen, lächelnd
Jetzt, da er ruhet, den Kühnen.

they need that man; but their rule is that he break his own house and curse
like an enemy what he loves most and bury his father and child under the
rubble, if he wishes to be like them and jibe at inequality, the fantast.
Therefore happy he who has found a well-allotted fate, where on firmly
built shores still the memory of his travels and, sweetly, of his sufferings
rings out from below, so that there and yonder he will be glad to look as far
as the bounds which at birth God has drawn for his sojourn. Then he's at
rest, blissfully modest, for all that he desired, heavenly things, of them-
selves and unforced surround the bold one, smiling, now that he is at
rest.

Halbgötter denk' ich jetzt
Und kennen muß ich die Teuern,
Weil oft ihr Leben so
Die sehnende Brust mir beweget.
Wem aber, wie, Rousseau, dir,
Unüberwindlich die Seele,
Die starkausdauernde ward,
Und sicherer Sinn
Und süße Gabe zu hören,
Zu reden so, daß er aus heiliger Fülle
Wie der Weingott, törig göttlich
Und gesetzlos sie, die Sprache der Reinesten gibt
Verständlich den Guten, aber mit Recht
Die Achtungslosen mit Blindheit schlägt,
Die entweihenden Knechte, wie nenn ich den Fremden?

Die Söhne der Erde sind, wie die Mutter,
Alliebend, so empfangen sie auch
Mühlos, die Glücklichen, Alles.
Drum überraschet es auch
Und schröckt den sterblichen Mann,
Wenn er den Himmel, den
Er mit den liebenden Armen
Sich auf die Schultern gehäuft,
Und die Last der Freude bedenket;

Of demi-gods now I think and I must know these dear ones, because
often their lives so move my yearning heart. But that man whose soul,
Rousseau, like yours, the strongly enduring, became invincible, whose
mind was sure and who had a sweet gift of hearing, of speaking so that
from holy profusion like the wine-god he foolishly, divinely, and lawlessly
lavished it, the language of the most pure, comprehensible to the good, but
rightly struck with blindness the irreverent, the profaning slaves, what
should I call the stranger?

The sons of Earth, like their mother, are all-loving, and so without
effort, these fortunate ones, receive all things. That also is why it surprises
and startles the mortal man when he considers the heaven which on his
own shoulders with loving arms he has heaped, and the burden of joy;

Dann scheint ihm oft das Beste
Fast ganz vergessen da,
Wo der Strahl nicht brennt,
Im Schatten des Walds
Am Bielersee in frischer Grüne zu sein,
Und sorglos arm an Tönen,
Anfängern gleich, bei Nachtigallen zu lernen.

Und herrlich ists, aus heiligem Schlafe dann
Erstehen und aus Waldes Kühle
Erwachend, Abends nun
Dem milderen Licht entgegenzugehn,
Wenn, der die Berge gebaut
Und den Pfad der Ströme gezeichnet,
Nachdem er lächelnd auch
Der Menschen geschäftiges Leben,
Das othemarme, wie Segel
Mit seinem Lüften gelenkt hat,
Auch ruht und zu der Schülerin jetzt,
Der Bildner, Gutes mehr
Denn Böses findend,
Zur heutigen Erde der Tag sich neiget. –

then often it seems to him best almost wholly forgotten to be where the beam does not sear, in the shade of the forest, by Lake Bienne amidst fresh verdure, and, lightheartedly poor in music, like beginners to learn from nightingales.

And it is glorious then to rise up from holy sleep and, awakening from the coolness of the wood, now at evening to walk towards the milder light, when he who built the mountains and drafted the paths of the rivers after, smiling, he had also steered the busy life of men, so poor in breath, like sails with his breezes, is also at rest, and to his pupil now, finding more good than evil, the shaping one, Day, bows down to present Earth. –

Dann feiern das Brautfest Menschen und Götter,
Es feiern die Lebenden all,
Und ausgeglichen
Ist eine Weile das Schicksal.
Und die Flüchtlinge suchen die Herberg,
Und süßen Schlummer die Tapfern,
Die Liebenden aber
Sind, was sie waren; sie sind
Zu Hause, wo die Blume sich freuet
Unschädlicher Glut und die finsteren Bäume
Der Geist umsäuselt, aber die Unversöhnten
Sind umgewandelt und eilen,
Die Hände sich ehe zu reichen,
Bevor das freundliche Licht
Hinuntergeht und die Nacht kommt.

Doch einigen eilt
Dies schnell vorüber, andere
Behalten es länger.
Die ewigen Götter sind
Voll Lebens allzeit; bis in den Tod
Kann aber ein Mensch auch
Im Gedächtnis doch das Beste behalten,
Und dann erlebt er das Höchste.

Then men and gods celebrate their nuptials, all the living celebrate, and
Fate for a while is levelled. And the fugitives seek lodging, and sweet
slumber the brave, but the lovers are what they were, at home where the
flower takes delight in harmless ardour and the spirit rustles around the
darkling trees; but the unreconciled are transformed and hasten to hold out
their hands to one another before the kind light goes down and Night
comes.
    Yet for some this quickly passes, others retain it longer. The eternal
gods are full of life at all times; but until death even a man in his memory
can preserve what is best, and then he experiences the utmost. Only each

Nur hat ein jeder sein Maß.
Denn schwer ist zu tragen
Das Unglück, aber schwerer das Glück.
Ein Weiser* aber vermocht es
Vom Mittag bis in die Mitternacht,
Und bis der Morgen erglänzte,
Beim Gastmahl helle zu bleiben.

Dir mag auf heißem Pfade unter Tannen oder
Im Dunkel des Eichwalds gehüllt
In Stahl, mein Sinklair! Gott erscheinen oder
In Wolken, du kennst ihn, da du kennest, jugendlich,
Des Guten Kraft, und nimmer ist dir
Verborgen das Lächeln des Herrschers
Bei Tage, wenn
Es fieberhaft und angekettet das
Lebendige scheinet oder auch
Bei Nacht, wenn alles gemischt
Ist ordnungslos und wiederkehrt
Uralte Verwirrung.

one has his measure. For misfortune is hard to bear, but good fortune still harder. Yet from noon to midnight, and till morning shone forth, a wise man* was able to remain lucid at the banquet.

To you, my Sinclair, on a hot path under fir-trees or in the oak forest's darkness, wrapped in steel, God may appear, or in clouds; you know Him, since youthfully you know the Good One's power and never from you the Ruler's smile is hidden by day, when all that lives seems febrile and all chained up, or also by night, when all is mingled chaotically and primeval confusion returns.

---

* Socrates in Plato's *Symposium*.

[*Vorstufen zur* FRIEDENSFEIER]

VERSÖHNENDER der du nimmergeglaubt
Nun da bist, Freundesgestalt mir
Annimmst Unsterblicher, aber wohl
Erkenn ich ... das Hohe
Das mir die Knie beugt,
Und fast wie ein Blinder muß ich
Dich, himmlischer fragen wozu du mir,
Woher du seiest, seliger Friede!
Dies Eine weiß ich, sterbliches bist du nichts,
Denn manches mag ein Weiser oder
Treuanblickenden Freunde einer erhellen, wenn aber
Ein Gott erscheint, auf Himmel und Erde und Meer
Kömmt allerneuende Klarheit.

(Einst freueten wir uns auch,
Zur Morgenstunde wo stille die Werkstatt war
Am Feiertag, und die Blumen in der Stille,
Wohl blühten schöner auch sie und helle quillten lebendigen
    Brunnen.
Fern rauschte der Gemeinde schauerlicher Gesang,
Wo heiligen Wein gleich, die geheimeren Sprüche
Gealtert aber gewaltiger einst, aus Gottes

[*Preliminary drafts for* CELEBRATION OF PEACE]

CONCILIATOR, who never believed now are here, assuming the shape of
a friend, immortal one, yet truly I recognize ... the exalted power that
bends my knees, and like a blind man almost I must ask you heavenly one
for what and whence you have come to me, blessed Peace! This one thing
I know, you are no mortal power, for much a wise man or one of the faith-
fully gazing friends may elucidate, but when a God appears, on Heaven
and earth and sea all-renewing clarity reigns.

(Once too, we were glad, at the morning hour when the workshop was
silent, on a holiday, and indeed in that stillness the flowers more beautifully
bloomed, and brightly the living source welled up. Far away the com-
munity's shuddering song flowed on, where like holy wine the more mys-
terious responses, aged but more mighty once, grown up in summer out of
God's thunderstorms, still could allay my griefs and my doubts, but never

Gewittern im Sommer gewachsen,
Die Sorgen doch mir stillten
Und die Zweifel aber nimmer wußt ich, wie mir geschah,
Denn kaum geboren, warum breitetet
Ihr mir schon über die Augen eine Nacht,
Daß ich die Erde nicht sah, und mühsam
Euch atmen mußt, ihr himmlischen Lüfte.

Zuvorbestimmt wars. Und es lächelt Gott,
Wenn unaufhaltsam aber von seinen Bergen gehemmt
Ihm zürnend in den ehernen Ufern brausen die Ströme,
Tief wo kein Tag die begrabenen nennt.
Und o, daß immer allerhaltender, du auch mich
So haltest, und leichtentfliehende Seele mir sparest)
Drum hab ich heute das Fest, und abendlich in der Stille
Blüht rings der Geist und wär auch silbergrau mir die Locke,
Doch würd ich raten, daß wir sorgten ihr Freunde
Für Gastmahl und Gesang, und Kränze genug und Töne
Bei solcher Zeit unsterblichen Jünglingen gleich.

Und manchen möcht' ich laden, aber o du,
Der freundlichernst den Menschen zugetan
Dort unter syrischer Palme
Wo nahe lag die Stadt am Brunnen gerne weiltest,

I knew how it was with me, for why, when I had scarcely been born, did
you cover my eyes with night, so that I could not see the Earth and with
an effort only could breathe you, you winds of Heaven.

Pre-ordained it was. And God smiles when, not to be stopped but
hemmed in by His mountains, in their adamant banks the rivers roar at
Him furious, deep down where no day calls these buried ones by their
names. And oh, that ever, Upholder of All, thus you may hold me too, and
spare my volatile soul) therefore today I celebrate, and vespertine now in
the stillness all round the spirit blossoms, and though my hair were silver-
grey, yet I'd advise you, friends, to prepare both banquet and song, and
garlands enough and music at such a time like immortal youths.

And there are many I would invite, but O you that benignly, gravely
inclined towards men, there beneath the Syrian palm-tree, where the town

Das Kornfeld rauschte rings, still atmete die Kühlung
Vom Dunkel des geweiheten Gebirgs,
Und die lieben Freunde, das treue Gewölk
Umschatteten dich auch, damit der reine, kühne
Durch Wildnis mild der Strahl von oben kam o Jüngling!
Ach! aber dunkler umschattete, mitten im Wort dich
Furchtbarentscheidend ein tödlich Verhängnis. So ist schnell
Vergänglich alles Himmlische; aber umsonst nicht.

Denn schonend rührt, des Maßes allzeit kundig
Nur einen Augenblick die Wohnungen der Menschen
Ein Gott an, unversehn, und keiner weiß es, wer?
Und drüber hin darf alles Freche gehn,
Und kommen muß zum heilgen Ort das Wilde
Von Enden fern, und blindbetastend übt den Wahn
Am Göttlichen, und trifft darin ein Schicksal. Aber Dank
Folgt niemals auf dem Fuße solchem Geschenke.
Zu schwer ist jenes zu fassen,
Denn wäre der es gibt, nicht sparsam
Längst wäre vom Segen des Herds
Uns Gipfel und Boden entzündet.

lay near, by the well were disposed to linger, round about the cornfield
rustled, calmly the coolness breathed from the shade of the hallowed
mountains, and your dear friends, the faithful cloud, cast their shadows
upon you also, so that the pure, the bold, the beam through wilderness
gently would come to men from above, O youth! But, alas, more darkly
in the midst of your speech, dreadfully determining, a deadly doom over-
shadowed you. Thus speedily fleeting is all that is heavenly; but not in
vain.

For sparing, at all times sure of the measure, for a moment only does a
God touch the dwellings of men, unforeseen, and no one knows it, who?
And, over it, all insolence may pass, and to the holy place must come the
savage from ends remote, and blindly fingering it proves his delusion upon
the divine, and thereby meets a fate. But thankfulness never at once fol-
lows upon such a gift. This is too hard to grasp, for if He who gives it were
not sparing, long ago the blessings upon our hearths would have set fire to
both roof and floor.

Des Göttlichen aber empfingen wir
Doch viel. Es ward die Flamm uns
In die Hände gegeben, und Boden und Meersflut.
Vielmehr denn nur auf menschliche Weise, nimmer mehr
Sind jene mit uns, die fremden Kräfte vertrauet,
Und es lehret das Gestirn dich, das
Vor Augen dir ist, doch nimmer kannst du ihm gleichen.
Dem Allebendigen aber von dem
Viel Freuden sind und Gesänge,
Ist einer ein Sohn, ein Ruhigmächtiger ist er,
Denn nun erkennen wir ihn,
Jetzt da wir kennen den Vater,
Und Feiertage zu halten
Der Hohe sich, der Geist der Welt
Sich froh zu Menschen geneigt hat.

Zur Herrschaft war der immer zu groß
Und geringer denn er, so weit es gereichet sein Feld.
Es mag ein Gott auch, gleich Sterblichen
Erwählen ein Tagewerk und teilen alles Schicksal
Daß alle sich einander erfahren, und wenn
Die Stille wiederkehret, eine Sprache unter Lebenden
Sei. Wie der Meister tritt er dann, aus der
Werkstatt, und anderes Gewand nicht denn ein festliches ziehet
        er an.

But of the divine we received much nonetheless. The flame was put in our hands, and the soil and ocean flood. Much more than only in human fashion these, the alien powers, never again are intimate with us. And you are taught by the stars that are in front of your eyes, though never you can be like them. Yet of the All-Living from whom many joys and songs have sprung, One is the Son, he is calmly powerful, for now we recognize him, now that we know the Father, and, to keep holidays the exalted, the Spirit of the World, has gladly condescended to men.

For dominion He has always been too great, and smaller than He, far though it extends, His field. Even a God, like mortals, may choose the mere daily task and share all manner of fate, so that all shall know of all others and, when silence comes again, there may be a language among the living.

Die Gesetze aber, die unter Liebenden gelten
Die schönausgleichenden sie sind dann allgeltend
Von der Erde bis hoch in den Himmel.

Denn siehe es ist der Abend der Zeit
Und der Vater thront nun nimmer oben allein.
Und andere sind noch bei ihm.
Viel hat erfahren der Mensch. Der Himmlischen viele genannt,
Seit ein Gespräch wir sind
Und hören können voneinander.

Sei gegenwärtig Jüngling, jetzt erst, denn noch ehe du aus-
    geredet
Rief es herab, und schnell verhüllt war jenes Freudige, das
Du reichtest, und weitumschattend breitete sich über dir
Und furchtbar ein Verhängnis,
So ist schnellvergänglich alles Himmlische, aber umsonst nicht.
Des Maßes allzeit kundig rührt mit schonender Hand
Die Wohnungen der Menschen
Ein Gott an, einen Augenblick nur
Und sie wissen es nicht, doch lange
Gedenken sie des, und fragen, wer es gewesen.
Wenn aber eine Zeit vorbei ist, kennen sie es.

Then like the master he steps out of the workshop, and none but a festive
garment he puts on. But the laws that prevail among lovers, the gently
levelling laws, then are all-prevailing from Earth to high up in Heaven
    For, behold, it is the Evening of Time and no longer alone the Father
sits enthroned above. And others yet are with him. Much mankind has
learnt. Named many of the Heavenly, since we have been a discourse and
can hear from one another.
    Be present, youth, only now, for before you had finished speaking, you
were called below, and quickly that joy was obscured which you proffered,
and overshadowing far and wide and dreadful, a doom descended upon
you, so speedily fleeting is all that is heavenly, but not in vain. At all times
sure of the measure, with a sparing hand, a God touches the dwellings of
men, for a moment only, and they do not know it, yet long they remember
it and ask who it had been. But when a certain time has passed they know it.

Und menschlicher Wohltat folget der Dank,
Auf göttliche Gabe aber jahrlang
Das Leid erst und das Irrsal
Daß milder auf die folgende Zeit
Der hohe Strahl
Durch heilige Wildnis scheine.
Darum, o Göttlicher! sei gegenwärtig,
Und schöner, wie sonst, o sei
Versöhnender nun versöhnt daß wir des Abends
Mit den Freunden dich nennen, und singen
Von den Hohen, und neben dir noch andere sein.


Denn versiegt fast, all in Opferflammen
War ausgeatmet das heilige Feuer
Da schickte schnellentzündend der Vater
Das liebendste, was er hatte, herab
Damit entbrennend,
Und wenn fortzehrend von Geschlecht zu Geschlecht
Die Menschen wären des Segens zu voll,
Daß jeder sich genügt und übermütig vergäße des Himmels,

And thankfulness follows upon human beneficence, but upon the god-sent gift for years at first there follow suffering and confusion, so that more mildly in the subsequent period the lofty beam shall shine through holy wilderness. Therefore, divine one, be present and more than before, O Conciliator, now be reconciled, so that at Evening with the friends we may name you, and sing of the Exalted ones, and there may be others beside you.

For almost exhausted, all breathed out in sacrificial flames, was the sacred fire, when, swiftly kindling, the Father sent down the most loving He had, blazing up therewith; and when, consuming it generation after generation, men should be too full of blessings, so that each was sufficient unto himself and, arrogant, forgot Heaven, then, He said, a new age shall begin. And,

Dann sprach er soll ein neues beginnen,
Und siehe! was du verschwiegest,
Der Zeiten Vollendung hat es gebracht.
Wohl wußtest du es, aber nicht zu leben, zu sterben warst du
    gesandt,
Und immer größer, denn sein Feld, wie der Götter Gott
Er selbst, muß einer der anderern auch sein.

Wenn aber die Stunde schlägt,
Wie der Meister tritt er, aus der Werkstatt,
Und ander Gewand nicht, denn
Ein festliches ziehet er an
Zum Zeichen, daß noch anderes auch
Im Werk ihm übrig gewesen.
Geringer und größer erscheint er.
Und so auch du
Und gönnest uns, den Söhnen der liebenden Erde,
Daß wir, so viel herangewachsen
Der Feste sind, sie alle feiern und nicht
Die Götter zählen, Einer ist immer für alle.
Mir gleich dem Sonnenlichte! göttlicher sei
Am Abend deiner Tage gegrüßet.
Und mögen bleiben wir nun.

behold, what you left unspoken, the end of the ages has made manifest. And well you know it, but not to live, to die, you were sent, and ever greater than his field, like the God of gods Himself, one of the others also must be.

But when the hour strikes, like the master he steps out of the workshop and none but a festive garment he puts on, as a sign that something different too remained for him in his work. Smaller and greater he appears. And likewise you, and you grant us, the sons of loving Earth, that numerous as are the holidays that have been established, we may observe them all and not count the gods; one always stands for all. To me like the sunlight, divine one, let me greet you at the Evening of your days! And may we now remain!

## FRIEDENSFEIER

*Ich bitte dieses Blatt nur gutmütig zu lesen. So wird es sicher nicht unfaßlich, noch weniger anstößig sein. Sollten aber dennoch einige eine solche Sprache zu wenig konventionell finden, so muß ich ihnen gestehen; ich kann nicht anders. An einem schönen Tage läßt sich ja fast jede Sangart hören, und die Natur, wovon es her ist, nimmts auch wieder.*

*Der Verfasser gedenkt dem Publikum eine ganze Sammlung von dergleichen Blättern vorzulegen, und dieses soll irgend eine Probe sein davon.*

Der himmlischen, still wiederklingenden,
Der ruhigwandelnden Töne voll,
Und gelüftet ist der altgebaute,
Seliggewohnte Saal; um grüne Teppiche duftet
Die Freudenwolk' und weithinglänzend stehn,
Gereiftester Früchte voll und goldbekränzter Kelche,
Wohlangeordnet, eine prächtige Reihe,
Zur Seite da und dort aufsteigend über dem
Geebneten Boden die Tische.

## CELEBRATION OF PEACE

*All I ask is that the reader be kindly disposed towards these pages. In that case he will certainly not find them incomprehensible, far less objectionable. But if, nonetheless, some should think such a language too unconventional, I must confess to them: I cannot help it. On a fine day – they should consider – almost every mode of song makes itself heard: and Nature, whence it originates, also receives it again.*

*The author intends to offer the public an entire collection of similar pieces, and this one should be regarded as a kind of sample.*

With heavenly, softly re-echoing, with calmly modulating music filled, and aired is the hall raised in ancient times, the blessèdly familiar; about green carpets there wafts the fragrant cloud of joy and, widely gleaming, full of most mellow fruit and chalices wreathed with gold, set out in seemly order, a splendid array, rising on either side above the levelled floor, the

177

Denn ferne kommend haben
Hieher, zur Abendstunde,
Sich liebende Gäste beschieden.

    Und dämmernden Auges denk' ich schon,
Vom ernsten Tagwerk lächelnd,
Ihn selbst zu sehn, den Fürsten des Festes.
Doch wenn du schon dein Ausland gern verleugnest,
Und als vom langen Heldenzuge müd,
Dein Auge senkst, vergessen, leichtbeschattet,
Und Freundesgestalt annimmst, du Allbekannter, doch
Beugt fast die Knie das Hohe. Nichts vor dir,
Nur Eines weiß ich, Sterbliches bist du nicht.
Ein Weiser mag mir manches erhellen; wo aber
Ein Gott noch auch erscheint,
Da ist doch andere Klarheit.

    Von heute aber nicht, nicht unverkündet ist er;
Und einer, der nicht Flut noch Flamme gescheuet,
Erstaunet, da es stille worden, umsonst nicht, jetzt,
Da Herrschaft nirgend ist zu sehn bei Geistern und Menschen.
Das ist, sie hören das Werk,

tables stand. For hither, travelling far, at the evening hour, loving guests have repaired.

    And with dusk-dim eyes already, smiling with the grave daily task now done, I think that I see him in person, the prince of the feast-day. But though you like to disavow your foreign land, and, as though weary after long heroic war, cast down your eyes, oblivious, lightly shaded, and assume the shape of a friend, you known to all men, yet almost such greatness forces knees to bend. Nothing I know before you, but one thing, you are no mortal power. Much a wise man may elucidate for me; but where a God as well appears, a different clarity reigns.

    Yet not sprung up today, not unproclaimed he comes; and one who did not balk at either flood or flame not without reason astonishes now that all has grown silent, and dominion is visible nowhere, not among spirits or mortals. That is, not till now do they hear the work, though long it has

Längst vorbereitend, von Morgen nach Abend, jetzt erst,
Denn unermeßlich braust, in der Tiefe verhallend,
Des Donnerers Echo, das tausendjährige Wetter,
Zu schlafen, übertönt von Friedenslauten, hinunter.
Ihr aber, teuergewordne, o ihr Tage der Unschuld,
Ihr bringt auch heute das Fest, ihr Lieben! und es blüht
Rings abendlich der Geist in dieser Stille;
Und raten muß ich, und wäre silbergrau
Die Locke, o ihr Freunde!
Für Kränze zu sorgen und Mahl, jetzt ewigen Jünglingen
ähnlich.

Und manchen möcht' ich laden, aber o du,
Der freundlichernst den Menschen zugetan,
Dort unter syrischer Palme,
Wo nahe lag die Stadt, am Brunnen gerne war;
Das Kornfeld rauschte rings, still atmete die Kühlung
Vom Schatten des geweiheten Gebirges,
Und die lieben Freunde, das treue Gewölk,
Umschatteten dich auch, damit der heiligkühne
Durch Wildnis mild dein Strahl zu Menschen kam, o Jüngling!

prepared them, from Orient to Occident, for immeasurably now, subsiding
in the depths, the Thunderer's echo, the millennial storm rumbles down to
sleep, almost lost in peaceful music. But to you, grown dear to us, O days
of innocence, today's celebration also is due, belovèd ones, and vespertine
all around the spirit flowers in this stillness; and I must advise you, friends,
though our hair were silver-grey, to provide both banquet and garlands,
now resembling eternal youths.
    And there are many I would invite, but O you that benignly, gravely
inclined towards men, there beneath the Syrian palm-tree, where the town
lay near, by the well were disposed to linger; round about the cornfield
rustled, calmly the coolness breathed from the shade of the hallowed moun-
tains, and your dear friends, the faithful cloud, cast their shadows about
you also, so that the divinely bold, the beam through wilderness gently
would come to men, O youth! But, alas, more darkly in the midst of your

Ach! aber dunkler umschattete, mitten im Wort, dich
Furchtbarentscheidend ein tödlich Verhängnis. So ist schnell
Vergänglich alles Himmlische; aber umsonst nicht;

Denn schonend rührt des Maßes allzeit kundig
Nur einen Augenblick die Wohnungen der Menschen
Ein Gott an, unversehn, und keiner weiß es, wenn?
Auch darf alsdann das Freche drüber gehn,
Und kommen muß zum heilgen Ort das Wilde
Von Enden fern, übt rauhbetastend den Wahn,
Und trifft daran ein Schicksal, aber Dank,
Nie folgt der gleich hernach dem gottgegebnen Geschenke;
Tiefprüfend ist es zu fassen.
Auch wär' uns, sparte der Gebende nicht
Schon längst vom Segen des Herds
Uns Gipfel und Boden entzündet.

Des Göttlichen aber empfingen wir
Doch viel. Es ward die Flamm' uns
In die Hände gegeben, und Ufer und Meersflut.
Viel mehr, denn menschlicher Weise
Sind jene mit uns, die fremden Kräfte, vertrauet.

speech, dreadfully determining, a deadly doom overshadowed you. Thus
speedily fleeting is all that is heavenly; but not in vain;
　For sparing, at all times sure of the measure, for a moment only does a
God touch the dwellings of men, unforeseen, and no one knows when.
And over it henceforth the insolent may pass, and to the holy place must
come the savage from ends remote, and coarsely fingering it, proves his
delusion, and thereby meets a fate; but thankfulness, never at once does
this follow upon the god-sent gift; deeply probing, this must be grasped.
For were not the giver sparing, long ago the blessings upon our hearths
would have set fire to both roof and floor.
　But of the divine we received much nonetheless. The flame was put in
our hands, and shore and ocean flood. Much more than in human fashion
these, the alien powers, are intimate with us. And you are taught by the

Und es lehret Gestirn dich, das
Vor Augen dir ist, doch nimmer kannst du ihm gleichen.
Vom Alllebendigen aber, von dem
Viel Freuden sind und Gesänge,
Ist einer ein Sohn, ein Ruhigmächtiger ist er,
Und nun erkennen wir ihn,
Nun, da wir kennen den Vater
Und Feiertage zu halten
Der hohe, der Geist
Der Welt sich zu Menschen geneigt hat.

Denn längst war der zum Herrn der Zeit zu groß
Und weit aus reichte sein Feld, wann hats ihn aber erschöpfet?
Einmal mag aber ein Gott auch Tagewerk erwählen,
Gleich Sterblichen und teilen alles Schicksal.
Schicksalgesetz ist dies, daß Alle sich erfahren,
Daß, wenn die Stille kehrt, auch eine Sprache sei.
Wo aber wirkt der Geist, sind wir auch mit, und streiten,
Was wohl das Beste sei. So dünkt mir jetzt das Beste,
Wenn nun vollendet sein Bild und fertig ist der Meister,
Und selbst verklärt davon aus seiner Werkstatt tritt,
Der stille Gott der Zeit und nur der Liebe Gesetz,
Das schönausgleichende gilt von hier an bis zum Himmel.

---

stars that are in front of your eyes, though never you can be like them. Yet of the All-Living, from whom many joys and songs have sprung, One is the Son, he is calmly powerful, and Him now we recognize, now that we know the Father, and to keep holidays, the exalted, the Spirit of the World, has condescended to men.

For long now He had been too great to rule as the Lord of Time, and wide his field extended; yet when did this exhaust him? Yet for once a God himself may choose the mere daily task, like mortals, and share all manner of fate. This is the law of fate, that each shall know of all others, that, when silence comes again, there may be a language too. But where the Spirit is active, we too will stir and dispute what course might be the best. Thus what now seems best to me is that now the master completes his image, and is ready, and, himself transfigured by it, steps out of his workshop, the quiet God of Time, and only the law of love, the gently levelling, reigns from here right up to Heaven.

Viel hat von Morgen an,
Seit ein Gespräch wir sind und hören voneinander,
Erfahren der Mensch; bald sind [wir] aber Gesang.
Und das Zeitbild, das der große Geist entfaltet,
Ein Zeichen liegts vor uns, das[s] zwischen ihm und andern
Ein Bündnis zwischen ihm und andern Mächten ist.
Nicht er allein, die Unerzeugten, Ew'gen
Sind kennbar alle daran, gleichwie auch an den Pflanzen
Die Mutter Erde sich und Licht und Luft sich kennet.
Zuletzt ist aber doch, ihr heiligen Mächte, für euch
Das Liebeszeichen, das Zeugnis
Daß ihrs noch seiet, der Festtag,

Der Allversammelnde, wo Himmlische nicht
Im Wunder offenbar, noch ungesehn im Wetter,
Wo aber bei Gesang gastfreundlich untereinander
In Chören gegenwärtig, eine heilige Zahl
Die Seligen in jeglicher Weise
Beisammen sind, und ihr Geliebtestes auch,
An dem sie hängen, nicht fehlt; denn darum rief ich
Zum Gastmahl, das bereitet ist,
Dich, Unvergeßlicher, dich, zum Abend der Zeit,

Much, from morning onwards, since we have been a discourse, hearing from one another, mankind has learnt; but soon we shall be song. And that temporal image which the great Spirit unfolds as a token lies before us that between Him and others, Himself and other powers, there is a pact of peace. Not He alone, the Unconceived, Eternal are all to be known by this, as likewise by the plants our Mother Earth and light and air are known. But ultimately, O holy powers, our token of love for you, our testimony that still you are holy to us, is the feast-day,

The all-assembling, where the heavenly powers in miracles are not manifest, nor unseen in thunderstorms, but where in song hospitably conjoined, present in choirs, a holy number, the blessèd in every way meet and forgather, and He whom most they love, devoted to Him, is not missing; and that is why I called you to the banquet, now prepared, called you, the unforgettable you, at the Evening of Time, called you, O youth, to the prince

O Jüngling, dich zum Fürsten des Festes; und eher legt
Sich schlafen unser Geschlecht nicht,
Bis ihr Verheißenen all,
All ihr Unsterblichen, uns
Von eurem Himmel zu sagen,
Da seid in unserem Hause.

   Leichtatmende Lüfte
Verkünden euch schon,
Euch kündet das rauchende Tal
Und der Boden, der vom Wetter noch dröhnet,
Doch Hoffnung rötet die Wangen,
Und vor der Türe des Hauses
Sitzt Mutter und Kind,
Und schauet den Frieden
Und wenige scheinen zu sterben
Es hält ein Ahnen die Seele,
Vom goldnen Lichte gesendet,
Hält ein Versprechen die Ältesten auf.

   Wohl sind die Würze des Lebens,
Von oben bereitet und auch
Hinausgeführet, die Mühen.
Denn Alles gefällt jetzt,
Einfältiges aber
Am meisten, denn die langgesuchte,

of the feast-day; nor shall our nation ever lie down to sleep until all you
that were prophesied, all you Immortals, to tell us news of your Heaven,
are here in our own house.

Lightly wafting breezes proclaim you already, the smoking valley pro-
claims you, and the ground still resounding with the thunderstorm, yet
hope flushes our cheeks and in front of the door of their house sit mother
and child and gaze upon peace, and few appear to be dying; for now a fore-
boding, transmitted by golden light, holds back their souls, a promise
holds back the most aged.

True, it is travails, designed from above and completed too, that are the
spice of life. For now all things are pleasing, but most of all the ingenuous,

Die goldne Frucht,
Uraltem Stamm
In schütternden Stürmen entfallen,
Dann aber, als liebstes Gut, vom heiligen Schicksal selbst,
Mit zärtlichen Waffen umschützt,
Die Gestalt der Himmlischen ist es.

   Wie die Löwin, hast du geklagt,
O Mutter, da du sie,
Natur, die Kinder verloren.
Denn es stahl sie, Allzuliebende, dir
Dein Feind, da du ihn fast
Wie die eigenen Söhne genommen,
Und Satyren die Götter gesellt hast.
So hast du manches gebaut,
Und manches begraben,
Denn es haßt dich, was
Du, vor der Zeit
Allkräftige, zum Lichte gezogen.
Nun kennest, nun lässest du dies;
Denn gerne fühllos ruht,
Bis daß es reift, furchtsamgeschäftiges drunten.

for it is the long-sought, the golden fruit fallen in shattering gales from the ancient stem, but then, the most loved of possessions, girt about with tender weapons by holy Fate herself, the shape of the Heavenly it is.

   Like the lioness you lamented, O Mother, when you lost, Nature, your children. For these, all too loving one, your enemy stole from your care when almost like your own sons you would tend him, and with satyrs would join the gods. So you built much and buried much, for you are hated by that which too soon, all-powerful one, you reared to the light of day. Now you know your error, and cease; for fain the fearfully active, until grown ripe, unfeeling reposes below.

## DER EINZIGE

*Erste Fassung*

WAS ist es, das
An die alten seligen Küsten
Mich fesselt, daß ich mehr noch
Sie liebe, als mein Vaterland?
Denn wie in himmlische
Gefangenschaft verkauft
Dort bin ich, wo Apollo ging
In Königsgestalt,
Und zu unschuldigen Jünglingen sich
Herabließ Zeus und Söhn' in heiliger Art
Und Töchter zeugte
Der Hohe unter den Menschen?

Der hohen Gedanken
Sind nämlich viel
Entsprungen des Vaters Haupt
Und große Seelen
Von ihm zu Menschen gekommen.
Gehöret hab' ich
Von Elis und Olympia, bin


## THE ONLY ONE

*First Version*

WHAT is it that binds me to the ancient blessèd shores, so that I love them still more than my fatherland? For, as though sold into heavenly bondage, there I am where Apollo walked in the guise of a king, and Zeus condescended to innocent youths, and in holy fashion begot sons and daughters, the exalted, among mankind.

For from the Father's head many lofty thoughts have sprung, and great souls descended from Him to mortals. I have heard of Elis and Olympia,

Gestanden oben auf dem Parnaß,
Und über Bergen des Isthmus,
Und drüben auch
Bei Smyrna und hinab
Bei Ephesos bin ich gegangen;

Viel hab' ich schönes gesehn,
Und gesungen Gottes Bild,
Hab' ich, das lebet unter
Den Menschen, aber dennoch
Ihr alten Götter und all
Ihr tapfern Söhne der Götter
Noch Einen such ich, den
Ich liebe unter euch,
Wo ihr den letzten eures Geschlechts
Des Hauses Kleinod mir
Dem fremden Gaste verberget.

Mein Meister und Herr!
O du, mein Lehrer!
Was bist du ferne
Geblieben? und da
Ich fragte unter den Alten,
Die Helden und
Die Götter, warum bliebest
Du aus? Und jetzt ist voll

have stood on the top of Parnassus and above mountains of the Isthmus,
and yonder also, by Smyrna, and down to Ephesus I have walked;
    Have seen much that is beautiful and have sung the image of God that
lives among mankind, and yet, you ancient gods and all you brave sons of
the gods, there is One other I seek whom I love among you, where you
keep hidden from me, from the foreign guest, the last of your kind, the
jewel of your house.
    My Master and Lord! O you, my teacher! Why did you always keep far
away? And when I inquired among the ancients, questioned the heroes and
the gods, why were you absent? And now my soul is full of sadness as if

Von Trauern meine Seele
Als eifertet, ihr Himmlischen, selbst
Daß, dien' ich einem, mir
Das andere fehlet.

Ich weiß es aber, eigene Schuld
Ists! Denn zu sehr,
O Christus! häng' ich an dir,
Wiewohl Herakles Bruder
Und kühn bekenn' ich, du
Bist Bruder auch des Eviers, der
An den Wagen spannte
Die Tiger und hinab
Bis an den Indus
Gebietend freudigen Dienst
Den Weinberg stiftet und
Den Grimm bezähmte der Völker.

Es hindert aber eine Scham
Mich dir zu vergleichen
Die weltlichen Männer. Und freilich weiß
Ich, der dich zeugte, dein Vater,
Derselbe der, ...
.....
Denn nimmer herrscht er allein.
.....

you Heavenly yourself excitedly cried that if I serve one, I must lack the
other.

But I know, it is my own fault. For too greatly, O Christ, I am devoted
to you, although Heracles' brother, and boldly I confess, you are the
brother also of Evius, who harnessed tigers to his chariot and down as far
as the Indus, commanding joyful service, founded the vineyard and tamed
the wrath of the peoples.

Yet a feeling of shame forbids me to compare the worldly men with you.
And indeed I know that He who begot you, the Father, the same who ...
for never He reigns alone. ...

Es hänget aber an Einem
Die Liebe. Diesesmal
Ist nämlich vom eigenen Herzen
Zu sehr gegangen der Gesang,
Gut machen will ich den Fehl
Wenn ich noch andere singe.
Nie treff ich, wie ich wünsche,
Das Maß. Ein Gott weiß aber
Wenn kommet, was ich wünsche das Beste.
Denn wie der Meister
Gewandelt auf Erden
Ein gefangener Aar,

   Und viele, die
Ihn sahen, fürchteten sich,
Dieweil sein Äußerstes tat
Der Vater und sein Bestes unter
Den Menschen wirkete wirklich,
Und sehr betrübt war auch
Der Sohn so lange, bis er
Gen Himmel fuhr in den Lüften,
Dem gleich ist gefangen die Seele der Helden.
Die Dichter müssen auch
Die geistigen weltlich sein.

But to One does love attach. For this time the song has come too much from my own heart, and I will make good the fault if I sing others yet. Never I strike the right measure, as I wish to do. But a god knows when it comes, what I wish for, the best. For as the Master moved about on earth, a captive eagle,

And many who saw Him were afraid, while the Father did His utmost and in reality wrought His best among men, and the Son too was greatly distressed until to Heaven He rose in the breezes, so too the souls of the heroes are captive. The poets, even the spiritual, must be worldly.

## DER EINZIGE

*Zweite Fassung*

WAS ist es, das
An die alten seligen Küsten
Mich fesselt, daß ich mehr noch
Sie liebe, als mein Vaterland?
Denn wie in himmlischer
Gefangenschaft gebückt, in flammender Luft
Dort bin ich, wo, wie Steine sagen Apollo ging
In Königsgestalt,
Und zu unschuldigen Jünglingen sich
Herabließ Zeus und Söhn in heiliger Art
Und Töchter zeugte
Der Hohe unter den Menschen?

Der hohen Gedanken
Sind nämlich viel
Entsprungen des Vaters Haupt
Und große Seelen
Von ihm zu Menschen gekommen.
Gehöret hab' ich
Von Elis und Olympia, bin

## THE ONLY ONE

*Second Version*

WHAT is it that binds me to the ancient, blessèd shores, so that I love them
still more than my fatherland? For as though bowed in heavenly bondage,
in flaming air I am there where, the stones tell, Apollo walked in the guise
of a king, and Zeus condescended to innocent youths and in holy fashion
begot sons and daughters, the exalted, among mankind.

For from the Father's head many lofty thoughts have sprung, and great
souls descended from Him to mortals. I have heard of Elis and Olympia,

Gestanden oben auf dem Parnaß,
Und über Bergen des Isthmus,
Und drüben auch
Bei Smyrna und hinab
Bei Ephesos bin ich gegangen;

Viel hab' ich schönes gesehn,
Und gesungen Gottes Bild
Hab' ich, das lebet unter
Den Menschen, denn sehr dem Raum gleich ist
Das Himmlische reichlich in
Der Jugend zählbar, aber dennoch
O du der Sterne Leben und all
Ihr tapfern Söhne des Lebens
Noch Einen such ich, den
Ich liebe unter euch,
Wo ihr den letzten eures Geschlechts
Des Hauses Kleinod mir
Dem fremden Gaste verberget.

Mein Meister und Herr!
O du, mein Lehrer!
Was bist du ferne
Geblieben? und da
Ich fragte unter den Alten,

have stood on the top of Parnassus, and above mountains of the Isthmus, and yonder also by Smyrna, and down by Ephesus I have walked;

Have seen much that is beautiful, and sung the image of God that lives among mankind, for very much like space is the heavenly, plentiful, numerable in youth, and yet, O you the life of stars and all you brave sons of life, there is One other I seek whom I love among you, where you keep hidden from me, from the foreign guest, the last of your kind, the jewel of your house.

My Master and Lord! O you, my teacher! Why did you always keep far away? And when I inquired among the ancients, questioned the heroes and

Die Helden und
Die Götter, warum bliebest
Du aus? Und jetzt ist voll
Von Trauern meine Seele
Als eifertet, ihr Himmlischen, selbst
Daß, dien' ich einem, mir
Das andere fehlet.

Ich weiß es aber, eigene Schuld ists! Denn zu sehr
O Christus! häng' ich an dir, wiewohl Herakles Bruder
Und kühn bekenn' ich, du bist Bruder auch des Eviers, der
Die Todeslust der Völker aufhält und zerreißet den Fallstrick,
Fein sehen die Menschen, daß sie
Nicht gehn den Weg des Todes und hüten das Maß, daß einer
Etwas für sich ist, den Augenblick
Das Geschick der großen Zeit auch
Ihr Feuer fürchtend, treffen sie, und wo
Des Wegs ein anderes geht, da sehen sie
Auch, wo ein Geschick sei, machen aber
Das sicher, Menschen gleichend oder Gesetzen.

Es entbrennet aber sein Zorn; daß nämlich
Das Zeichen die Erde berührt, allmählich
Aus Augen gekommen, als an einer Leiter.

the gods, why were you absent? And now my soul is full of sadness as if
you Heavenly yourself excitedly cried that if I serve one, I must lack the
other.
    But I know, it is my own fault. For too greatly, O Christ, I am devoted
to you, although Heracles' brother, and boldly I confess, you are the
brother also of Evius, who restrains the death-wish of peoples and tears up
the gin and snare, well men can see, that they will not follow the way of
death and maintain the measure, that a man shall be something in himself,
fearing the moment, the fate of great eras and also their fire, they strike,
and where another goes that way, there too they see where there is a fate,
but make it safe, resembling human beings or laws.
    Yet his anger flares up; that is, so that the sign shall touch the earth,
gradually loosed from eyes, as though by a ladder. This time. Self-willed

Diesmal. Eigenwillig sonst, unmäßig
Grenzlos, daß der Menschen Hand
Anficht das Lebende, mehr auch, als sich schicket
Für einen Halbgott, heiliggesetztes übergeht
Der Entwurf. Seit nämlich böser Geist sich
Bemächtiget des glücklichen Altertums, unendlich,
Langher währt Eines, gesangsfeind, klanglos, das
In Maßen vergeht, des Sinnes gewaltsames. Ungebundenes aber
Hasset Gott. Fürbittend aber

Hält ihn der Tag von dieser Zeit, stillschaffend,
Des Weges gehend, die Blüte der Jahre.
Und Kriegsgetön, und Geschichte der Helden unterhält,
                         hartnäckig Geschick,
Die Sonne Christi, Gärten der Büßenden, und
Der Pilgrime Wandern und der Völker ihn, und des Wächters
Gesang und die Schrift
Des Barden oder Afrikaners. Ruhmloser auch
Geschick hält ihn, die an den Tag
Jetzt erst recht kommen, das sind väterliche Fürsten. Denn
                  viel ist der Stand

at other times, immoderate, unbounded, that the hands of men impugn the
living, more, too, than is fitting for a demi-god, the design transgresses
beyond the divinely appointed. For since an evil spirit has taken possession
of happy antiquity, infinite, long now one thing has prevailed, hostile to
song, without resonance, that perishes in measures, the violence of the
mind. But God hates the unbound. Yet interceding
   The day holds him back from this age, silently creating, going its way,
the blossom of the years. And the din of war, and the story of heroes ...
stiff-necked fate, the sun of Christ, gardens of the penitent, and the wander-
ing of pilgrims and of the peoples maintain him, and the watchman's song
and the writings of the bard or the African. And the fate of the unillustrious
holds him too, who only now really have their day, that is, paternal
princes. For ... this rank has become much more godlike than before. For

Gottgleicher, denn sonst. Denn Männern mehr
Gehöret das Licht. Nicht Jünglingen.
Das Vaterland auch. Nämlich frisch

Noch unerschöpfet und voll mit Locken.
Der Vater der Erde freuet nämlich sich des
Auch, daß Kinder sind, so bleibet eine Gewißheit
Des Guten. So auch freuet
Das ihn, daß eines bleibet.
Auch einige sind, gerettet, als
Auf schönen Inseln. Gelehrt sind die.
Versuchungen sind nämlich
Grenzlos an die gegangen.
Zahllose gefallen. Also ging es, als
Der Erde Vater bereitet ständiges
In Stürmen der Zeit. Ist aber geendet.

## PATMOS

### DEM LANDGRAFEN VON HOMBURG

Nᴀʜ ist
Und schwer zu fassen der Gott.
Wo aber Gefahr ist, wächst
Das Rettende auch.

now more to men does light belong. Not to youths. The fatherland too.
For fresh
  Still unexhausted and full of curls. For the Father of Earth is glad of this
too, that there are children, so that the certainty of goodness remains. So
too he is glad of this, that one remains. And some too have been saved, as
though on lovely islands. These are learnèd. For they have been subject to
boundless temptations. Countless fallen. So it went when the Father of
Earth wrought what is constant in the storms of the age. But that is ended.

## PATMOS

### FOR THE LANDGRAVE OF HOMBURG

Nᴇᴀʀ is, and difficult to grasp, the God. But where there is danger the
saving powers also grow. In darkness dwell the eagles, and fearless over

Im Finstern wohnen
Die Adler und furchtlos gehn
Die Söhne der Alpen über den Abgrund weg
Auf leichtgebaueten Brücken.
Drum, da gehäuft sind rings
Die Gipfel der Zeit,
Und die Liebsten nahe wohnen, ermattend auf
Getrenntesten Bergen,
So gib unschuldig Wasser,
O Fittiche gib uns, treuesten Sinns
Hinüberzugehn und wiederzukehren.

So sprach ich, da entführte
Mich schneller, denn ich vermutet,
Und weit, wohin ich nimmer
Zu kommen gedacht, ein Genius mich
Vom eigenen Haus. Es dämmerten
Im Zwielicht, da ich ging,
Der schattige Wald
Und die sehnsüchtigen Bäche
Der Heimat; nimmer kannt'ich die Länder;
Doch bald, in frischem Glanze,
Geheimnisvoll
Im goldenen Rauche, blühte
Schnell aufgewachsen,
Mit Schritten der Sonne,
Mit tausend Gipfeln duftend,

the chasm walk the sons of the Alps on bridges lightly built. Therefore, since all around the summits of Time are heaped, and the most loved live near, growing faint on most separate mountains, give us innocent water, then, oh give us pinions, most faithful in mind to cross over and to return.

Thus I spoke, when more swiftly than ever I had surmised, and far as never I thought I should come, a Spirit bore me away from my own house. There glimmered in twilight, as I went, the shadowy forest and the yearning streams of home; no longer I knew these lands; but soon, in her primal radiance, mysteriously, in the golden vapours quickly grown up with strides of the sun, fragrant with a thousand peaks.

Mir Asia auf, und geblendet sucht'
Ich eines, das ich kennete, denn ungewohnt
War ich der breiten Gassen, wo herab
Vom Tmolus fährt
Der goldgeschmückte Pactol
Und Taurus stehet und Messogis,
Und voll von Blumen der Garten,
Ein stilles Feuer; aber im Lichte
Blüht hoch der silberne Schnee;
Und Zeug unsterblichen Lebens
An unzugangbaren Wänden
Uralt der Epheu wächst und getragen sind
Von lebenden Säulen, Cedern und Lorbeern
Die feierlichen,
Die göttlichgebauten Paläste.

Es rauschen aber um Asias Tore
Hinziehend da und dort
In ungewisser Meeresebene
Der schattenlosen Straßen genug,
Doch kennt die Inseln der Schiffer.
Und da ich hörte
Der nahegelegenen eine
Sei Patmos,
Verlangte mich sehr,
Dort einzukehren und dort
Der dunklen Grotte zu nahn.

Asia unfurled for me, and dazzled I looked for something I might know, for I was unaccustomed to these wide streets where down from Tmolus drives Pactolus adorned with gold, and Taurus stands and Messogis, and full of flowers the garden, a quiet fire; but in the light high up there blossoms the silver snow; and, witness of immortal life, on inaccessible walls pristine the ivy grows, and supported on living pillars, cedars, and laurels, are the festive, the divinely constructed palaces.

But around Asia's gates there murmur, extending this way and that in the uncertain plain of the sea, shadowless roads enough. Yet the boatman knows the islands. And when I heard that one of the nearest was Patmos, I greatly desired to sojourn there, and there to approach the dark grotto.

Denn nicht, wie Cypros,
Die quellenreiche, oder
Der anderen eine
Wohnt herrlich Patmos,

　Gastfreundlich aber ist
Im ärmeren Hause
Sie dennoch
Und wenn vom Schiffbruch oder klagend
Um die Heimat oder
Den abgeschiedenen Freund
Ihr nahet einer
Der Fremden, hört sie es gern, und ihre Kinder
Die Stimmen des heißen Hains,
Und wo der Sand fällt, und sich spaltet
Des Feldes Fläche, die Laute
Sie hören ihn und liebend tönt
Es wieder von den Klagen des Manns. So pflegte
Sie einst des gottgeliebten,
Des Sehers, der in seliger Jugend war

　Gegangen mit
Dem Sohne des Höchsten, unzertrennlich, denn
Es liebte der Gewittertragende die Einfalt
Des Jüngers und es sahe der achtsame Mann
Das Angesicht des Gottes genau,

For not like Cyprus, the rich in sources, nor like any of the others, magnificently, does Patmos dwell,
　But in the poorer house nonetheless she is hospitable, and when, after shipwreck or lamenting his homeland or his departed friend, some stranger approaches, she is glad of the news, and her children, the voices of the hot orchard, and where the sand falls, and the field's surface cracks, the sounds, these hear him and lovingly all echoes with the man's lament. So once she tended the God-beloved, the seer, who in blessèd youth
　Had walked with the Son of the Highest, inseparable, for the bearer of thunder loved the disciple's ingenuousness, and the attentive man clearly saw the face of the God when, over the mystery of the vine, they sat to-

Da, beim Geheimnisse des Weinstocks, sie
Zusammensaßen, zu der Stunde des Gastmahls,
Und in der großen Seele, ruhigahnend den Tod
Aussprach der Herr und die letzte Liebe, denn nie genug
Hatt' er von Güte zu sagen
Der Worte, damals, und zu erheitern, da
Ers sahe, das Zürnen der Welt.
Denn alles ist gut. Drauf starb er. Vieles wäre
Zu sagen davon. Und es sahn ihn, wie er siegend blickte
Den Freudigsten die Freunde noch zuletzt,

    Doch trauerten sie, da nun
Es Abend worden, erstaunt,
Denn Großentschiedenes hatten in der Seele
Die Männer, aber sie liebten unter der Sonne
Das Leben und lassen wollten sie nicht
Vom Angesichte des Herrn
Und der Heimat. Eingetrieben war,
Wie Feuer im Eisen, das, und ihnen ging
Zur Seite der Schatte des Lieben.
Drum sandt' er ihnen
Den Geist, und freilich bebte
Das Haus und die Wetter Gottes rollten

gether, at the hour of the communal meal, and in His great soul, calmly
foreknowing, the Lord pronounced death, and ultimate love, for never at
that time He could find words enough to speak about kindness, and to
brighten, when He saw it, the wrath of the world. For all things are good.
Thereupon He died. Much could be said about this. And at the very last
the friends beheld Him as he gazed triumphantly, the gladdest of all.
    Yet now they mourned, since evening had come, astonished, since in
their souls these men harboured greatly determined things, but under the
sun they loved life and did not wish to part from the face of the Lord and
their homeland. Driven in, as fire into iron, was this, and at their side
walked the loved one's shade. Therefore He sent them the Spirit, and the
house trembled greatly and the storms of God rumbled, distantly thundering

Ferndonnernd über
Die ahnenden Häupter, da, schwersinnend
Versammelt waren die Todeshelden,

   Izt, da er scheidend
Noch einmal ihnen erschien.
Denn izt erlosch der Sonne Tag
Der Königliche und zerbrach
Den geradestrahlenden,
Den Zepter, göttlichleidend, von selbst,
Denn wiederkommen sollt es
Zu rechter Zeit. Nicht wär es gut
Gewesen, später, und schroffabbrechend, untreu,
Der Menschen Werk, und Freude war es
Von nun an,
Zu wohnen in liebender Nacht, und bewahren
In einfältigen Augen, unverwandt
Abgründe der Weisheit. Und es grünen
Tief an den Bergen auch lebendige Bilder,

   Doch furchtbar ist, wie da und dort
Unendlich hin zerstreut das Lebende Gott.
Denn schon das Angesicht
Der teuern Freunde zu lassen
Und fernhin über die Berge zu gehn
Allein, wo zweifach

over their divining heads, when, deep in thought, the heroes of death
were assembled,
   Now that, departing, once more He appeared to them. For now the
Kingly One put out the Day of the sun and, divinely suffering, broke the
straight-beaming, the sceptre of His own will, for it was to return when the
time was due. It would not have been good if it had been later and abruptly,
disloyally had broken off the work of men, and joy it was henceforth to
dwell in loving Night and in fixed ingenuous eyes to preserve abysses of
wisdom. And down at the foot of the mountains, too, living images grow,
   But it is terrible how here and there unendingly God disperses the living.
For only to leave the sight of their dear friends and go far off across the

Erkannt, einstimmig
War himmlischer Geist; und nicht geweissagt war es, sondern
Die Locken ergriff es, gegenwärtig,
Wenn ihnen plötzlich
Ferneilend zurück blickte
Der Gott und schwörend,
Damit er halte, wie an Seilen golden
Gebunden hinfort
Das Böse nennend, sie die Hände sich reichten –

   Wenn aber stirbt alsdenn
An dem am meisten
Die Schönheit hing, daß an der Gestalt
Ein Wunder war und die Himmlischen gedeutet
Auf ihn, und wenn, ein Rätsel ewig füreinander
Sie sich nicht fassen können
Einander, die zusammenlebten
Im Gedächtnis, und nicht den Sand nur oder
Die Weiden es hinwegnimmt und die Tempel
Ergreift, wenn die Ehre
Des Halbgotts und der Seinen
Verweht und selber sein Angesicht
Der Höchste wendet

mountains alone, when doubly recognized heavenly spirit was unambiguous; and it had not been prophesied, but seized them by the hair, present when suddenly, hastening away, the God looked back at them and conjuring Him to stay, calling evil goldenly bound henceforth as with ropes, they clasped one another's hands –

   But when thereupon he dies to whom beauty most adhered, so that a miracle had been wrought in his person and the Heavenly had pointed at him, and when, an eternal enigma to one another, they cannot grasp one another who lived together in remembrance, and not only the sand or the willows it takes away, and seizes the temples, but even the demi-god's honour and that of His friends is borne away by the wind and the Highest

Darob, daß nirgend ein
Unsterbliches mehr am Himmel zu sehn ist oder
Auf grüner Erde, was ist dies?

Es ist der Wurf des Säemanns, wenn er faßt
Mit der Schaufel den Weizen,
Und wirft, dem Klaren zu, ihn schwingend über die Tenne.
Ihm fällt die Schale vor den Füßen, aber
Ans Ende kommet das Korn,
Und nicht ein Übel ists, wenn einiges
Verloren gehet und von der Rede
Verhallet der lebendige Laut,
Denn göttliches Werk auch gleichet dem unsern,
Nicht alles will der Höchste zumal.
Zwar Eisen träget der Schacht,
Und glühende Harze der Ätna,
So hätt' ich Reichtum,
Ein Bild zu bilden, und ähnlich
Zu schaun, wie er gewesen, den Christ,

Wenn aber einer spornte sich selbst,
Und traurig redend, unterwegs, da ich wehrlos wäre
Mich überfiele, daß ich staunt' und von dem Gotte
Das Bild nachahmen möcht' ein Knecht —

Himself averts His countenance because nowhere now an immortal is to be seen in the skies or on the green earth, what is that?

It is the sower's throw when he picks up the wheat with his shovel and throws it, towards the open, swinging it over the thrashing floor. The husks fall at his feet, but the grain reaches its end, and there is no harm if some of it is lost and the living sound of the speech dies away, for divine work too resembles our own, not all things at once does the Highest will. The pit bears iron, though, and glowing resins Etna, and thus I should have material in plenty with which to fashion an image and see Christ much as He was,

But if someone spurred himself on and, talking sadly, on the road, when I was defenceless, attacked me, so that I marvelled and, a slave, desired to imitate the image of the God — visible in anger, once I saw the Lord of

Im Zorne sichtbar sah' ich einmal
Des Himmels Herrn, nicht, daß ich sein sollt etwas, sondern
Zu lernen. Gütig sind sie, ihr Verhaßtestes aber ist,
So lange sie herrschen, das Falsche, und es gilt
Dann Menschliches unter Menschen nicht mehr.
Denn sie nicht walten, es waltet aber
Unsterblicher Schicksal und es wandelt ihr Werk
Von selbst, und eilend geht es zu Ende.
Wenn nämlich höher gehet himmlischer
Triumphgang, wird genennet, der Sonne gleich
Von Starken der frohlockende Sohn des Höchsten,

   Ein Losungszeichen, und hier ist der Stab
Des Gesangs, niederwinkend,
Denn nichts ist gemein. Die Toten wecket
Er auf, die noch gefangen nicht
Vom Rohen sind. Es warten aber
Der scheuen Augen viele
Zu schauen das Licht. Nicht wollen
Am scharfen Strahle sie blühn,
Wiewohl den Mut der goldene Zaum hält.
Wenn aber, als
Von schwellenden Augenbrauen

Heaven, not that I should be something, but to learn. Benign they are, but what they most abhor, as long as they reign, is that which is false, and then what is human no longer counts among human kind. For they do not rule, but the fate of immortals rules, and their work moves of itself and hurrying reaches its end. For when the Heavenly go farther in their triumphal procession, the jubilant Son of the Highest is called like the sun by the strong,
   As a secret sign, and here is the baton of song, beckoning down, for nothing is common. The dead He awakens who are not yet made captive by coarseness. But many timid eyes are waiting to see the light. They do not wish to flower under the searing beam, although it is the golden bridle that checks their courage. But when, as if by swelling eyebrows made oblivious

Der Welt vergessen
Stilleuchtende Kraft aus heiliger Schrift fällt, mögen
Der Gnade sich freuend, sie
Am stillen Blicke sich üben.

   Und wenn die Himmlischen jetzt
So, wie ich glaube, mich lieben
Wie viel mehr Dich,
Denn Eines weiß ich,
Daß nämlich der Wille
Des ewigen Vaters viel
Dir gilt. Still ist sein Zeichen
Am donnernden Himmel. Und Einer stehet darunter
Sein Leben lang. Denn noch lebt Christus.
Es sind aber die Helden, seine Söhne
Gekommen all und heilige Schriften
Von ihm und den Blitz erklären
Die Taten der Erde bis izt,
Ein Wettlauf unaufhaltsam. Er ist aber dabei. Denn seine
      Werke sind
Ihm alle bewußt von jeher.

   Zu lang, zu lang schon ist
Die Ehre der Himmlischen unsichtbar.
Denn fast die Finger müssen sie

of the world, quietly glowing strength falls from holy scripture, then, glad
of grace, they may practise upon the quiet gaze.
   And if the Heavenly now, as I believe, love me, how much more must
they love you, for one thing I know, that the eternal Father's will counts
much with you. Silent is His sign on thundering heaven. And there is One
who stands beneath it His whole life long. For Christ lives yet. But all the
heroes, His sons, have come, and holy scripture about Him and the deeds
of the world until now explain His lightning, a race that cannot be stopped.
But He is present in it. For known unto Him are all His works from the
beginning.
   Too long, too long now the honour of the Heavenly has been invisible.
For almost they must guide our fingers, and shamefully a power is wresting

Uns führen und schmählich
Entreißt das Herz uns eine Gewalt.
Denn Opfer will der Himmlischen jedes,
Wenn aber eines versäumt ward,
Nie hat es Gutes gebracht.
Wir haben gedienet der Mutter Erd'
Und haben jüngst dem Sonnenlichte gedient,
Unwissend, der Vater aber liebt,
Der über allen waltet,
Am meisten, daß gepfleget werde
Der feste Buchstab, und bestehendes gut
Gedeutet. Dem folgt deutscher Gesang.

## PATMOS

*Bruchstücke der späteren Fassung*

VOLL Güt' ist; keiner aber fasset
Allein Gott.
Wo aber Gefahr ist, wächst
Das Rettende auch.
Im Finstern wohnen
Die Adler, und furchtlos gehn
Die Söhne der Alpen über den Abgrund weg
Auf leichtgebaueten Brücken.

away our hearts. For sacrifices all the Heavenly demand, and when one was omitted, good never came of it. We have served Mother Earth and lately have served the sunlight, unknowingly, but what the Father who reigns over all loves most is that the solid letter should be maintained, and the existing be well construed. This German song observes.

## PATMOS

*Fragments of the Later Version*

FULL of goodness is, but no one by himself can grasp God. Yet where there is danger the saving powers also grow. In darkness dwell the eagles, and fearless over the chasm walk the sons of the Alps, on bridges flimsily built. Therefore, since all around the summits of Time are heaped, around

Drum, da gehäuft sind rings, um Klarheit,
Die Gipfel der Zeit,
Und die Liebsten nahe wohnen, ermattend auf
Getrenntesten Bergen,
So gib unschuldig Wasser,
O Fittige gib uns, treuesten Sinns
Hinüberzugehn und wiederzukehren.

So sprach ich, da entführte
Mich künstlicher, denn ich vermutet
Und weit, wohin ich nimmer
Zu kommen gedacht, ein Genius mich
Vom eigenen Haus. Es kleideten sich
Im Zwielicht, Menschen ähnlich, da ich ging
Der schattige Wald
Und die sehnsüchtigen Bäche
Der Heimat; nimmer kannt' ich die Länder.
Viel aber mitgelitten haben wir, viel Male. So
In frischem Glanze, geheimnisvoll,
In goldenem Rauche blühte
Schnellaufgewachsen,
Mit Schritten der Sonne,
Von tausend Tischen duftend, jetzt,

clearness, and the most loved live near, growing faint on most separate mountains, give us innocent water, then, O give us pinions, most faithful in mind to cross over and to return.

Thus I spoke, when more ingeniously than ever I had surmised, and far as I never thought I should come, a Spirit bore me away from my own house. There arrayed themselves in twilight as I went, resembling human beings, the shadowy forest and the yearning streams of home; no longer I knew these lands. Yet much we have suffered with them, many times. So, in her primal radiance, mysteriously in the golden vapours, quickly grown up with strides of the sun, fragrant with many tables, now

Mir Asia auf und geblendet ganz
Sucht' eins ich, das ich kennete, denn ungewohnt
War ich der breiten Gassen, wo herab
Vom Tmolus fährt
Der goldgeschmückte Pactol
Und Taurus stehet und Messogis,
Und schläfrig fast von Blumen der Garten,
.....

O Insel des Lichts!
Denn wenn erloschen ist der Ruhm die Augenlust und gehalten
    nicht mehr
Von Menschen, schattenlos, die Pfade zweifeln und die Bäume,
Und Reiche, das Jugendland der Augen sind vergangen
Athletischer,
Im Ruin, ... und Unschuld angeborne
Zerrissen ist. Von Gott aus nämlich kommt gediegen
Und gehet das Gewissen, Offenbarung, die Hand des Herrn
Reich winkt aus richtendem Himmel, dann und eine Zeit ist
Unteilbar Gesetz, und Amt, und die Hände
Zu erheben, das, und das Niederfallen
Böser Gedanken, los, zu ordnen. Grausam nämlich hasset

Asia unfurled for me and, wholly dazzled, I looked for something I might know, for I was unaccustomed to these wide streets where down from Tmolus drives Pactolus adorned with gold, and Taurus stands, and Messogis, and almost drowsy with flowers the garden, ...

O island of light! For when fame is extinguished, the delight of eyes, and no longer maintained by men, shadowless, the paths succumb to doubt, and the trees and kingdoms, the youthful land of eyes, are perished, more athletic in ruin ... and inborn innocence is torn to shreds. For from God, unalloyed, does conscience come, and go, revelation, the hand of the Lord richly beckons from judging Heaven; then, and for a time, there is indivisible law and office and the raising of hands; that, and the ridding oneself of the falling down of evil thoughts, and imposing order on them.

Allwissende Stirnen Gott. Rein aber bestand
Auf ungebundnem Boden Johannes. Wenn einer
Für irdisches prophetisches Wort erklärt
.....

Vom Jordan und von Nazareth
Und fern vom See, an Capernaum,
Und Galiläa die Lüfte, und von Cana.
Eine Weile bleib ich, sprach er. Also mit Tropfen
Stillt er das Seufzen des Lichts, das durstigem Wild
War ähnlich in den Tagen, als um Syrien
Jammert der getöteten Kindlein heimatliche
Anmut im Sterben, und das Haupt
Des Täufers gepflückt, war unverwelklicher Schrift gleich
Sichtbar auf weilender Schüssel. Wie Feuer
Sind Stimmen Gottes. Schwer ists aber
Im Großen zu behalten das Große.
Nicht eine Waide. Daß einer
Bleibet im Anfang. Jetzt aber
Geht dieses wieder, wie sonst.

Johannes. Christus. Diesen möcht'
Ich singen, gleich dem Herkules, oder
Der Insel, welche festgehalten und gerettet, erfrischend

For cruelly God hates omniscient brows. But pure, on a site unbound, did
John remain. When someone interprets prophetic words as earthly ...
   From Jordan and from Nazareth and far from the lake, by Capernaum,
and Galilee the breezes, and from Canaan. Yet a while I am with you, he
said. So with drops he quenched the sighing of the light, which in those
days was like thirsty wild beasts, when the native grace of murdered in-
fants lamented for Syria, and the Baptist's head, just picked, was visible
like an unwithering script on the abiding platter. Like fire are voices of
God. Yet it is hard in great events to preserve what is great. Not a pasture.
That a man may remain at the beginning. But now this proceeds again as
before.
   John. Christ. This latter now I would sing, as Hercules once, or the
island which was held and rescued, refreshing the neighbouring one with

Die benachbarte mit kühlen Meereswassern aus der Wüste
Der Flut, der weiten, Peleus. Das geht aber
Nicht. Anders ists ein Schicksal. Wundervoller.
Reicher, zu singen. Unabsehlich
Seit jenem die Fabel. Und jetzt
Möcht' ich die Fahrt der Edelleute nach
Jerusalem, und das Leiden irrend in Canossa,
Und den Heinrich singen. Daß aber
Der Mut nicht selber mich aussetze. Begreifen müssen
Dies wir zuvor. Wie Morgenluft sind nämlich die Namen
Seit Christus. Werden Träume. Fallen, wir Irrtum
Auf das Herz und tötend, wenn nicht einer

    Erwäget, was sie sind und begreift.
Es sah aber der achtsame Mann
Das Angesicht des Gottes,
Damals, da, beim Geheimnisse des Weinstocks sie
Zusammensaßen, zu der Stunde des Gastmahls,
Und in der großen Seele, wohlauswählend, den Tod
Aussprach der Herr, und die letzte Liebe, denn nie genug
Hatt er, von Güte, zu sagen
Der Worte, damals, und zu bejahn bejahendes. Aber sein Licht
    war
Tod. Denn karg ist das Zürnen der Welt.

cool sea waters drawn from the ocean's desert, the vast, Peleus. But that
cannot be. A different fate it is. More marvellous. Richer to sing. Im-
measurable the fable ever since. And now I would sing the journey of the
nobles to Jerusalem, and anguish wandering at Canossa, and Heinrich him-
self. If only courage itself does not expose me. This first we must grasp.
For like morning air since Christ the names have been. Become dreams.
Fall on the heart like error, killing, if no one
    Considers well what they are and understands. Yet the attentive man
saw the face of God, when over the mystery of vine, they sat together, at
the banqueting hour, and choosing well, in his great soul the Lord pro-
nounced death, and ultimate love, for never at that time he could find
words enough to speak about kindness, and to affirm that which affirms.
But his light was death. For niggardly is the wrath of the world. But this he

Das aber erkannt' er. Alles ist gut. Drauf starb er.
Es sahen aber, gebückt, des ungeachtet, vor Gott die Gestalt
Des Verleugnenden, wie wenn
Ein Jahrhundert sich biegt, nachdenklich, in der Freude der
    Wahrheit
Noch zuletzt die Freunde,

  Doch trauerten sie, da nun
Es Abend worden. Nämlich rein
Zu sein, ist Geschick, ein Leben, das ein Herz hat,
Vor solchem Angesicht', und dauert über die Hälfte.
Zu meiden aber ist viel. Zu viel aber
Der Liebe, wo Anbetung ist,
Ist gefahrreich, triffet am meisten. Jene wollten aber
Vom Angesichte des Herrn
Nicht lassen und der Heimat. Eingeboren
Wie Feuer war in dem Eisen das, und ihnen
Zur Seite ging, wie eine Seuche, der Schatte des Lieben.
Drum sandt er ihnen
Den Geist, und freilich bebte
Das Haus und die Wetter Gottes rollten
Ferndonnernd, Männer schaffend, wie wenn Drachenzähne,
... prächtigen Schicksals,
.....

perceived. All things are good. Thereupon he died. Yet nevertheless the
friends, bowed down, before God at the very last saw the denier's shape,
as when a century bends, pensive, with the joy of truth,
  Yet now they mourned, since evening had come. For to be pure is a skill,
a life that has a heart, in the presence of such a face, and it lasts longer than
the middle. But much is to be avoided. Too much of love, where there is
idolatry, is dangerous, strikes home most. But those men would not part
from the face of the Lord and their homeland. Driven in, as fire into the
iron was this, and at their side, like a plague, walked the loved one's shade.
Therefore he sent them the Spirit, and the house trembled greatly and the
storms of God rumbled distantly thundering, creating men, as when
dragon's teeth ... of glorious fate, ...

## ANDENKEN

Der Nordost wehet,
Der liebste unter den Winden
Mir, weil er feurigen Geist
Und gute Fahrt verheißet den Schiffern.
Geh aber nun und grüße
Die schöne Garonne,
Und die Gärten von Bordeaux
Dort, wo am scharfen Ufer
Hingehet der Steg und in den Strom
Tief fällt der Bach, darüber aber
Hinschauet ein edel Paar
Von Eichen und Silberpappeln;

Noch denket das mir wohl und wie
Die breiten Gipfel neiget
Der Ulmwald, über die Mühl',
Im Hofe aber wächset ein Feigenbaum.
An Feiertagen gehn
Die braunen Frauen daselbst
Auf seidnen Boden,
Zur Märzenzeit,
Wenn gleich ist Nacht und Tag,

## REMEMBRANCE

The north-easterly blows, of winds the dearest to me, because it promises fiery spirit and a good voyage to mariners. But now go and greet the lovely Garonne and the gardens of Bordeaux, where along the rugged bank the path extends, and into the river deep falls the brook, but, above, a noble pair of oaks and white poplars gaze;

Still I remember this, and how the wood inclines its wide crests over the mill, but in the court-yard a fig-tree grows. But on holidays the brown women walk in that place on a silken floor, in the month of March, when

Und über langsamen Stegen,
Von goldenen Träumen schwer,
Einwiegende Lüfte ziehen.

Es reiche aber,
Des dunklen Lichtes voll,
Mir einer den duftenden Becher,
Damit ich ruhen möge; denn süß
Wär' unter Schatten der Schlummer.
Nicht ist es gut
Seellos von sterblichen
Gedanken zu sein. Doch gut
Ist ein Gespräch und zu sagen
Des Herzens Meinung, zu hören viel
Von Tagen der Lieb',
Und Taten, welche geschehen.

Wo aber sind die Freunde? Bellarmin
Mit dem Gefährten? Mancher
Trägt Scheue, an die Quelle zu gehn;
Es beginnet nämlich der Reichtum
Im Meere. Sie,

night and day are equal, and over slow highways, heavy with golden dreams, lulling breezes travel.

But someone pass me the fragrant cup full of dark light, so that I may rest; for it would be sweet to drowse in the shade. It is not good to be soulless with mortal thoughts. But a conversation is good, and to speak the heart's opinion, to hear much about days of love and deeds that occurred.

But where are the friends? Bellarmine and his companion? Many a man is shy of going to the source; for wealth begins in the sea. They, like

Wie Maler, bringen zusammen
Das Schöne der Erd' und verschmähn
Den geflügelten Krieg nicht, und
Zu wohnen einsam, jahrlang, unter
Dem entlaubten Mast, wo nicht die Nacht durchglänzen
Die Feiertage der Stadt,
Und Saitenspiel und eingeborener Tanz nicht.

Nun aber sind zu Indiern
Die Männer gegangen,
Dort an der luftigen Spitz'
An Traubenbergen, wo herab
Die Dordogne kommt
Und zusammen mit der prächt'gen
Garonne meerbreit
Ausgehet der Strom. Es nehmet aber
Und gibt Gedächtnis die See,
Und die Lieb' auch heftet fleißig die Augen,
Was bleibet aber, stiften die Dichter.

painters, assemble the beauty of Earth and do not disdain winged war, and
to live lonely for years beneath the defoliate mast, where the city's holidays
do not gleam through the night, nor the music of strings and indigenous
dancing.

But now to Indians these men have gone, there on the airy summit on
vine-covered hills where down comes the Dordogne and together with the
splendid Garonne, wide as an ocean the waters move out. But it is the sea
that gives memory, and takes it away, and love also zealously fixes our
eyes, but what is lasting the poets provide.

## MNEMOSYNE*

*Dritte Fassung*

Reif sind, in Feuer getaucht, gekochet
Die Frücht und auf der Erde geprüfet und ein Gesetz ist
Daß alles hineingeht, Schlangen gleich,
Prophetisch, träumend auf
Den Hügeln des Himmels. Und vieles
Wie auf den Schultern eine
Last von Scheitern ist
Zu behalten. Aber bös sind
Die Pfade. Nämlich unrecht,
Wie Rosse, gehn die gefangenen
Element' und alten
Gesetze der Erd. Und immer
Ins Ungebundene gehet eine Sehnsucht. Vieles aber ist
Zu behalten. Und Not die Treue.


## MNEMOSYNE*

*Third Version*

Ripe are, dipped in fire, cooked the fruit and tried on the earth, and it is a law that all must enter in, like serpents, prophetically, dreaming upon the mounds of Heaven. And much, as on the shoulders a load of logs, must be retained. But evil are the paths, for crookedly, like horses, go the restricted elements and ancient laws of the earth. And always there is a yearning that seeks the unbound. But much must be retained. And faithfulness is needed.

---

* The last of Hölderlin's hymns to be completed; after it came fragments, then his madness and his return to rhymed verse. Mnemosyne means 'memory', and she was the mother of the Muses. Mourning for the past is not permitted to the poet, who must 'collect his soul' for a different task, that of interpreting the 'signs of day', what is present and actual. 'Cooking' denotes the natural process of ripening, as distinct from roasting or burning – a distinction observed in ancient sacrificial rites. Paracelsus wrote: 'The ripening of fruit is natural cookery: therefore what nature has in her, she cooks, and when it is cooked, then nature is whole.' Snakes are prophetic creatures; since they slough their skins, they are also symbols of renewal.

Vorwärts aber und rückwärts wollen wir
Nicht sehn. Uns wiegen lassen, wie
Auf schwankem Kahne der See.

Wie aber liebes? Sonnenschein
Am Boden sehen wir und trockenen Staub
Und heimatlich die Schatten der Wälder und es blühet
An Dächern der Rauch, bei alter Krone
Der Türme, friedsam; gut sind nämlich
Hat gegenredend die Seele
Ein Himmlisches verwundet, die Tageszeichen.
Denn Schnee, wie Maienblumen
Das Edelmütige, wo
Es seie, bedeutend, glänzet auf,
Der grünen Wiese
Der Alpen, hälftig, da, vom Kreuze redend, das
Gesetzt ist unterwegs einmal
Gestorbenen, auf hoher Straß
Ein Wandersmann geht zornig,
Fern ahnend mit
Dem andern, aber was ist dies?

Am Feigenbaum ist mein
Achilles mir gestorben,
Und Ajax liegt

Forward, however, and back we will not look. Be lulled and rocked, as on a swaying skiff of the sea.

But how, my dear one? On the ground sunshine we see and the dry dust and, a native sight, the shade of forests, and on the roof-tops there blossoms smoke, near ancient crests of the turrets, peaceful; for good, when contradicting, the soul has wounded one of the Heavenly, are the signs of day. For snow, like lilies of the valley, by indicating where the noble-minded is, shines brightly on the green meadow of the Alps, half melted, where, discoursing of the cross that once was placed there on the way-side for the dead, high up, in anger, a traveller walks, distantly divining with the other, but what is this?

Beside the fig-tree my Achilles has died and is lost to me, and Ajax lies

An den Grotten der See,
An Bächen, benachbart dem Skamandros.
An Schläfen Sausen einst, nach
Der unbewegten Salamis steter
Gewohnheit, in der Fremd', ist groß
Ajax gestorben
Patroklos aber in des Königes Harnisch. Und es starben
Noch andere viel. Am Kithäron aber lag
Elevtherä, der Mnemosyne Stadt. Der auch als
Ablegte den Mantel Gott, das abendliche nachher löste
Die Locken. Himmlische nämlich sind
Unwillig, wenn einer nicht die Seele schonend sich
Zusammengenommen, aber er muß doch; dem
Gleich fehlet die Trauer.

## DEUTSCHER GESANG

WENN der Morgen trunken begeisternd heraufgeht
Und der Vogel sein Lied beginnt,
Und Strahlen der Strom wirft, und rascher hinab
Die rauhe Bahn geht über den Fels,
Weil ihn die Sonne gewärmet.

beside the grottoes of the sea, beside the brooks that neighbour Scamandros. Of a rushing noise in his temples once, according to the changeless custom of unmoved Salamis, in foreign parts great Ajax died, not so Patroclus, dead in the king's own armour. And many others too have died. But by Cithaeron there stood Eleutherae, Mnemosyne's town. From her, when God laid down His festive cloak, soon after did the powers of Evening sever a lock of hair. For the Heavenly, when someone has not collected his soul, to spare it, are angry, for still he must; like him, here mourning is at fault.

## GERMAN SONG

WHEN drunkenly inspiring, the morning rises and the bird begins his tune, and the river flashes beams of light and more quickly takes its rough course over the rock, because the sun has warmed it. ... And the ... wishing

.....
Und der ...
Verlangend in anders Land
Die Jünglinge ...
.....
Und das Tor erwacht und der Marktplatz,
Und von heiligen Flammen des Herds
Der rötliche Duft steigt, dann schweigt er allein,
Dann hält er still im Busen das Herz,
Und sinnt in einsamer Halle.

    Doch wenn ...
.....
... dann sitzt im tiefen Schatten,
Wenn über dem Haupt die Ulme säuselt,
Am kühlatmenden Bache der deutsche Dichter
Und singt, wenn er des heiligen nüchternen Wassers
Genug getrunken, fernhin lauschend in die Stille,
Den Seelengesang.
Und noch, noch ist er des Geistes zu voll,
Und die reine Seele ...

to go to another land ... the youths. ... And the gate awakens and the market-place, and the reddish odour rises from sacred flames of the hearth, then he alone is silent, then quiet in his breast he keeps his heart, and ponders in the lonely hall.

But when ... then in the deep shade, when above his head the elm-tree rustles, by the coolly breathing stream the German poet sits and, when he has drunk enough of the holy, sober water, listening far into the distance, sings the song of the soul. And still, still he is too full of the spirit, and his pure soul ...

HÖLDERLIN

.....
Bis zürnend er ...
Und es glühet ihm die Wange vor Scham,
Unheilig jeder Laut des Gesangs.


   Doch lächeln über des Mannes Einfalt,
Die Gestirne, wenn vom Orient her
Weissagend über den Bergen unseres Volks
Sie verweilen
Und wie des Vaters Hand ihm über den Locken geruht,
In Tagen der Kindheit,
So krönet, daß er schaudernd es fühlt
Ein Segen das Haupt des Sängers,
Wenn dich, der du
Um deiner Schöne willen, bis heute,
Namlos geblieben, o göttlichster!
O guter Geist des Vaterlands
Sein Wort im Liede dich nennet.

Until in anger he ... and his cheek glows with shame, every note of his
song unholy.
   Yet the stars smile at the man's ingenuousness, when, come from the
Orient, prophesying they linger above the mountains of our people, and
as the Father's hand had rested upon his locks in the days of childhood,
thus now a blessing, so that with a shudder he feels it, crowns the head of
the singer when you, who for the sake of your beauty have been kept name-
less until today, O most divine, O the good spirit of our fatherland, you his
word names in song.

216

## HEIMAT

UND niemand weiß ...
.....
Indessen laß mich wandeln
Und wilde Beeren pflücken
Zu löschen die Liebe zu dir
An deinen Pfaden, o Erd'

Hier wo ...
... und Rosendornen
Und süße Linden duften neben
Den Buchen, des Mittags, wenn im falben Kornfeld
Das Wachstum rauscht, an geradem Halm,
Und den Nacken die Ähre seitwärts beugt
Dem Herbste gleich, jetzt aber unter hohem
Gewölbe der Eichen, da ich sinn
Und aufwärts frage, der Glockenschlag
Mir wohlbekannt
Fernher tönt, goldenklingend, um die Stunde, wenn
Der Vogel wieder wacht. So gehet es wohl.

## HOMELAND

AND no one knows. ... Meanwhile let me walk and pick wild berries to quench my love for you upon your paths, O Earth.

Here where ... and the thorns of roses and sweet lime-trees give out their fragrance beside the beeches, at noon, when in the pale yellow corn-field there is a whisper of growth, by the straight stalk, and the ear inclines its neck to one side like autumn, but now beneath the high vault of the oaks, where I ponder and question skywards, the stroke of the bell, familiar to me, sounds from afar, with a golden ring, at the hour when the bird is awake once more. Then all is well.

HÖLDERLIN

AN DIE MADONNA*

V I E L hab' ich dein
Und deines Sohnes wegen
Gelitten, o Madonna,
Seit ich gehöret von ihm
In süßer Jugend;
Denn nicht der Seher allein,
Es stehen unter einem Schicksal
Die Dienenden auch. Denn weil ich

. . . . .

Und manchen Gesang, den ich
Dem höchsten zu singen, dem Vater
Gesonnen war, den hat
Mir weggezehret die Schwermut.


TO THE VIRGIN MARY*

MUCH I have suffered on your account and on your son's, O Madonna,
since first in my sweet youth I heard of him; for not only over the seer but
even over those who serve, a destiny rules. Because I ... and many a song
which to the Highest, the Father, I once was minded to sing, was lost to
me, consumed by sadness.

* 'A lowly man or a king' refers to Herod, who had John the Baptist
decapitated, but also to those responsible for the death of Christ, and to
Creon in Sophocles' *Antigone*, whose laws are contrasted with the 'unwrit-
ten, unalterable laws of Heaven'. 'Spiritual waters' is ambiguous, since in
contemporary German it denoted mineral water. Hölderlin was thinking of
the mineral springs of Bad Driburg in Westphalia, where he spent part of
the year 1796, not far from the *Knochenberg* (Mountain of Bones), which he
associates with the Thessalian mountain Ossa. This region was also the site
of the battle between the Romans and the German tribes under Arminius,
hence the allusion to Teutoburg.

Once again Hölderlin is concerned with the poet's temptation to com-
mune with the dead ('the shades'), a mode of personal happiness which
conflicts with his true mission. Instead, he praises the Virgin, God's repre-
sentative on earth in the present transitional age of Night or 'wilderness'.
It is she who desires that the coming age, the 'burgeoning days', shall be
greater than the transitional era of her reign.

Doch Himmlische, doch will ich
Dich feiern und nicht soll einer
Der Rede Schönheit mir
Die heimatliche, vorwerfen,
Dieweil ich allein
Zum Felde gehe, wo wild
Die Lilie wächst, furchtlos,
Zum unzugänglichen,
Uralten Gewölbe
Des Waldes, ...
... das Abendland,
.....
... und gewaltet über
Den Menschen hat, statt anderer Gottheit sie
Die allvergessende Liebe.


Denn damals sollt es beginnen
Als ...
.....
Geboren dir im Schoße
Der göttliche Knabe und um ihn
Der Freundin Sohn, Johannes genannt
Vom stummen Vater, der kühne
Dem war gegeben
Der Zunge Gewalt,


Yet, heavenly one, yet you I'll celebrate and let no one reproach me with the beauty of native speech, now that alone I go to the field where wild the lily grows, fearless, to the inaccessible, primordial vault of the forest, ... the Occident, ... and over mankind in place of other destinies there reigned the all-oblivious Love.

For then it was to begin, when ... born from within you, the divine boy, and when about him the son of your friend, named John by his dumb father, he, the bold one to whom was given the power of the tongue to

Zu deuten
. . . . .
Und die Furcht der Völker und
Die Donner und
Die stürzenden Wasser des Herrn.

Denn gut sind Satzungen, aber
Wie Drachenzähne, schneiden sie
Und töten das Leben, wenn im Zorne sie schärft
Ein Geringer oder ein König.
Gleichmut ist aber gegeben
Den Liebsten Gottes. So dann starben jene.
Die Beiden, ... so auch sahst
Du göttlichtrauernd in der starken Seele sie sterben.
Und wohnst deswegen ...
. . . . .
... und wenn in heiliger Nacht
Der Zukunft einer gedenkt und Sorge für
Die sorglosschlafenden trägt
Die frischaufblühenden Kinder
Kommst lächelnd du, und fragst, was er, wo du
Die Königin seiest, befürchte.

interpret ... and the fear of the peoples and the thunder and the rushing
waters of the Lord.

For good are statutes, but like dragons' teeth they cut and kill the living,
when in anger whetted by a lowly man or a king. But equanimity is given
to those most loved by God. So then they died, those two, ... so you also
saw them die, divinely mourning in your mighty soul. And for that reason
dwell ... and when in holy Night of coming ages someone remembers and
is troubled on their account who untroubled sleep, the freshly unfolding
children, then smiling you come and ask him what, where you are Queen,
he could fear.

Denn nimmer vermagst du es
Die keimenden Tage zu neiden,
Denn lieb ist dirs, von je,
Wenn größer die Söhne sind,
Denn ihre Mutter. Und nimmer gefällt es dir
Wenn rückwärtsblickend
Ein Älteres spottet des Jüngern.
Wer denkt der teuern Väter
Nicht gern und erzählet
Von ihren Taten,
. . . . .
... wenn aber Verwegnes geschah,
Und Undankbare haben
Das Ärgernis ... gegeben
Zu gerne blickt ...
Dann ... zum
Und tatenscheu
Unendliche Reue und es haßt das Alte die Kinder.

Darum beschütze
Du Himmlische sie
Die jungen Pflanzen und wenn
Der Nord kommt oder giftiger Tau weht oder
Zu lange dauert die Dürre
Und wenn sie üppigblühend

For never you could be moved to envy the burgeoning days, but always have been pleased when the sons are greater than their mother. And never you approve when looking back, an older man mocks at the younger. Who does not like to think of the dear fathers, and tell about their deeds ... but when reckless, arrogant deeds were done, and ungrateful men gave cause for ... annoyance, too gladly then ... looks ... to ... and, shy of action, unending remorse, and the old will hate the children.

Therefore protect them, O heavenly one, those tender plants, and when the north wind comes or poisonous dew wafts, or too long a drought has lasted, and when in copious flower they sink beneath the scythe, the all too

Versinken unter der Sense
Der allzuscharfen, gib erneuertes Wachstum.
Und daß nur niemals nicht
Vielfältig, in schwachem Gezweige
Die Kraft mir vielversuchend
Zerstreue das frische Geschlecht, stark aber sei
Zu wählen aus Vielem das beste.

Nichts ists, das Böse. Das soll
Wie der Adler den Raub
Mir Eines begreifen.
Die Andern dabei. Damit sie nicht
Die Amme, die
Den Tag gebieret
Verwirren, falsch anklebend
Der Heimat und der Schwere spottend
Der Mutter ewig sitzen
Im Schoße. Denn groß ist
Von dem sie erben den Reichtum.
Der ...

Vor allem, daß man schone
Der Wildnis göttlichgebaut
Im reinen Gesetze, woher
Es haben die Kinder
Des Gotts, lustwandelnd unter
Den Felsen und Haiden purpurn blühn

sharp, then grant them renewal of growth. And never, above all, attempt-
ing much and multifarious in feeble branches, let a power disperse the new
generation, but strong let it be out of many to choose the best.

A mere nothing is Evil. This, as an eagle his prey, let One man grasp.
The others no less. So that they do not perplex the nurse who gives birth
to Day, wrongly sticking to home and mocking at hardship, endlessly sit
on their mother's lap. For great is he whose wealth they inherit. He ...

Above all, let them spare the wilderness divinely built in the spirit of
pure law, whence the God's children have it, pleasantly strolling among the
rocks; and.heaths are in purple flower, and dark the sources for you, O

Und dunkle Quellen
Dir, o Madonna und
Dem Sohne, aber den anderen auch
Damit nicht, als von Knechten,
Mit Gewalt das ihre nehmen
Die Götter.

An den Grenzen aber, wo stehet
Der Knochenberg, so nennet man ihn
Heut, aber in alter Sprache heißet
Er Ossa, Teutoburg ist
Daselbst auch und voll geistigen Wassers
Umher das Land, da
Die Himmlischen all
Sich Tempel ...
.....
Ein Handwerksmann. ...
.....
Uns aber die wir ...
Daß ...
.....
Und zu sehr zu fürchten die Furcht nicht!
Denn du nicht, holde
.... aber es gibt
Ein finster Geschlecht, das weder einen Halbgott

Madonna, and for the Son, but for the others also, lest as from slaves by
force the gods should take what is theirs.

But near the frontiers, where lies the Knochenberg, so now it is called,
but in the ancient language its name was Ossa, Teutoburg also is there and
full of spiritual waters the country round about, where the Heavenly all
(built) themselves temples ... an artisan ... But to us who ... that ... nor
be too much afraid of fear! For, gracious one, not you ... but there is a
sinister race which does not like to hear either a demi-god or when with

Gern hört, oder wenn mit Menschen ein Himmlisches oder
In Wogen erscheint, gestaltlos, oder das Angesicht
Des reinen ehrt, des nahen
Allgegenwärtigen Gottes.
. . . . .


Denn wenn unheilige schon
... in Menge
... und frech
. . . . .
Was kümmern sie dich
O Gesang den Reinen, ich zwar
Ich sterbe, doch du
Gehest andere Bahn, umsonst
Mag dich ein Neidisches hindern.
. . . . .
Wenn dann in kommender Zeit
Du einem Guten begegnest
So grüß ihn, und er denkt,
Wie unsere Tage wohl
Voll Glücks, voll Leidens gewesen.
Von einem gehet zum andern
. . . . .


mortals a heavenly being appears, or in waves, amorphous, nor will honour
the face of Him, the pure, the near and omnipresent God. ...
   But even if the unholy ... in masses ... and insolent. ... What do they
matter to you, O song, that are pure; indeed, I die but you follow a differ-
ent course; in vain shall the envious try to obstruct you. ... And if in a
coming age, you should meet with a good man, then greet him, and he will
think how once our days were full of joy, of suffering. From one it will go
to another ...

Noch Eins ist aber
Zu sagen. Denn es wäre
Mir fast zu plötzlich
Das Glück gekommen,
Das Einsame, daß ich unverständig
Im Eigentum
Mich an die Schatten gewandt,
Denn weil du gabst
Den Sterblichen
Versuchend Göttergestalt,
Wofür ein Wort? so meint' ich, denn es hasset die Rede,
    wer
Das Lebenslicht das herzernährende sparet.
Es deuteten vor Alters
Die Himmlischen sich, von selbst, wie sie
Die Kraft der Götter hinweggenommen.

Wir aber zwingen
Dem Unglück an und hängen die Fahnen
Dem Siegesgott, dem befreienden auf, darum auch
Hast du Rätsel gesendet. Heilig sind sie
Die Glänzenden, wenn aber alltäglich
Die Himmlischen und gemein
Das Wunder scheinen will, wenn nämlich
Wie Raub Titanenfürsten die Gaben
Der Mutter greifen, hilft ein Höherer ihr.

Yet one thing remains to be said. For almost too suddenly this happiness
would have been granted, this lonely happiness: that foolish in ownership
to the shades I would have turned, for since you gave to mortals the tenta-
tive shape of gods, of what use is a word? So then I thought, for he hates
speech who husbands the light of life that nourishes the heart. In ancient
times the Heavenly for themselves interpreted how the might of the Gods
had snatched them away.

But we wrest from misfortune and hang the banners upon the god of
victory, the liberator, and that is why you sent enigmas. Holy are they, the
shining, but when the Heavenly would seem but workaday, and common-
place the miracle, and when indeed like stolen booty Titanic princes seize
the Mother's gifts, then One who is higher comes to her aid.

## DER ADLER

Mᴇɪɴ Vater ist gewandert, auf dem Gotthard,
Da wo die Flüsse, hinab,
Wohl nach Hetruria seitwärts,
Und des geraden Weges
Auch über den Schnee,
Zu dem Olympos und Hämos
Wo den Schatten der Athos wirft,
Nach Höhlen in Lemnos.
Anfänglich aber sind
Aus Wäldern des Indus
Starkduftenden
Die Eltern gekommen.
Der Urahn aber
Ist geflogen über der See
Scharfsinnend, und es wunderte sich
Des Königs goldnes Haupt
Ob dem Geheimnis der Wasser,
Als rot die Wolken dampften
Über dem Schiff und die Tiere stumm
Einander schauend
Der Speise gedachten, aber
Es stehen die Berge doch still,
Wo wollen wir bleiben?


## THE EAGLE

Mʏ father went wandering, on the Gotthard, where the rivers are, downwards, and perhaps to Etruria, sideways, and by the straight way also over the snow, to Olympus and Haemus, where Athos casts its shadow, to caverns on Lemnos. But in the beginning my parents came out of the forests of the Indus, the strongly scented. But our first ancestor came flying over the sea, pondering sharply, and the golden head of that king marvelled at the mystery of the waters, when red the clouds were steaming above the ship and the animals, dumbly gazing at one another, gave thought to food; but nonetheless the mountains stand still, where shall we remain?

.....
Der Fels ist zu Weide gut,
Das Trockne zu Trank.
Das Nasse aber zu Speise.
Will einer wohnen,
So sei es an Treppen,
Und wo ein Häuslein hinabhängt
Am Wasser halte dich auf.
Und was du hast, ist
Atem zu holen.
Hat einer ihn nämlich hinauf
Am Tage gebracht,
Er findet im Schlaf ihn wieder.
Denn wo die Augen zugedeckt,
Und gebunden die Füße sind,
Da wirst du es finden.
Denn wo erkennest, ...

## GRIECHENLAND
### *Erste Fassung*

... Wege des Wanderers!
Denn ... Schatten der Bäume
Und Hügel, sonnig, wo
Der Weg geht
Zur Kirche,
... Regen, wie Pfeilenregen

... The rock is good for pasture, what is dry, for drink. But what is wet, for food. If someone wishes to dwell, let it be on steps, and where a small house hangs down near water, there spend your days. And what is yours is to take breath. For if someone has brought it to the top by day, in sleep he finds it again. For where our eyes are covered and our feet are bound, there you shall find it. For where will you recognize. ...

## GREECE
### *First Version*
... Ways of the wanderer! For ... shadows of the trees and hills, sunny, where the path leads to church, ... rain, like a shower of arrows, and trees

227

Und Bäume stehen, schlummernd, doch
Eintreffen Schritte der Sonne,
Denn eben so, wie sie heißer
Brennt über der Städte Dampf
So gehet über des Regens
Behangne Mauern die Sonne

Wie Efeu nämlich hänget
Astlos der Regen herunter. Schöner aber
Blühn Reisenden die Wege
... im Freien ... wechselt wie Korn.
Avignon waldig über den Gotthardt
Tastet das Roß, Lorbeern
Rauschen um Virgilius und daß
Die Sonne nicht
Unmännlich suchet, das Grab. Moosrosen
Wachsen
Auf den Alpen. Blumen fangen
Vor Toren der Stadt an, auf geebneten Wegen unbegünstiget
Gleich Kristallen in der Wüste wachsend des Meers.
Gärten wachsen um Windsor. Hoch
Ziehet, aus London,
Der Wagen des Königs.
Schöne Gärten sparen die Jahrzeit.
Am Canal. Tief aber liegt
Das ebene Weltmeer, glühend.

stand, drowsing, yet strides of the sun arrive, for just as more hotly it burns above the smoke of cities, so does the sun go above the hung walls of the rain
For, like ivy, branchless the rain hangs down. But more beautifully to travellers the roads blossom ... in the open air ... changes like corn. Avignon woody over the Gotthard the horse gropes its way, laurels rustle around Vergil and, so that not unmanfully the sun shall search, the grave. Moss roses grow on the Alps. Flowers begin before the gates of the city, on levelled paths, unfavoured like crystals growing in the desert of the sea. Gardens grow around Windsor. High up, from London, the King's coach drives on. Beautiful gardens save up the season. By the canal. But deep down lies the level ocean, glowing.

# NACHTGESÄNGE

# CHIRON

Wo bist du, Nachdenkliches! das immer muß
Zur Seite gehn, zu Zeiten, wo bist du, Licht?
    Wohl ist das Herz wach, doch mir zürnt, mich
        Hemmt die erstaunende Nacht nun immer.

Sonst nämlich folgt' ich Kräutern des Walds und lauscht'
Ein weiches Wild am Hügel; und nie umsonst.
    Nie täuschten, auch nicht einmal deine
        Vögel; denn allzubereit fast kamst du,

So Füllen oder Garten dir labend ward,
Ratschlagend, Herzens wegen; wo bist du, Licht?
    Das Herz ist wieder wach, doch herzlos
        Zieht die gewaltige Nacht mich immer.

Ich war's wohl. Und von Krokus und Thymian
Und Korn gab mir die Erde den ersten Strauß.
    Und bei der Sterne Kühle lernt' ich,
        Aber das Nennbare nur. Und bei mir

---

## CHIRON

WHERE are you, the thoughtful that always must go at my side, at this time, where are you, light? Indeed, the heart is awake, but I rage and always now astonishing Night constricts me.

For once I followed herbs of the wood and on the hillside listened for a soft animal: and never in vain. Never I was deceived, not even by your birds; for almost too promptly you came

When foal or garden invited you, advising, for the heart's sake; where are you, light? My heart is awake once more, but heartless always powerful Night allures me.

Once I was different indeed. And of crocus and thyme and corn, Earth would gather her first gift to me. And I learned in the coolness of the stars. but only what can be named. And, disenchanting

Das wilde Feld entzaubernd, das traur'ge, zog
   Der Halbgott,* Zeus Knecht, ein, der gerade Mann;
     Nun sitz' ich still allein, von einer
       Stunde zur anderen, und Gestalten

Aus frischer Erd' und Wolken der Liebe schafft,
   Weil Gift ist zwischen uns, mein Gedanke nun;
     Und ferne lausch' ich hin, ob nicht ein
       Freundlicher Retter vielleicht mir komme.

Dann hör' ich oft den Wagen des Donnerers
   Am Mittag, wenn er naht, der bekannteste,
     Wenn ihm das Haus bebt und der Boden
       Reiniget sich, und die Qual Echo wird.

Den Retter hör' ich dann in der Nacht, ich hör'
   Ihn tötend, den Befreier, und drunten voll
     Von üpp'gem Kraut, als in Gesichten
       Schau ich die Erd', ein gewaltig Feuer;

The wild field for me, the mournful, came the demi-god,* the servant of Zeus, the upright man, installing himself; now I sit alone in silence, from one hour to the next, and my thought devises

Shapes out of earth still fresh and the clouds of love, because there is poison between us; and far into the distance I listen, wondering whether perhaps a kindly deliverer is coming to me.

Then often I hear the Thunderer's chariot at noon, when he draws near, the best known of all, when his head is trembling and the ground is purged, and anguish becomes an echo.

Then in the night I hear the deliverer, hear him killing, the liberator, and down below full of rank vegetation, as though in visions, I see Earth, a powerful fire;

---

\* Hercules.

Die Tage aber wechseln, wenn einer dann
   Zusiehet denen, lieblich und bös', ein Schmerz,
      Wenn einer zweigestalt ist, und es
         Kennet kein einziger nicht das Beste;

Das aber ist der Stachel des Gottes; nie
   Kann einer lieben göttliches Unrecht sonst.
      Einheimisch aber ist der Gott dann
         Angesichts da, und die Erd' ist anders.

Tag! Tag! Nun wieder atmet ihr recht; nun trinkt,
   Ihr meiner Bäche Weiden! ein Augenlicht,
      Und rechte Stapfen gehn, und als ein
         Herrscher, mit Sporen, und bei dir selber

Örtlich, Irrstern des Tages, erscheinest du,
   Du auch, o Erde, friedliche Wieg', und du
      Haus meiner Väter, die unstädtisch
         Sind, in den Wolken des Wilds, gegangen.

Nimm nun ein Roß, und harnische dich und nimm
   Den leichten Speer, o Knabe! Die Wahrsagung
      Zerreißt nicht, und umsonst nicht wartet,
         Bis sie erscheinet, Herakles Rückkehr.

---

But, changing, then, both lovely and evil, the days go by, and when one observes them, an agony when one is twofold, and no single man can know what is best;

But that is the sting of the god; otherwise no one could ever love divine injustice. But then the god is present, indigenous there and visible, and Earth is different.

Day! Day! Now truly you breathe again; now you drink, O willows of my stream, a radiant sight, and proper hoofbeats go, and as a ruler, with spurs, and located in your

Own place, planet of Day, you appear, and you also, O Earth, you peaceful cradle, and you, house of my fathers, who walked unurban in the clouds of savage creatures.

Now take a horse and put on your armour and take the light spear, O youth! The prophecy shall not tear, and not in vain Heracles' return awaits its fulfilment.

## TRÄNEN

Himmlische Liebe! zärtliche! wenn ich dein
Vergäße, wenn ich, o ihr geschicklichen,
Ihr feur'gen, die voll Asche sind und
Wüst und vereinsamet ohnedies schon,

Ihr lieben Inseln, Augen der Wunderwelt!
Ihr nämlich geht nun einzig allein mich an,
Ihr Ufer, wo die abgöttische
Büßet, doch Himmlischen nur, die Liebe.

Denn allzudankbar haben die Heiligen
Gedienet dort in Tagen der Schönheit und
Die zorn'gen Helden; und viel Bäume
Sind, und die Städte daselbst gestanden,

Sichtbar, gleich einem sinnigen Mann; izt sind
Die Helden tot, die Inseln der Liebe sind
Entstellt fast. So muß übervorteilt,
Albern doch überall sein die Liebe.

## TEARS

Heavenly Love, you the tender! If I should forget you, if ever I should,
O you fateful ones, you fiery ones that are full of ashes and even before
were deserted and lonely,

Beloved islands, eyes of the world of marvels! For you have become my
one and only concern, your shores where the idolatrous, where Love does
penance, but to the Heavenly alone.

For, all too thankful, there the holy ones served in the days of beauty, and
the wrathful heroes; and many trees, and the cities, stood in that place,

Visible, like a pondering man; now the heroes are dead, the islands of
Love are almost disfigured. Thus everywhere must Love be tricked and
exploited, silly.

Ihr weichen Tränen, löschet das Augenlicht
Mir aber nicht ganz aus; ein Gedächtnis doch,
    Damit ich edel sterbe, laßt ihr
        Trügrischen, Diebischen, mir nachleben.

## AN DIE HOFFNUNG

O HOFFNUNG! holde! gütiggeschäftige!
Die du das Haus der Trauernden nicht verschmähst,
    Und gerne dienend, Edle! zwischen
        Sterblichen waltest und Himmelsmächten,

Wo bist du? wenig lebt' ich; doch atmet kalt
Mein Abend schon. Und stille, den Schatten gleich,
    Bin ich schon hier; und schon gesanglos
        Schlummert das schaudernde Herz im Busen.

Im grünen Tale, dort, wo der frische Quell
Vom Berge täglich rauscht, und die liebliche
    Zeitlose mir am Herbsttag aufblüht,
        Dort, in der Stille, du Holde, will ich

But O you soft tears, do not quite extinguish the light of my eyes; let
one sole memory, so that nobly I shall die, you deceitful, thievish tears,
only one outlive me.

## TO HOPE

O HOPE, you the gracious, benignly active, who do not disdain the house
of the sorrowing, and, gladly serving, noble one, between mortals and the
powers of Heaven mediate,
    Where are you? Little I have lived; but already cold my evening
breathes. And silent, like shades, already I am here; and already songless
my shuddering heart grows drowsy within my bosom.
    In the green valley, yonder where the fresh brook daily purls down from
the mountain, and the lovely late crocus opens for me on an autumn day,
there, in the stillness, gracious one, I shall

Dich suchen, oder wenn in der Mitternacht
Das unsichtbare Leben im Haine wallt,
Und über mir die immerfrohen
Blumen, die blühenden Sterne, glänzen,

O du des Äthers Tochter! erscheine dann
Aus deines Vaters Gärten, und darfst du nicht
Ein Geist der Erde, kommen, schröck', o
Schröcke mit anderem nur das Herz mir.

## VULKAN

Jetzt komm und hülle, freundlicher Feuergeist,
Den zarten Sinn der Frauen in Wolken ein,
In goldne Träum' und schütze sie, die
Blühende Ruhe der Immerguten.

Dem Manne laß sein Sinnen, und sein Geschäft,
Und seiner Kerze Schein, und den künftgen Tag
Gefallen, laß des Unmuts ihm, der
Häßlichen Sorge zu viel nicht werden,

Look for you, or when at midnight invisible life is teeming in the orchard, and up above me the ever-joyous flowers, the blossoming stars, are gleaming,
Then Aether's daughter, O then appear out of your father's gardens, and if you may not come as a spirit of Earth, frighten, O frighten my heart with a different vision.

## VULCAN

Now come, benevolent spirit of fire, and wrap in clouds the delicate minds of women, wrap them in golden dreams and protect it, the flowering peace of the ever-kindly.
Leave the man content with his pondering, and with his business, and with his candle's brightness, and with the day that's to come, and do not let him be burdened with too much annoyance and ugly cares,

Wenn jetzt der immerzürnende Boreas,
　Mein Erbfeind, über Nacht mit dem Frost das Land
　　Befällt, und spät, zur Schlummerstunde,
　　　Spottend der Menschen, sein schröcklich Lied singt,

Und unsrer Städte Mauren und unsern Zaun,
　Den fleißig wir gesetzt, und den stillen Hain
　　Zerreißt, und selber im Gesang die
　　　Seele mir störet, der Allverderber,

Und rastlos tobend über den sanften Strom
　Sein schwarz Gewölk ausschüttet, daß weit umher
　　Das Tal gärt, und, wie fallend Laub, vom
　　　Berstenden Hügel herab der Fels fällt.

Wohl frömmer ist, denn andre Lebendige,
　Der Mensch; doch zürnt es draußen, gehöret der
　　Auch eigner sich, und sinnt und ruht in
　　　Sicherer Hütte, der Freigeborne.

Und immer wohnt der freundlichen Genien
　Noch einer gerne segnend mit ihm, und wenn
　　Sie zürnten all', die ungelehrgen
　　　Geniuskräfte, doch liebt die Liebe.

---

If now the ever-wrathful, Boreas, my enemy from birth, overnight attacks the land with frost, and late, at the drowsy hour, mocking at men, sings his terrible song,
　And tears up the walls of our cities and our fence, which laboriously we put up, and the quiet orchard, and even disturbs my soul as it sings, he the spoiler of all,
　And restlessly raging pours his black bunches of clouds over the gentle river, so that far and wide the valley seethes, and like falling leaves the rocks tumble down from the bursting hill-side.
　No doubt, more pious than other living creatures is Man; but when it rages outside, he too is more himself, and ponders and rests in his well-built cottage, the free-born.
　And one benevolent spirit always will bless him and dwell with him still, and even if all were angry, all those indocile spiritual powers, still Love will be loving.

## BLÖDIGKEIT

Sɪɴᴅ denn dir nicht bekannt viele Lebendigen?
  Geht auf Wahrem dein Fuß nicht, wie auf Teppichen?
    Drum, mein Genius! tritt nur
      Bar in's Leben, und sorge nicht!

Was geschiehet, es sei alles gelegen dir!
  Sei zur Freude gereimt, oder was könnte denn
    Dich beleidigen, Herz, was
      Da begegnen, wohin du sollst?

Denn, seit Himmlischen gleich Menschen, ein einsam Wild
  Und die Himmlischen selbst führet, der Einkehr zu,
    Der Gesang und der Fürsten
      Chor, nach Arten, so waren auch

Wir, die Zungen des Volks, gerne bei Lebenden,
  Wo sich vieles gesellt, freudig und jedem gleich,
    Jedem offen, so ist ja
      Unser Vater, des Himmels Gott,

## DIFFIDENCE

Aʀᴇ not many of the living known to you? Does not your foot walk
upon truth, as though upon carpets? Well, then, my genius, boldly step
into life, and never fear!

Whatever happens, let all be welcome to you, be disposed for joy, or
what could offend you, heart, what affront you in that place where you
must go?

For, since the Heavenly were like men, a lonely woodland beast, and,
each according to its kind, song and the choirs of princes led the Heavenly
themselves, towards communion, so also we,

The tongues of the people, were glad to be with the living, where much
is conjoined, joyous, and equal to, open to, all, because such is our Father,
Heaven's God,

Der den denkenden Tag Armen und Reichen gönnt,
Der, zur Wende der Zeit, uns die Entschlafenden
Aufgerichtet an goldnen
Gängelbanden, wie Kinder, hält.

Gut auch sind und geschickt* einem zu etwas wir,
Wenn wir kommen, mit Kunst, und von den Himmlischen
Einen bringen. Doch selber
Bringen schickliche * Hände wir.

## GANYMED

Was schläfst du, Bergsohn, liegest in Unmut, schief,
Und frierst am kahlen Ufer, Gedultiger!
Denkst nicht der Gnade du, wenn's an den
Tischen die Himmlischen sonst gedürstet?

Who grants the thinking day to poor and rich alike, who, at the turning-point of Time, keeps us, the sleepy, upright as one keeps children, with golden leading-strings.
We too are good and sent* to someone for something, when we come, with art, and bring one of the Heavenly with us. Yet we ourselves bring competent* hands.

## GANYMEDE

Why are you sleeping, son of the mountains, why do you lie discontented, crookedly, and freeze on the bare bank, you patient one? Do you not remember grace, when once at the tables of the Heavenly there was thirst?

---

* The words *geschickt* and *schicklich* are ambiguous, since Hölderlin is aware of the etymological link between *schicken* (to send), *Schicksal* (fate), *geschickt* (skilful), and *schicklich* (fitting, seemly); the implication is that skill is predestined, that the poet's skill is also the proof of his mission, and that anything which is fated or predestined is also fitting.

Kennst drunten du vom Vater die Boten nicht,
  Nicht in der Kluft der Lüfte geschärfter Spiel?
    Trifft nicht das Wort dich, das voll alten
      Geists ein gewanderter Mann dir sendet?

Schon tönet's aber ihm in der Brust. Tief quillt's,
  Wie damals, als hoch oben im Fels er schlief,
    Ihm auf. Im Zorne reinigt aber
      Sich der Gefesselte nun, nun eilt er

Der Linkische; der spottet der Schlacken nun,
  Und nimmt und bricht und wirft die Zerbrochenen
    Zorntrunken, spielend, dort und da zum
      Schauenden Ufer und bei des Fremdlings

Besondrer Stimme stehen die Herden auf,
  Es regen sich die Wälder, es hört tief Land
    Den Stromgeist fern, und schaudernd regt im
      Nabel der Erde der Geist sich wieder.

Der Frühling kömmt. Und jedes, in seiner Art,
  Blüht. Der ist aber ferne; nicht mehr dabei.
    Irr ging er nun; denn allzugut sind
      Genien; himmlisch Gespräch ist sein nun.

Do you not recognize the Father's messengers there below, nor in the chasms the breezes' more vigorous play? Does not the word strike home which, full of ancient spirit, a travelled man sends you?

But already it sounds in his breast. Deeply, as before, when he slept high up in the rocks, it wells up in him. But now the fettered in anger purifies himself, now he hastens,

The clumsy one; now he laughs at the slag and takes and breaks and throws the broken pieces, drunk with rage, playing, here and there at the watching banks, and at the stranger's

Peculiar voice the herds rise to their feet, the forests begin to stir, and deep inland far off the river-spirit is heard, and shuddering now in the navel of Earth the spirit awakens.

Spring comes. And everything, in its own way, blossoms. But he is distant; no longer part of it. Now he has gone astray; for all too good are genii; heavenly conversation is his now.

NACHTGESÄNGE

## LEBENSALTER

Ihr Städte des Euphrats!
Ihr Gassen von Palmyra!
Ihr Säulenwälder in der Eb'ne der Wüste,
Was seid Ihr?
Euch hat die Kronen,
Dieweil ihr über die Grenze
Der Odmenden seid gegangen,
Von Himmlischen der Rauchdampf und
Hinweg das Feuer genommen;
Jetzt aber sitz' ich unter Wolken (deren
Ein jedes eine Ruh' hat eigen) unter
Wohleingerichteten Eichen, auf
Der Heide des Rehs, und fremd
Erscheinen und gestorben mir
Der Seligen Geister.

## THE AGES OF LIFE

You cities of the Euphrates! You streets of Palmyra! You forests of pillars
in the desert plain, what are you? Your crests, as you passed beyond the
bounds of the breathing, the smoke of the Heavenly and fire has taken
away from you; but now I sit under clouds (each of which has a peculiar
peace of its own) under well-arranged oak-trees, on the heath of the deer,
and strange to me seem, and dead, the spirits of the blessed.

## HÄLFTE DES LEBENS

Mit gelben Birnen hänget
Und voll mit wilden Rosen
Das Land in den See,
Ihr holden Schwäne,
Und trunken von Küssen
Tunkt ihr das Haupt
Ins heilignüchterne Wasser.

Weh mir, wo nehm' ich, wenn
Es Winter ist, die Blumen, und wo
Den Sonnenschein
Und Schatten der Erde?
Die Mauern stehn
Sprachlos und kalt, im Winde
Klirren die Fahnen.

## THE MIDDLE OF LIFE

With yellow pears and full of wild roses the land hangs down into the
lake, you lovely swans, and drunken with kisses you dip your heads into
the holy and sober water.

Alas, where shall I find, when winter comes, the flowers, and where the
sunshine and shadows of earth? The walls loom speechless and cold, in the
wind weathercocks clatter.

# POEMS OF HIS
# LATER YEARS

In lieblicher Bläue blühet mit dem metallenen Dache der Kirch-
turm. Den umschwebet Geschrei der Schwalben, den umgibt die
rührendste Bläue. Die Sonne gehet hoch darüber und färbet das
Blech, im Winde aber oben stille krähet die Fahne. Wenn einer
unter der Glocke dann herabgeht, jene Treppen, ein stilles Leben
ist es, weil, wenn abgesondert so sehr die Gestalt ist, die Bild-
samkeit herauskommt dann des Menschen. Die Fenster, daraus
die Glocken tönen, sind wie Tore an Schönheit. Nämlich, weil
noch der Natur nach sind die Tore, haben diese die Ähnlichkeit
von Bäumen des Walds. Reinheit aber ist auch Schönheit. Innen
aus Verschiedenem entsteht ein ernster Geist. So sehr einfältig
aber die Bilder, so sehr heilig sind die, daß man wirklich oft
fürchtet, die zu beschreiben. Die Himmlischen aber, die immer
gut sind, alles zumal, wie Reiche, haben diese, Tugend und
Freude. Der Mensch darf das nachahmen. Darf, wenn lauter
Mühe das Leben, ein Mensch aufschauen und sagen: so will ich
auch sein? Ja. So lange die Freundlichkeit noch am Herzen, die
Reine, dauert, misset nicht unglücklich der Mensch sich mit der
Gottheit. Ist unbekannt Gott? Ist er offenbar wie der Himmel?

IN lovely blueness with its metal roof the steeple blossoms. Around it the
crying of swallows hovers, most moving blueness surrounds it. The sun
hangs high above it and colours the sheets of tin, but up above in the wind
silently crows the weathercock. If now someone comes down beneath the
bell, comes down those steps, a still life it is, because, when the figure is so
detached, the man's plasticity is brought out. The windows from which
the bells are ringing are like gates in beauty. That is, because gates still
conform to nature, these have a likeness to trees of the wood. But purity
too is beauty. Within, out of diversity a serious mind is formed. Yet these
images are so simple, so very holy are these, that really often one is afraid
to describe them. But the Heavenly, who are always good, all things at
once, like the rich, have these, virtue and pleasure. This men may imitate.
May, when life is all hardship, may a man look up and say: I, too, would
like to resemble these? Yes. As long as kindliness, which is pure, remains
in his heart not unhappily a man may compare himself with the divinity. Is
God unknown? Is he manifest as the sky? This rather I believe. It is the

dieses glaub' ich eher. Des Menschen Maß ist's. Voll Verdienst,
doch dichterisch, wohnet der Mensch auf dieser Erde. Doch
reiner ist nicht der Schatten der Nacht mit den Sternen, wenn
ich so sagen könnte, als der Mensch, der heißet ein Bild der
Gottheit.*

GIBT es auf Erden ein Maß? Es gibt keines. Nämlich es
hemmen den Donnergang nie die Welten des Schöpfers. Auch
eine Blume ist schön, weil sie blühet unter der Sonne. Es findet
das Aug' oft im Leben Wesen, die viel schöner noch zu nennen
wären als die Blumen. O! ich weiß das wohl! Denn zu bluten an
Gestalt und Herz, und ganz nicht mehr zu sein, gefällt das Gott?
Die Seele aber, wie ich glaube, muß rein bleiben, sonst reicht an

---

measure of man. Full of acquirements, but poetically, man dwells on this
earth. But the darkness of night with all the stars is not purer, if I could
put it like that, than man, who is called the image of God.

Is there a measure on earth? There is none. For never the Creator's
worlds constrict the progress of thunder. A flower too is beautiful, be-
cause it blooms under the sun. Often in life the eye discovers beings that
could be called much more beautiful still than flowers. Oh, well I know it!
For to bleed both in body and heart, and wholly to be no more, does that
please God? Yet the soul, it is my belief, must remain pure, else on pinions

---

\* Though not an authentic work of Hölderlin's, this piece is included
here because it is undoubtedly based on Hölderlin's written and oral utter-
ances during his madness. It is taken from the novel *Phaeton* (1823), by
Wilhelm Waiblinger, who was in close contact with Hölderlin and drew
on his knowledge of him for the character of Phaeton, a sculptor. In 1822
Waiblinger mentioned in his diary that he had access to Hölderlin's un-
published work, and the above extract from his novel is introduced as
follows: '... At that time he covered with writing all the paper he could get
hold of. Here are a few pages from his papers, which at the same time give
a deep insight into the terrible state of his confused mind. In the original
they are divided into lines like verses in the Pindaric manner.' The most
likely assumption is that Waiblinger adapted this piece from one or more
poems given to him by Hölderlin, and now lost, possibly adding and sup-
pressing passages in the process. In 1827 Waiblinger wrote an early
account of Hölderlin's *Life, Work, and Madness*.

das Mächtige auf Fittigen der Adler mit lobendem Gesange und der Stimme so vieler Vögel. Es ist die Wesenheit, die Gestalt ist's. Du schönes Bächlein, du scheinest rührend, indem du rollest so klar, wie das Auge der Gottheit, durch die Milchstraße. Ich kenne dich wohl, aber Tränen quillen aus dem Auge. Eine heiteres Leben seh' ich in den Gestalten mich umblühen der Schöpfung, weil ich es nicht unbillig vergleiche den einsamen Tauben auf dem Kirchhof. Das Lachen aber scheint mich zu grämen der Menschen, nämlich ich hab' ein Herz. Möcht' ich ein Komet sein? Ich glaube. Denn sie haben die Schnelligkeit der Vögel; sie blühen an Feuer, und sind wie Kinder an Reinheit. Größeres zu wünschen, kann nicht des Menschen Natur sich vermessen. Der Tugend Heiterkeit verdient auch gelobt zu werden vom ernsten Geiste, der zwischen den drei Säulen wehet des Gartens. Eine schöne Jungfrau muß das Haupt umkränzen mit Myrthenblumen, weil sie einfach ist ihrem Wesen nach und ihrem Gefühl. Myrthen aber gibt es in Griechenland.

WENN einer in den Spiegel siehet, ein Mann, und siehet darin sein Bild, wie abgemalt; es gleicht dem Manne. Augen hat des

---

the eagle reaches far as the Mighty with songs of praise and the voice of so many birds. It is the essence, the form it is. You beautiful little stream, you seem touching, as you flow so clear, clear as the eye of divinity, through the Milky Way. I know you well, but tears gush out of my eyes. A serene life I see blossom around me in the shapes of creation, because not unfittingly I compare it to the solitary doves of the churchyard. But the laughter of men seems to grieve me, for I have a heart. Would I like to be a comet? I think so. For they possess the swiftness of birds; they blossom with fire and are like children in purity. To desire more than that, human nature cannot presume. The serenity of virtue also deserves to be praised by the serious spirit which wafts between the garden's three columns. A beautiful virgin must wreathe her-head with myrtle, because she is simple both in her nature and in her feelings. But myrtles are to be found in Greece.

IF someone looks into the mirror, a man, and in it sees his image, as though it were a painted likeness; it resembles the man. The image of man

Menschen Bild, hingegen Licht der Mond. Der König Oedipus hat ein Auge zuviel vielleicht. Diese Leiden dieses Mannes, sie scheinen unbeschreiblich, unaussprechlich, unausdrücklich. Wenn das Schauspiel ein solches darstellt, kommt's daher. Wie ist mir's aber, gedenk' ich deiner jetzt? Wie Bäche reißt das Ende von Etwas mich dahin, welches sich wie Asien ausdehnet. Natürlich dieses Leiden, das hat Oedipus? Natürlich ist's darum. Hat auch Herkules gelitten? Wohl. Die Dioskuren in ihrer Freundschaft haben die nicht Leiden auch getragen? Nämlich wie Herkules mit Gott zu streiten, das ist Leiden. Und die Unsterblichkeit im Neide dieses Lebens, diese zu teilen, ist ein Leiden auch. Doch das ist auch ein Leiden, wenn mit Sommer-flecken ist bedeckt ein Mensch, mit manchen Flecken ganz über-deckt zu sein! Das tut die schöne Sonne: nämlich die ziehet alles auf. Die Jünglinge führt die Bahn sie mit Reizen ihrer Strahlen wie mit Rosen. Die Leiden scheinen so, die Oedipus getragen, als wie ein armer Mann klagt, daß ihm etwas fehle. Sohn Laios, armer Fremdling in Griechenland! Leben ist Tod, und Tod ist auch ein Leben.

has eyes, whereas the moon has light. King Oedipus has an eye too many perhaps. The sufferings of this man, they seem indescribable, unspeakable, inexpressible. If the drama represents something like this, that is why. But what comes over me if I think of you now? Like brooks the end of some-thing sweeps me away, which expands like Asia. Of course, this affliction, Oedipus has it too? Of course, that is why. Did Hercules suffer too? In-deed. The Dioscuri in their friendship, did not they bear afflictions too? For to fight with God, like Hercules, that is an affliction. And immortality amidst the envy of this life, to share in that, is an affliction too. But this also is an affliction, when a man is covered with freckles, to be wholly covered with many a spot! The beautiful sun does that: for it rears up all things. It leads young men along their course with the allurements of its beams as though with roses. The afflictions that Oedipus bore seem like this, as when a poor man complains that there is something he lacks. Son of Laios, poor stranger in Greece! Life is death, and death is a kind of life.

WENN aus der Ferne, da wir geschieden sind,
Ich dir noch kennbar bin, die Vergangenheit
O du Teilhaber meiner Leiden!
Einiges Gute bezeichnen dir kann,*

So sage, wie erwartet die Freundin dich?
In jenen Gärten, da nach entsetzlicher
Und dunkler Zeit wir uns gefunden?
Hier an den Strömen der heilgen Urwelt.

Das muß ich sagen, einiges Gutes war
In deinen Blicken, als in den Fernen du
Dich einmal fröhlich umgesehen
Immer verschlossener Mensch, mit finstrem

Aussehn. Wie flossen Stunden dahin, wie still
War meine Seele über der Wahrheit daß
Ich so getrennt gewesen wäre?
Ja! ich gestand es, ich war die deine.

---

IF from the distance where we went separate ways still I am recognizable
to you, the past, O you the sharer of my sufferings, still can mean some-
thing good to you,

Then tell me, how does the loved woman await you? In those gardens
where, after dark and gruelling years, we have met again? Here, by the
rivers of the holy primordial world.

This much I must say, something good there was in your glances, when
in the distance gaily once you looked back, you man for ever taciturn, of
gloomy

Appearance. How the hours flowed on, how quiet my soul became
when it dwelled on the truth that I had been so separate? Yes, I confessed I
was yours entirely.

---

* An imaginary letter addressed to Hölderlin by his 'Diotima', who had
been dead for some years when the poem was written, and the only poem
of this phase which alludes to his past life.

Wahrhaftig! wie du alles Bekannte mir
  In mein Gedächtnis bringen und schreiben willst,
    Mit Briefen, so ergeht es mir auch
      Daß ich Vergangenes alles sage.

Wars Frühling? war es Sommer? die Nachtigall
  Mit süßem Liede lebte mit Vögeln, die
    Nicht ferne waren im Gebüsche
      Und mit Gerüchen umgaben Bäum' uns.

Die klaren Gänge, niedres Gesträuch und Sand
  Auf dem wir traten, machten erfreulicher
    Und lieblicher die Hyazinthe
      Oder die Tulpe, Viole, Nelke.

Um Wänd und Mauern grünte der Efeu, grünt'
  Ein selig Dunkel hoher Alleen. Oft
    Des Abends, Morgens waren dort wir
      Redeten manches und sahn uns froh an.

In meinen Armen lebte der Jüngling auf,
  Der, noch verlassen, aus den Gefilden kam,
    Die er mir wies, mit einer Schwermut,
      Aber die Namen der seltnen Orte

---

Indeed! Just as you wish to recall to me and write all the familiar things, in letters, so I also find myself giving away the whole past.

Was it spring? Was it summer? The nightingale, delightfully singing, lived with birds that were not far away in the bushes, and trees surrounded us with odours.

The clear-cut pathways, low shrubs, and sand on which we trod were made more agreeable, more charming by the hyacinth or the tulip, violet, carnation.

Against the house and on walls green ivy grew, green too was the blissful gloom of high avenues. Often at evening, morning we were there, talked of this and that and happily looked at each other.

It was in my arms that the youth revived who, desolate still, came out of the fields to which he directed me, with such melancholy, but the names of those rare places

Und alles Schöne hatt' er behalten, das
   An seligen Gestaden, auch mir sehr wert
   Im heimatlichen Lande blühet
      Oder verborgen, aus hoher Aussicht,

Allwo das Meer auch einer beschauen kann,
   Doch keiner sein will. Nehme vorlieb, und denk
   An die, die noch vergnügt ist, darum
      Weil der entzückende Tag uns anschien,

Der mit Geständnis oder der Hände Druck
   Anhub, der uns vereinet. Ach! wehe mir!
   Es waren schöne Tage. Aber
      Traurige Dämmerung folgte nachher.

Du seiest so allein in der schönen Welt
   Behauptest du mir immer, Geliebter! das
   Weißt aber du nicht,
     . . . . .

He has retained, and all things beautiful that flower upon the blessèd shores, to me most precious too, in our native country, or hidden, from a high vantage point,

Where one may look at the open sea, but no one wants to be. Let that suffice, and think of her who is still happy because once we were brightened by that enchanting day

Which began with confessions or the pressure of hands, which united us. Oh, woe is me! Those were beautiful days. But they were followed by a grievous dusk.

That you're so utterly alone in this beautiful world, you always assert, beloved one! But you cannot be sure of that ...

## DER RUHM

Es knüpft an Gott der Wohllaut, der geleitet
Ein sehr berühmtes Ohr, denn wunderbar
Ist ein berühmtes Leben groß und klar,
Es geht der Mensch zu Fuße oder reitet.

Der Erde Freuden, Freundlichkeit und Güter,
Der Garten, Baum, der Weinberg mit dem Hüter,
Sie scheinen mir ein Wiederglanz des Himmels,
Gewähret von dem Geist den Söhnen des Gewimmels. –

Wenn Einer ist mit Gütern reich beglücket,
Wenn Obst den Garten ihm, und Gold ausschmücket
Die Wohnung und das Haus, was mag er haben
Noch mehr in dieser Welt, sein Herz zu laben?

Das Angenehme dieser Welt hab' ich genossen,
Die Jugendstunden sind, wie lang! wie lang! verflossen,
April und Mai und Julius sind ferne,
Ich bin nichts mehr, ich lebe nicht mehr gerne!

## FAME

The euphony that accompanies a very famous ear is a link with God, for a famous life is marvellously great and clear; men either go on foot or ride.

The pleasure, kindness, and possessions of this earth, the garden, tree, the vineyard with its keeper, these seem to me a refulgence of heaven, vouchsafed by the spirit to the sons of the teeming crowd. –

When a man is richly blessed with possessions, when fruit adorns his garden, and gold his dwelling place and house, what more could he have in this world to delight his heart?

The pleasant things of this world I've enjoyed; how long, how long ago the hours of youth went by; April and May and July are now remote, I'm nothing any more, and I am no longer glad to be alive.

## AN ZIMMERN

Die Linien des Lebens sind verschieden
Wie Wege sind, und wie der Berge Grenzen.
Was hier wir sind, kann dort ein Gott ergänzen
Mit Harmonien und ewigem Lohn und Frieden.

Wenn aus dem Himmel hellere Wonne sich
Herabgießt, eine Freude den Menschen kommt,
Daß sie sich wundern über manches
Sichtbares, Höheres, Angenehmes:

Wie tönet lieblich heilger Gesang dazu!
Wie lacht das Herz in Liedern die Wahrheit an,
Daß Freudigkeit an einem Bildnis –
Über dem Stege beginnen Schafe

Den Zug, der fast in dämmernde Wälder geht.
Die Wiesen aber, welche mit lautrem Grün
Bedeckt sind, sind wie jene Haide,
Welche gewöhnlicher Weise nah ist

## TO ZIMMER

The lines of life are various, as roads are, and the mountains' boundaries. What here we are, yonder a god can complete with harmonies, eternal recompense, and peace.

When down from heaven more radiant gladness pours, a joy approaches for human kind, so that they marvel at much that is visible, higher, agreeable:
  How beautifully with it does sacred song combine! How laughingly in hymns does the heart dwell upon the truth that in an image is rejoicing – over the pathway sheep set out on
  Their track, that takes them almost to glimmering woods. The meadows, however, which are covered with flawless green, are like that heath which habitually is to be found

Dem dunklen Walde. Da, auf den Wiesen auch
 Verweilen diese Schafe. Die Gipfel, die
  Umher sind, nackte Höhen sind mit
   Eichen bedecket und seltnen Tannen.

Da, wo des Stromes regsame Wellen sind,
 Daß einer, der vorüber des Weges kommt,
  Froh hinschaut, da erhebt der Berge
   Sanfte Gestalt und der Weinberg hoch sich.

Zwar gehn die Treppen unter den Reben hoch
 Herunter, wo der Obstbaum blühend darüber steht
  Und Duft an wilden Hecken weilet,
   Wo die verborgenen Veilchen sprossen;

Gewässer aber rieseln herab, und sanft
 Ist hörbar dort ein Rauschen den ganzen Tag;
  Die Orte aber in der Gegend
   Ruhen und schweigen den Nachmittag durch.

Near the dark wood. There, on the meadows too these sheep remain.
The peaks that are round about, bare heights, are covered with oaks and
with rare pine-trees.

There, where the river's lively wavelets are, so that someone passing
there on his way looks at them happily, there the gentle shape of the moun-
tains and the vineyard rises high.

True, amidst the grape-vines the steps steeply descend, where the fruit-
tree stands above it in blossom, and fragrance lingers upon wild hedges,
where the hidden violets burgeon;

But waters come trickling down, and a rustling is faintly audible there all
day long: the villages in that region, however, rest and are silent through-
out the afternoon.

## AN ZIMMERN

Von einem Menschen sag ich, wenn der ist gut
Und weise, was bedarf er? Ist irgend eins
Das einer Seele gnüget? ist ein Halm, ist
Eine gereifteste Reb' auf Erden

Gewachsen, die ihn nähre? Der Sinn ist des
Also. Ein Freund ist oft die Geliebte, viel
Die Kunst. O Teurer, dir sag ich die Wahrheit.
Dädalus Geist und des Walds ist deiner.

## ÜBERZEUGUNG*

Als wie der Tag die Menschen hell umscheinet,
Und mit dem Lichte, das den Höh'n entspringet,
Die dämmernden Erscheinungen vereinet,
Ist Wissen, welches tief der Geistigkeit gelinget.

## TO ZIMMER

Of a man I say, if he is good and wise, what does he lack? Is there any-
thing that suffices a soul? Is there a blade of corn, is there a ripest grape-
vine grown on this earth
    That could nourish him? The sense of this is as follows. A friend is
often the belovèd, art is much. O dear one, I'll tell you the truth. The spirit
of Daedalus and the forest is yours.

## CONVICTION

As day surrounds men with bright radiance, and with that light which has
its origin on high unites all the dim objects of perception, such is know-
ledge deeply attained by the human intellect.

---

* Inscribed in Christopher Schwab's copy of Hölderlin's first collection
of poems, *Gedichte* (1826), edited by Ludwig Uhland and Gustav Schwab;
the lines were written and entered there at Christopher Schwab's request,
preceded by four lines of prose.

## DER SPAZIERGANG

Ihr Wälder schön an der Seite,
Am grünen Abhang gemalt,
Wo ich umher mich leite,
Durch süße Ruhe bezahlt
Für jeden Stachel im Herzen,
Wenn dunkel mir ist der Sinn,
Den Kunst und Sinnen hat Schmerzen
Gekostet von Anbeginn.
Ihr lieblichen Bilder im Tale,
Zum Beispiel Gärten und Baum,
Und dann der Steg der schmale,
Der Bach zu sehen kaum,
Wie schön aus heiterer Ferne
Glänzt Einem das herrliche Bild
Der Landschaft, die ich gerne
Besuch' in Witterung mild.
Die Gottheit freundlich geleitet
Uns erstlich mit Blau,
Hernach mit Wolken bereitet,
Gebildet wölbig und grau,

## THE WALK

You forests beautifully painted on the side, on the green slope, where I make my way, recompensed by sweet repose for every thorn in the heart, when my mind is dark, for from the beginning art and thought cost it pain. You lovely pictures in the valley, for instance gardens and tree, and then the path, the narrow, the brook hardly to be seen, how beautifully from the distance the splendid picture of that landscape gleams at one which I like to visit when the weather is mild. The divinity escorts us kindly, at first with blue, later with clouds prepared for us, vaulted and grey

Mit sengenden Blitzen und Rollen
Des Donners, mit Reiz des Gefilds,
Mit Schönheit, die gequollen
Vom Quell ursprünglichen Bilds.

## DER SOMMER

Noch ist die Zeit des Jahrs zu sehn, und die Gefilde
Des Sommers stehn in ihrem Glanz, in ihrer Milde;
Des Feldes Grün ist prächtig ausgebreitet,
Allwo der Bach hinab mit Wellen gleitet.

So zieht der Tag hinaus durch Berg und Tale,
Mit seiner Unaufhaltsamkeit und seinem Strahle,
Und Wolken ziehn in Ruh', in hohen Räumen,
Es scheint das Jahr mit Herrlichkeit zu säumen.

Mit Untertänigkeit<br>Scardanelli

d. 9<sup>ten</sup> März
1940

---

in shape, with lightning flashes that sear and the rumbling of thunder, with the charm of the meadow land, with beauty that has welled from the source of primal image.

## SUMMER

Still the time of year is to be seen, and the meadows of summer stand in their radiance, in their mildness; the green of the field extends gloriously where the brook glides down with its wavelets.

So the day wanders out through mountains and valleys, with its irresistible progress and its beam, and clouds drift on quietly, in higher spaces it seems as though the year holds back with its splendour.

Your humble and obedient servant<br>Scardanelli

9 March 1940

## DER HERBST

Die Sagen, die der Erde sich entfernen,
Vom Geiste, der gewesen ist und wiederkehret,
Sie kehren zu der Menschheit sich, und vieles lernen
Wir aus der Zeit, die eilends sich verzehret.

Die Bilder der Vergangenheit sind nicht verlassen
Von der Natur, als wie die Tag' verblassen
Im hohen Sommer, kehrt der Herbst zur Erde nieder,
Der Geist der Schauer findet sich am Himmel wieder.

In kurzer Zeit hat vieles sich geendet,
Der Landmann, der am Pfluge sich gezeiget,
Er siehet, wie das Jahr sich frohem Ende neiget,
In solchen Bildern ist des Menschen Tag vollendet.

Der Erde Rund mit Felsen ausgezieret
Ist wie die Wolke nicht, die Abends sich verlieret,
Es zeigt sich mit einem goldnen Tage,
Und die Vollkommenheit ist ohne Klage.

## AUTUMN

The legends which are departing from the earth, of the spirit that has
been and returns again, these turn to human kind, and we learn much from
time that speedily consumes itself.

The images of the past are not abandoned by nature; as the days grow
pale at the height of summer, autumn returns down to earth, the spirit of
the showers gathers again in the sky.

In a short period much has ended; the countryman who appeared at his
plough sees the year incline towards a happy end; in such images the day
of men completes itself.

The sphere of earth adorned with rocks is not like the cloud that loses
itself at night; it reveals itself with a golden day, and perfection is without
complaint.

## DER WINTER

Wenn ungesehn und nun vorüber sind die Bilder
Der Jahreszeit, so kommt des Winters Dauer,
Das Feld ist leer, die Ansicht scheinet milder,
Und Stürme wehn umher und Regenschauer.

Als wie ein Ruhetag, so ist des Jahres Ende,
Wie einer Frage Ton, daß dieser sich vollende,
Alsdann erscheint des Frühlings neues Werden,
So glänzet die Natur mit ihrer Pracht auf Erden.

Mit Untertänigkeit
Scardanelli

d. 24 April
1849

## WINTER

When the season's images are unseen and now past, the winter's duration comes; the field is empty, the view seems milder, and gales blow about, and showers.

Like a day of rest is the end of the year, like a question's tone that seeks completion; then spring's new becoming appears. Thus nature with her splendour shines on earth.

Your humble and obedient servant
Scardanelli

24 April 1849

## DER FRÜHLING*

WENN aus der Tiefe kommt der Frühling in das Leben,
Es wundert sich der Mensch, und neue Worte streben
Aus Geistigkeit, die Freude kehret wieder
Und festlich machen sich Gesang und Lieder.

Das Leben findet sich aus Harmonie der Zeiten,
Daß immerdar den Sinn Natur und Geist geleiten,
Und die Vollkommenheit ist Eines in dem Geiste,
So findet vieles sich, und aus Natur das Meiste.

Mit Untertänigkeit<br>Scardanelli

d. 24 Mai
1758

## SPRING

WHEN from the depths spring enters into life, men marvel, and new words aspire out of their intelligence, joy returns, and festively poetry and songs arise.

    Life comes to itself out of the harmony of the seasons, so that always nature and spirit accompany our consciousness, and perfection is One in our minds; in this way much comes to itself, and most of it out of nature.

Your most humble and obedient servant<br>Scardanelli

24 May 1758

* Believed to have been written on Hölderlin's last birthday, 20 March 1843.

# INDEX OF TITLES AND
# FIRST LINES

# INDEX OF TITLES

263

# INDEX OF FIRST LINES

Johann Wolfgang von Goethe
POEMS AND EPIGRAMS
*translated and introduced by Michael Hamburger*

Goethe (1749–1832) is mainly known in the English-speaking world as the poet of *Faust*. His other poetry, for all its richness and variety, has received comparatively little attention.

This book collects translations made over many years by Michael Hamburger. His selection and his critical introduction provide a valuable account of 'a writer so many-sided as to constitute a whole literature'. Here are poems from all periods of Goethe's creative life, including a complete version of the erotic *Roman Elegies* and poems and epigrams from *West-Eastern Divan*.

'The translations are uniformly excellent...' – STAND

'Michael Hamburger ... has opened the door for anybody curious enough to break through the ring of awe that surrounds the Great German Classic and enter.'
– THE IRISH TIMES

(USA hardback edition: *Roman Elegies* published by Black Swan Books)

Friedrich Nietzsche
## DITHYRAMBS OF DIONYSUS
*translated and introduced by R. J. Hollingdale*

Friedrich Nietzsche wrote the nine poems called *Dithyrambs of Dionysus* over a six-year period between 1883 and 1888. The collection, which he assembled for publication shortly before his breakdown in January 1889, forms a coda to his life's work; it represents the ultimate visionary poetic style which he developed during the years following *Thus Spoke Zarathustra*. In its completed form it was his last book.

In these poems Nietzsche fashioned a strongly cadenced and densely metaphorical free-verse style in which he was able to express his sense of remoteness from his times even more convincingly than in the famous celebrations of solitude in *Zarathustra*. R. J. Hollingdale's bilingual edition of the poems contains a full introduction and notes.

'This is an excellent sample of the work of such an influential writer and a translation which can well be recommended.' – ANGLO-WELSH REVIEW

(USA hardback edition published by Black Swan Books)

Rainer Maria Rilke
AN UNOFFICIAL RILKE
*translated and introduced by Michael Hamburger*

*An Unofficial Rilke* is Michael Hamburger's choice from
the many miscellaneous poems which Rilke wrote
between 1912, when the *Duino Elegies* began to take
shape in his mind, and his death in 1926. From Rilke's
crisis and post-crisis years Michael Hamburger has trans-
lated poems in which Rilke confronted energies or
realities that endangered his mastery, or those in which
he ventured into territory that was new to him. Some of
these poems will seem uncharacteristic to readers whose
view of Rilke is based on his more official canon; Rilke's
failure to recognize their worth can only be understood
in terms of his loss of faith and his sense of disorientation.

In his penetrating and sympathetic introduction
Michael Hamburger describes the nature of Rilke's
personal and artistic crisis, explores the tensions and
cross-currents of his later poetry, and argues persuasively
for the revaluation of his miscellaneous poems.

'The translations are admirable and capture well the
flavour of Rilke's sharp sensuousness . . .' – AMBIT

' . . . the collusion of Hamburger the German scholar and
Hamburger the poet gives the translations an unrivalled
distinction.' – PN REVIEW

(USA hardback edition, *Poems* 1912–1926, published by
Black Swan Books)

Johannes Bobrowski
SHADOW LANDS
*translated by Ruth & Matthew Mead*
*with an introduction by Michael Hamburger*

In the four years between the appearance of his first
collection of poems in 1961 and his death at the age of
forty-eight, Johannes Bobrowski gained lasting inter-
national recognition as the outstanding East German poet
of his time. He received major literary awards for his
poetry and fiction in Austria, Switzerland, East and West
Germany. The first selection of his poems in English
translation – *Shadow Land*, 1966 – was greeted with
enthusiasm by critics and readers alike, and was rapidly
reprinted. A second selection, *From the Rivers,* appeared
in 1975.

*Shadow Lands* demonstrates the range of Bobrowski's
poetic achievement by bringing together all the poems
which Ruth and Matthew Mead have been able to trans-
late. It revises and consolidates their earlier selections,
adding some fifty new poems. Michael Hamburger dis-
cusses the background and special qualities of Bobrowski's
work in his introductory essay.

'These are overwhelmingly moving and beautiful poems;
Bobrowski was clearly one of the great poets of this
century, and we are fortunate that the Meads have been
his English interpreters.' – THE LISTENER

'An essential book.' – THE GUARDIAN

Heinz Winfried Sabais
THE PEOPLE AND THE STONES
*translated by Ruth & Matthew Mead*

Sabais's distinctive gift lay in presenting the conflicts of
the post-war German experience without self-pity,
rhetoric, anger or blame; the 'matter-of-fact romanticism'
of his style is fully conveyed in these translations by a
poet of his own generation who has 'on occasion been
surprised to find myself writing down things which, even
allowing for the ventriloquist's-dummy aspect of trans-
lation, I might have written myself.'

*The People and the Stones* includes most of the poems
collected in the earlier book, together with two long
political poems written in the 1970s – 'Agenda' and
'Socialist Elegy' – and a selection from the posthumously
published *Self or Saxifrage*, a sequence of autobiographi-
cal and historical poems written shortly before his death
in 1981.

'Once again, the Meads have translated poetry into
genuine poetry.' – TIMES LITERARY SUPPLEMENT

'This is uncompromising, powerful and heart-rending
poetry.' – TRIBUNE